The Profitable AI Advantage

A business leader's guide to designing and delivering AI roadmaps for measurable results

Tobias Zwingmann

The Profitable AI Advantage

Portfolio Director: Gebin George
Relationship Lead: Gebin George
Program Manager: Prajakta Naik
Content Engineer: Vandita Grover
Technical Editor: Rahul Limbachiya
Copy Editor: Safis Editing
Indexer: Hemangini Bari
Proofreader: Vandita Grover
Production Designer: Salma Patel
Growth Lead: Nimisha Dua
Marketing Owner: Dipali Malwatkar

First published: October 2025
Production reference: 1180925

Published by Packt Publishing Ltd.
Grosvenor House
11 St Paul's Square
Birmingham
B3 1RB, UK.

ISBN 978-1-83620-589-0
www.packtpub.com

Foreword

We are living through one of the most profound transformations in the history of business. AI is no longer a niche technology confined to Silicon Valley research labs. It is rewriting the rules of competition, reshaping how decisions are made, and redefining what it means to work, lead, and build. In boardrooms around the world, AI has gone from a curiosity to the central strategic question: *How will this change us?* The conversations I have with leaders every week are strikingly similar. They want to know where to start, how to capture value before their competitors, and how to avoid being left behind. Beneath the excitement, there is also anxiety, because most organizations are still figuring out how to turn AI from potential into impact. The disruption is not just technological; it is organizational, cultural, and even personal. I have seen enterprises get stuck in two extremes: paralyzed by technical complexity or distracted by flashy demos that never scale. What is needed is not more hype and not another technical manual. What is needed is a pragmatic guide that connects vision to execution and helps leaders move from ideas to results.

That is why Tobias's work matters so much. I first discovered him through his writing and speaking, and what impressed me immediately was his ability to bridge two worlds. He understands both the technical depth of AI and the messy realities of business transformation. He knows where projects stall, how politics gets in the way, and what patterns consistently lead to success.

This book is what most leaders are searching for right now: a roadmap for action. It does not fall into the trap of being too abstract or too technical. It offers practical frameworks you can use, case studies you can learn from, and the confidence to take the next step no matter where you are in your journey. If there is one thing I want you to take away as you read, it is this: AI is not just a tool you add on top of existing processes. It is a catalyst for reimagining them completely. The way we work tomorrow will not look like today. Every function, every workflow, every role will be touched and transformed. This book will help you not just understand that future but also lead it. Read it with curiosity and courage. AI is the defining leadership challenge of our time. Tobias has given you a guide. The rest is up to you. Enjoy the journey.

Armand Ruiz

VP, AI Platforms, IBM

Contributors

About the author

Tobias Zwingmann is a leading AI expert and advisor. As Managing Partner at Germany-based **RAPYD.AI**, he helps companies adopt AI and machine learning faster while achieving meaningful business impact. Leveraging his background as a data scientist and over 15 years of experience at the intersection of business and technology, Tobias has led AI initiatives across a wide range of industries, from early-stage prototyping to full-scale deployment.

Beyond his consulting work, Tobias is a passionate educator who regularly delivers training, keynotes, and workshops. His work is followed by thousands of professionals looking to turn AI into real-world value.

I want to thank my family for their love, patience, and support through book number three. To my wife, Çiğdem, and our CTO crew: I love you. Without the joy you give, projects like this would never exist.

I am grateful to Gebin George for giving me the opportunity to write this book, and to the wonderful team at Packt Publishing who helped shape it. In particular, Prajakta Naik and Vandita Grover, who provided outstanding development and editorial support. I also want to acknowledge Amisha Vathare and Elliot R. Dallow for their guidance and help along the way.

Special thanks to my tech reviewers, especially Sumi Singh, for invaluable insights and expert feedback. Your sharp eye and comments pushed me to make this book clearer and more useful. I'm also thankful to everyone who shared ideas and comments during the process of developing this book over the last twelve months.

My wish is that this book helps make many people's AI journeys easier, clearer, and more rewarding.

About the reviewer

Dr. Sumi Singh is the Founder and CEO of **GAIL180**, a consulting and innovation lab pioneering AI-First transformation. She holds a PhD in Computer Science and brings more than 15 years of experience across enterprise AI, product development, research, and academia. Dr. Singh partners with CXOs, boards, and innovation leaders to accelerate the adoption, commercialization, and scale of AI across industries. A recognized thought leader, technologist, and educator, she leads GAIL180 in guiding Fortune 500 companies, universities, and SMBs to shape and execute AI-First strategies that deliver measurable business impact.

Table of Contents

Chapter 9: Scaling AI-Powered Systems and Workflows   185

Preface

When I first thought about writing this book, my initial instinct was: *no, not another AI book!*

I've seen dozens of them. Sometimes, a dozen in the same month. Most fall into one of two camps: either highly technical deep-dives that only AI people or data scientists could really appreciate, or fluffy business books that get you excited (sometimes even scared) but offer little in the way of action. Neither speaks to the people I meet every day in my consulting work: business leaders eager to understand AI and put it to work, but overwhelmed by the hype and struggling to make it real.

That's the gap this book is meant to fill.

I've spent the last five years in applied AI consulting, helping organizations of all shapes and sizes adopt AI in meaningful, pragmatic ways. Before that, I worked as a data scientist, where bringing machine learning models into production was part of my day job - long before ChatGPT made AI a household term. Today, my focus is less on training deep learning models from scratch and more on helping businesses apply accessible AI technology to real-world problems in ways that are practical and profitable.

When I talk about being *profitable*, I mean it in a managerial sense - expanding margins by reducing avoidable costs, increasing throughput, mitigating risks, or generating new revenue without adding proportional costs to the organization. I won't walk you through a discounted cash-flow analysis; instead, we'll use simple thresholds, cost caps, and quick sizing that you can plug into your own financials. The goal is straightforward: implement AI so that it shows up on your P&L.

This book distills the lessons, patterns, and pitfalls I've seen firsthand in a (hopefully) reader-friendly way. My work has taken me inside enterprise giants from industries such as automotive and insurance, mid-sized companies with 500–1,000 employees, and solopreneurs wanting to double their output, to small business owners uncovering $10k+ monthly savings in unexpected places. The contexts may differ wildly, but the underlying patterns of what makes AI succeed - and what makes it fail - remain surprisingly consistent.

Many of the ideas here began life as short pieces I shared in my weekly newsletter - read today by more than 10,000 professionals at companies like Google, Amazon, Gucci, Intercontinental Hotels, H&M, Santander, and Mercedes-Benz. What you'll find in these pages are the expanded, sharpened versions: frameworks, case studies, and strategies you can start using today in your business.

This book is designed to help you understand what AI means for your business and how to take the next step with clarity and confidence, so you can move forward toward ***profitable results***.

Starting now.

Who this book is for

This book is for business leaders, CTOs, entrepreneurs, managers, and professionals who want to understand AI in a way that's practical, actionable, and aligned with real business goals.

It's especially for those carrying the responsibility of pushing AI into their organization - whether you're a department head exploring use cases, a transformation lead tasked with building a roadmap, or an executive under pressure to turn hype into results.

You don't need to be a data scientist to benefit from this book. What you do need is curiosity, a willingness to rethink how work gets done, and the drive to bridge the gap between strategy and execution. If you've ever felt caught between technical jargon on one side and empty buzzwords on the other - this book was written for you.

If you're looking for a coding manual or a deep dive into algorithms, this isn't that book. There are already many others that do that well.

What this book covers

Chapter 1, Understanding the AI Revolution, cuts through the hype to show what's really happening with AI adoption in businesses, and why so many projects get stuck.

Chapter 2, Understanding Modern AI, breaks down today's AI technologies into simple, business-relevant concepts you can actually use.

Chapter 3, Approaches to Successful AI Adoption, explores proven strategies for adopting AI without falling into the trap of copying Silicon Valley.

Chapter 4, Getting Started on Your AI Journey, teaches you how to identify pain points and bottlenecks, and who should own the AI roadmap.

Chapter 5, Finding AI Opportunities in Processes and Products, walks you through mapping AI capabilities in your business.

Chapter 6, Designing AI Use Cases, gives you a structured framework to design, evaluate, and compare AI initiatives before committing resources.

Chapter 7, Building Your AI Roadmap, helps you turn a pile of use cases into a prioritized roadmap, find synergies, and align different stakeholders around a shared direction.

Chapter 8, Prototyping for Success, shows you how to test ideas quickly, avoid the prototype purgatory, and balance the make-versus-buy decision.

Chapter 9, Scaling AI-Powered Systems and Workflows, explores how to move from prototype to production successfully.

Chapter 10, Leveraging Your AI Toolkit, gives you a practical guide to assembling an AI technology stack that fits your requirements and helps you start building without getting overwhelmed.

To get the most out of this book

- *You don't need to read it cover to cover.* While chapters cross-reference earlier concepts, each one stands on its own. Feel free to jump straight to the part of the journey that matches where you are - whether that's identifying opportunities, building prototypes, or scaling.

- *Start with your context.* If you're new to AI in business, Part 1 gives you the foundations. If you're already running pilots, Part 2 and Part 3 will help you move from experiments to scale.

- *Blend it with what you already use.* If your organization already has frameworks or transformation models in place, treat mine as complementary field notes. Mix, match, and adapt - the value is in making it work for you.

- *Treat it like a playbook, not a theory book.* Don't just read the frameworks and checklists - pick one and try it this week. Test it with your team, learn from what happens, then come back for more. Progress comes from small, repeated actions - not from planning everything until it's perfect (a theme you'll see throughout this book).

Download the resource files

The resource files for the book are hosted on GitHub at https://github.com/PacktPublishing/The-Profitable-AI-Advantage. We also have other code bundles from our rich catalog of books and videos available at https://github.com/PacktPublishing. Check them out!

Download the color images

We also provide a PDF file that has color images of the screenshots/diagrams used in this book. You can download it here: https://packt.link/gbp/9781836205890.

Conventions used

There are a number of text conventions used throughout this book.

Bold: Indicates a new term, an important word, or words that you see on the screen. For instance, words in menus or dialog boxes appear in the text like this. For example: "To understand the impact of AI on competitive dynamics, let's talk about the classic **Five Forces framework**."

> Warnings or important notes appear like this.

> Tips and tricks appear like this.

Get in touch

Feedback from our readers is always welcome.

General feedback: If you have questions about any aspect of this book or have any general feedback, please email us at customercare@packt.com and mention the book's title in the subject of your message.

Errata: Although we have taken every care to ensure the accuracy of our content, mistakes do happen. If you have found a mistake in this book, we would be grateful if you reported this to us. Please visit http://www.packt.com/submit-errata, click **Submit Errata**, and fill in the form.

Piracy: If you come across any illegal copies of our works in any form on the internet, we would be grateful if you would provide us with the location address or website name. Please contact us at copyright@packt.com with a link to the material.

If you are interested in becoming an author: If there is a topic that you have expertise in and you are interested in either writing or contributing to a book, please visit http://authors.packt.com/.

Stay tuned

To keep up with the latest developments in the fields of Generative AI and LLMs, subscribe to our weekly newsletter, AI_Distilled, at `https://packt.link/80z6Y`.

Join our communities on Discord and Reddit

Have questions about the book or want to contribute to discussions on Generative AI and LLMs?

Join our Discord server at `https://packt.link/4Bbd9` and our Reddit channel at `https://packt.link/wcYOQ` to connect, share, and collaborate with like-minded enthusiasts.

Your Book Comes with Exclusive Perks - Here's How to Unlock Them

Unlock this book's exclusive benefits now

Scan this QR code or go to `https://packtpub.com/unlock`, then search this book by name. Ensure it's the correct edition.

UNLOCK NOW

Note: Keep your purchase invoice ready before you start.

Enhanced reading experience with our Next-gen Reader:

⌾ **Multi-device progress sync:** Learn from any device with seamless progress sync.

📖 **Highlighting and notetaking:** Turn your reading into lasting knowledge.

🔖 **Bookmarking:** Revisit your most important learnings anytime.

☀ **Dark mode:** Focus with minimal eye strain by switching to dark or sepia mode.

Learn smarter using our AI assistant (Beta):

✦ **Summarize it:** Summarize key sections or an entire chapter.

✦ **AI code explainers:** In the next-gen Packt Reader, click the **Explain** button above each code block for AI-powered code explanations.

> **Note:** The AI assistant is part of next-gen Packt Reader and is still in beta.

Learn anytime, anywhere:

Access your content offline with DRM-free PDF and ePub versions—compatible with your favorite e-readers.

Unlock Your Book's Exclusive Benefits

Your copy of this book comes with the following exclusive benefits:

⊙ Next-gen Packt Reader

✦ AI assistant (beta)

▣ DRM-free PDF/ePub downloads

Use the following guide to unlock them if you haven't already. The process takes just a few minutes and needs to be done only once.

How to unlock these benefits in three easy steps

Step 1

Keep your purchase invoice for this book ready, as you'll need it in *Step 3*. If you received a physical invoice, scan it on your phone and have it ready as either a PDF, JPG, or PNG.

For more help on finding your invoice, visit https://www.packtpub.com/unlock-benefits/help.

> **Note:** Did you buy this book directly from Packt? You don't need an invoice. After completing Step 2, you can jump straight to your exclusive content.

Step 2

Scan this QR code or go to https://packtpub.com/unlock.

On the page that opens (which will look similar to Figure 1 if you're on desktop), search for this book by name. Make sure you select the correct edition.

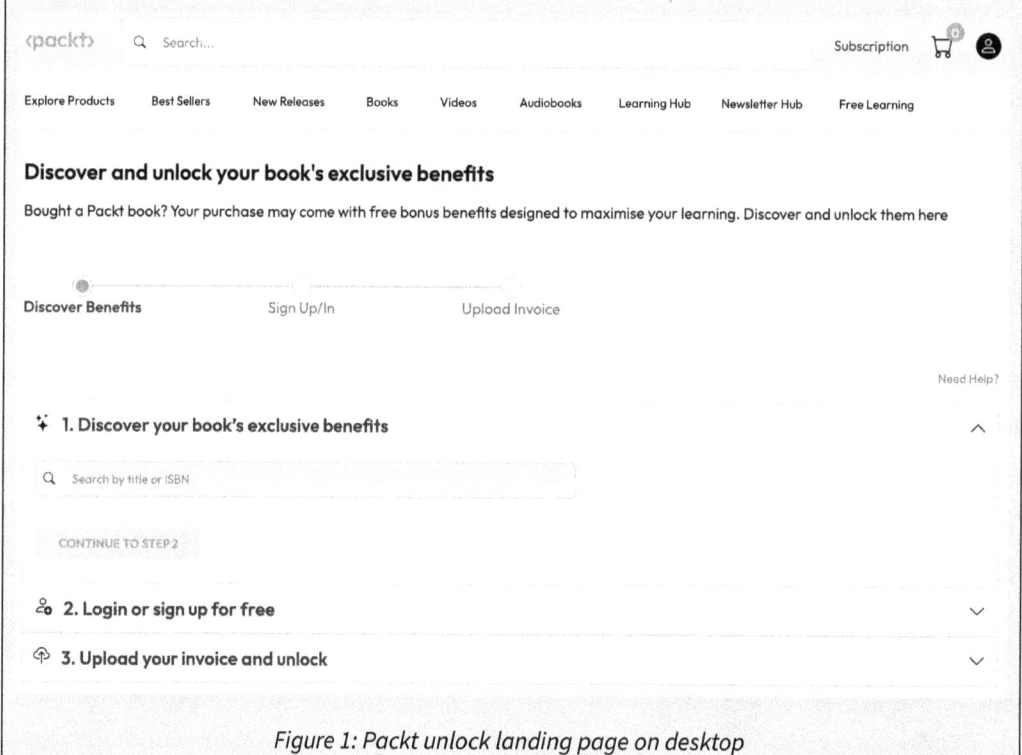

<packt>   Q Search...   Subscription 🛒 👤

Explore Products   Best Sellers   New Releases   Books   Videos   Audiobooks   Learning Hub   Newsletter Hub   Free Learning

Discover and unlock your book's exclusive benefits

Bought a Packt book? Your purchase may come with free bonus benefits designed to maximise your learning. Discover and unlock them here

Discover Benefits   Sign Up/In   Upload Invoice

Need Help?

✦ 1. Discover your book's exclusive benefits   ∧

Q Search by title or ISBN

CONTINUE TO STEP 2

⚲ 2. Login or sign up for free   ∨

☁ 3. Upload your invoice and unlock   ∨

Figure 1: Packt unlock landing page on desktop

Step 3

Sign in to your Packt account or create a new one for free. Once you're logged in, upload your invoice. It can be in PDF, PNG, or JPG format and must be no larger than 10 MB. Follow the rest of the instructions on the screen to complete the process.

Need help?

If you get stuck and need help, visit `https://www.packtpub.com/unlock-benefits/help` for a detailed FAQ on how to find your invoices and more. The following QR code will take you to the help page directly:

Note: If you are still facing issues, reach out to `customercare@packt.com`.

Share your thoughts

Once you've read *The Profitable AI Advantage*, we'd love to hear your thoughts! Scan the QR code below to go straight to the Amazon review page for this book and share your feedback.

`https://packt.link/r/1836205899`

Your review is important to us and the tech community and will help us make sure we're delivering excellent quality content.

Part 1

Preparing for the Journey

In the first part of the book, we'll set the stage for your AI journey. We'll explore the realities of the AI revolution, cut through the hype, and build a solid foundation for understanding modern AI concepts. You'll learn why copying Silicon Valley's playbook rarely works, and what successful adoption strategies look like in practice. By the end of this part, you'll have the context and fundamentals needed to start thinking about AI in a way that's grounded in business reality.

This part of the book includes the following chapters:

- *Chapter 1, Understanding the AI Revolution*
- *Chapter 2, Understanding Modern AI*
- *Chapter 3, Approaches to Successful AI Adoption*

1

Understanding the AI Revolution

Did you ever check your favorite social media app only to find your feed flooded with headlines like:

- *RIP product designers.*
- *This AI side hustle makes $1,579/day.*
- *This new AI will replace software engineers.*

At least in my AI bubble, that's what my feed looks like every day. A new model here. Another revolution there. Given the buzz on the web, you would bet your house that the AI revolution is in full swing.

However, my last few years of AI consulting have taught me that the reality is quite different. AI adoption remains a challenge and the vast majority of business leaders struggle to bring their (expensive) AI prototypes to (even more expensive) production scenarios.

Here's how a typical AI project runs for a typical, mid-sized, established B2B company.

The company hears about the potential of AI in optimizing a given process and decides to invest in an AI solution. They engage an IT consulting firm, which charges them $15,000 for an *AI strategy deck*. The deck outlines a vision of how AI could transform their business over the next 10 years in fluffy words. Excited by this vision, the CEO greenlights a prototype project. The consulting firm charges another $20,000 to develop a basic proof of concept using some historical (or perhaps even made-up) data. The prototype shows promising results and now everyone gets really excited.

But then comes the reality check. To put this prototype into production, the company needs to integrate the AI solution with its existing system landscape, which requires significant customization and new data pipelines. They would also need to train their staff on how to use and interpret the AI predictions. And finally, they would need to establish governance processes to monitor and maintain the AI system over time. With all these requirements in mind, the consulting firm presents a quote for this production implementation that is around 10 times the cost of the prototype.

The CEO no longer greenlights the project. Instead, they want to see a detailed ROI breakdown and proof that the solution will actually work as expected. Neither ever happens; the project stalls and becomes another casualty of what I call the *prototyping trap*.

This scenario is all too common. A survey by Gartner found that only 53% of AI prototypes make it to production. The rest get stuck in this *innovation theater*, where companies can point to their AI experiments as evidence of their digital transformation efforts but fail to translate these experiments into tangible business value.

So while companies are trying to figure it out, the hype around AI has filled the pockets of large IT consulting firms. Accenture predicted $900 million in additional revenue in a single quarter due to AI. BCG expected **Generative AI (GenAI)** to contribute 20% of its revenue in 2024. For McKinsey, AI was the top driver for business growth in 2024. These firms have capitalized on the AI gold rush, offering their (often expensive) services to help companies navigate the complex landscape of AI adoption.

But for many companies, the reality of AI adoption has been a sobering experience. When ChatGPT launched in late 2022, it felt as if AI development suddenly accelerated at an unimaginable pace. GPT-4's release in March 2023 set expectations sky-high for what was to come. Many anticipated that even more powerful models would quickly emerge, AI development would become unstoppable, and AI would rapidly transform every industry. The hype created an atmosphere of both excitement and fear, with many feeling that they were on the cusp of a transformation they couldn't control. (Does anyone still remember the big call to pause AI development?)

But the reality of AI's impact has been quite different from these big expectations. The gap between the AI revolution we were promised and the one that's actually unfolding is significant, and understanding this gap is crucial for navigating the true AI landscape.

When we dig deeper into the state of AI adoption, we find a paradox.

According to McKinsey, AI adoption in enterprises has surged from 33% in 2023 to 65% in 2024. On the surface, this looks like an impressive leap. But when we look at the depth of adoption, we see a different picture. Only 8% of companies have adopted AI in more than five business functions. The vast majority are only scratching the surface of AI's potential.

This shallow adoption is, to a large part, because of the *prototyping trap* I outlined above. It keeps companies stuck in the experimentation phase with AI. They've invested in pilots and proofs of concept, but struggle to scale these use cases to production. Even companies that have successfully navigated (or bought their way out of) the prototyping trap are not immune to setbacks.

McDonald's launched an automated chatbot that it had to pull back in 2024 following a viral TikTok video that highlighted errors, such as adding bacon to ice cream, mistakenly ordering hundreds of dollars worth of chicken nuggets, and confusing caramel ice cream with multiple stacks of butter.

A similar case happened to Air Canada, which decided to pull back its AI customer support chatbot after needing to take legal responsibility for the wrong answers this chatbot gave to a customer.

And it's not only chatbots. Back in 2021, the real estate platform Zillow shut down its AI-powered service **Zillow Offers** after its bad predictions contributed to a $500m loss and 2,000 laid-off employees.

Case studies like this have led to growing skepticism and, in some cases, budget cuts for AI initiatives. Gartner calls this the *trough of disillusionment* - the phase where initial hype gives way to disappointment as the technology fails to meet inflated expectations.

These challenges stem from several factors. We will further explore these throughout this book. But one of the most important reasons for gap between expectations and reality is that organizations lack the maturity to effectively adopt AI. They face hurdles on both the technical front, such as data quality and infrastructure readiness, and the non-technical front, particularly in terms of culture and skills. A survey by IBM found that the skills gap is the top barrier to AI adoption, cited by 33% of respondents. Besides that, the regulatory landscape around AI is starting to take shape, and it's already impacting implementation, especially in regions like the EU. The EU's AI Act, for example, classifies certain AI systems as *high-risk* and subject them to strict requirements around transparency, human oversight, and risk management. This adds another layer of complexity and cost to AI adoption.

Finally, measuring the progress and impact of AI initiatives remains a challenge. Unlike traditional software projects, the ROI of AI can be hard to quantify, especially in the short term. This makes it difficult for companies to justify large-scale investments in AI.

So, are AI projects doomed to failure?

Absolutely not! But real AI progress often comes in a shape that does not make the headlines. For example, biotech company Moderna publicly disclosed that over 750 AI-powered assistants are used by over 80% of the 5,000 employees in their organization to achieve an impact that would otherwise require a team of 100,000 if they operated in the old biopharmaceutical ways - a huge achievement that was left relatively unnoticed compared to other AI *breakthroughs* covered by media.

We will explore many more case studies like this throughout this book.

But let's first talk about *Why AI matters for non-tech business leaders?*

As you've seen and will continue to discover - AI adoption isn't as simple as buying a new IT tool. Adopting AI successfully is a journey, and this journey must be owned and driven by business leaders, not IT. In the next chapters, we'll explore how IT can be the enabler of AI-powered business transformation but not the key driver.

Instead, business leaders must take ownership of their AI roadmaps themselves. *How will AI impact work in their departments? What processes will be affected? How can they ensure every employee is onboard? Where's the profit?* This applies to every leader in an organization. AI roadmaps will be needed for marketing, legal, manufacturing, operations, and beyond. No one is building these roadmaps for these teams unless the business leaders themselves do. Business leaders understand the core needs of their area of responsibility - be it a large business unit, a small team, or a certain product of the company. While IT and engineering departments typically focus on implementation rather than vision, business leaders must bridge that gap to ensure AI initiatives align with strategic goals and the practical needs of the business.

This requires a critical assessment and ongoing iteration along the roadmap. This book will guide you in creating and executing such a roadmap. Without ownership of your AI roadmap, your company risks being stuck in the *shiny toy* phase-buying AI tools and launching small projects that have, at best, a minor impact on the business.

Owning your AI roadmap or failing to do so - will significantly impact your business's competitive position in the market. The world around you is in fast motion, so simply maintaining the status quo is no longer enough. If you don't act, you're effectively falling behind, even if your performance hasn't changed.

This is the insidious nature of AI's impact on competitiveness. It's not always about dramatic, disruptive innovation. Often, it's about the accumulation of lots of smaller gains across the whole organization in a way that they are compounding to a larger benefit, creating a widening gap between the AI haves and have-nots.

We'll explore all that in this chapter through the following sections:

- AI's impact on competitiveness
- The AI advantage: A new force

AI's impact on competitiveness

To understand the impact of AI on competitive dynamics, let's talk about the classic **Five Forces framework** (*Figure 1.1*), which is an excellent lens through which to examine these changes.

Developed by Harvard Business School professor Michael Porter back in 1979, the Five Forces framework is a tool for analyzing the competitive intensity of an industry by considering five key forces: the threat of new entrants, the bargaining power of suppliers, the bargaining power of buyers, the threat of substitute products or services, and the overall rivalry among existing competitors. The more forces there are, the harder it is to survive in a given market.

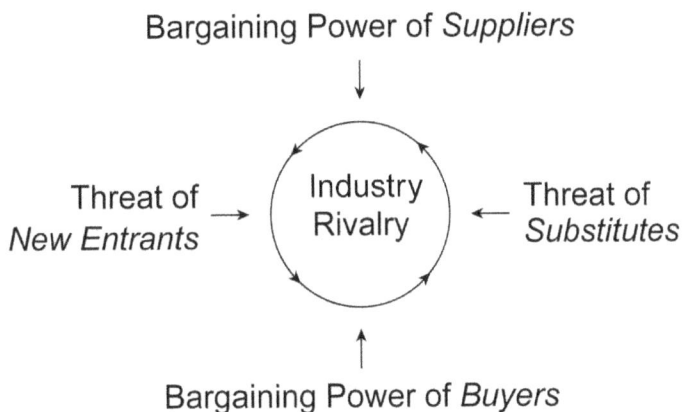

Bargaining Power of *Suppliers*

Threat of *New Entrants* → Industry Rivalry ← Threat of *Substitutes*

Bargaining Power of *Buyers*

Figure 1.1: Illustration of Porter's Five Forces, Wikipedia (`https://en.wikipedia.org/ wiki/Porter%27s_five_forces_analysis`*)*

By understanding how AI is changing each of these forces, we can gain a clearer picture of how AI is reshaping competitive landscapes across industries, and the potential to drive you (or even better, your competitors) out of business.

Force 1: Threat of new entrants

When it comes to the threat of new entrants, AI is a double-edged sword. On the one hand, the widespread availability of powerful AI services like GPT-4 and open source alternatives has lowered the barrier to entry for new players. Startups can now develop sophisticated AI solutions in a matter of weeks that would have been beyond imagination just a few years ago, allowing them to compete with more established companies on a more level playing field.

However, the successful application of AI often requires more than just access to the right tools. In many industries, the real value of AI comes from the combination of high-quality, proprietary data and skilled personnel who can turn that data into valuable insights and products. This is particularly true in many B2B sectors like healthcare, finance, and advanced manufacturing, where the data is often sensitive, regulated, or technically complex.

For new entrants in these industries, acquiring the necessary data and talent can be a significant challenge. Established players often have a head start in data collection and may have exclusive access to certain data streams. They also tend to have deeper pockets for hiring scarce AI talent. As a result, while AI has lowered some barriers to entry, it has heightened others.

Force 2: Threat of substitutes

In some industries, AI is not just enabling new competitors but also entirely new categories of substitutes. This is particularly evident in the creative industries, where AI-generated content is starting to compete with human-created work. From AI-written articles and scripts to AI-generated images and videos, the range of creative tasks that AI can handle is expanding rapidly.

We're seeing a similar trend in the service sector, where AI-powered chatbots and virtual assistants are augmenting workflows previously done exclusively by human workers. These AI agents can handle customer inquiries, provide recommendations, and even complete transactions, often at a fraction of the cost of their human counterparts.

This trend is likely to have a particularly significant impact on intermediaries across a range of industries. Whether it's travel agents, insurance brokers, real estate agents, or even agency business models that don't connect buyers and sellers but talent and clients, all are at risk of being disrupted by entirely new AI solutions. If your company currently occupies one of these middleman positions, you're in a market at a high risk of AI disruption.

Force 3: Bargaining power of suppliers

The impact of AI on supplier power can be significant when a company gains a monopoly-like position in a critical AI service. Consider a startup, for example, that develops an AI-powered system for optimizing supply chain logistics. By leveraging proprietary data from multiple industries, top AI talent, and custom algorithms, this company could offer a service that dramatically outperforms traditional logistics optimization. As more businesses realize the efficiency gains from this AI service, the startup quickly becomes the dominant player in the market, increasing their advantage through the continuous feedback loop. They have exclusive access to the data, talent, and technology that makes their offering so compelling, creating a high barrier to entry for potential competitors. With this level of market power, the AI logistics company has significant control over pricing. They can charge premium rates, knowing that customers have few alternatives that can match their level of performance. If customers can't absorb these high costs without eroding their own competitiveness, their profit margins will suffer. This dynamic gives the AI provider a great deal of bargaining power, potentially allowing them to capture a large portion of the value they create.

And if you now think that this sounds like a fantasy, then consider the story of Celonis, one of Germany's most valuable AI startups. Celonis has achieved rapid growth and a high valuation by providing AI-powered process mining services that help companies optimize their operations.

As AI becomes central to competition across industries, managing the bargaining power of AI service providers will be a critical strategic challenge.

Force 4: Bargaining power of buyers

Let's shift our focus from suppliers to buyers. In the B2C space, we've already seen how tools like comparison websites can empower consumers by helping them easily find the best deals on everything from insurance to hotels.

AI has the potential to bring a similar level of transparency to the more complex world of B2B transactions. By analyzing vast amounts of data on different vendors and their offerings, AI tools could help businesses quickly identify the best suppliers for their needs, at the optimal price point.

This could significantly disrupt traditional procurement processes, which often involve lengthy RFP cycles and manual comparisons of different vendors. With AI, these processes could be largely automated, with the AI system analyzing hundreds of potential suppliers and their nuanced offerings to recommend the optimal choice - giving buyers the ability to compare even more vendors and thus effectively secure better deals and streamline their purchasing processes. It also means that suppliers will need to work harder to differentiate their offerings beyond just price and basic feature sets.

Force 5: Rivalry among existing competitors

The impact of AI on rivalry among existing competitors is perhaps the most profound and multifaceted of all the five forces. AI is fundamentally reshaping the nature of competition in many industries, leading to a new era of AI-driven business strategy.

On one level, AI is enabling companies to achieve unprecedented levels of operational efficiency and customer understanding. This is putting pressure on all players in a market to adopt AI or risk being left behind.

However, the competitive advantages of AI often accrue disproportionately to the companies that understand best how to leverage AI to its fullest and how to avoid the biggest pitfalls - which often includes access to the best data and talent. This is leading to a widening gap between AI leaders and laggards in many industries. The AI frontrunners are able to continually improve their offerings and customer relationships, making it harder for rivals to catch up.

At the same time, the high costs and complexities of AI are driving many companies to seek out partnerships and collaborations, even with traditional competitors. We're seeing this in industries like automotive (with companies collaborating on autonomous driving technology) and healthcare (with rival firms sharing data to improve patient outcomes). These collaborations allow companies to share the risks and rewards of AI development.

The result is a complex and dynamic competitive landscape where companies must balance the imperatives of AI-driven competition (rapid innovation, proprietary data and algorithms, and top AI talent) with the potential benefits of AI-driven collaboration (shared costs and risks, larger datasets, and combined expertise). Navigating this landscape requires a nuanced understanding of the specific competitive dynamics in each industry and market - as well as a thorough understanding of where AI can give them the greatest competitive edge, where they may need to partner with others, and how they can build the internal capabilities and external relationships to succeed in an AI-driven world.

Hence, building a sound AI strategy is very important. It's not just about adopting AI tools or hiring AI talent; it's also about developing a comprehensive roadmap that leverages AI to reshape your company's value proposition, operational model, and competitive positioning.

The AI advantage: A new force

Given its impact on the existing forces we've seen in the preceding section, it's reasonable to call out AI as a new force in itself. The ability to effectively leverage AI is becoming a critical determinant of competitive advantage, cutting across all other forces - the AI advantage. This is the essence of the AI revolution.

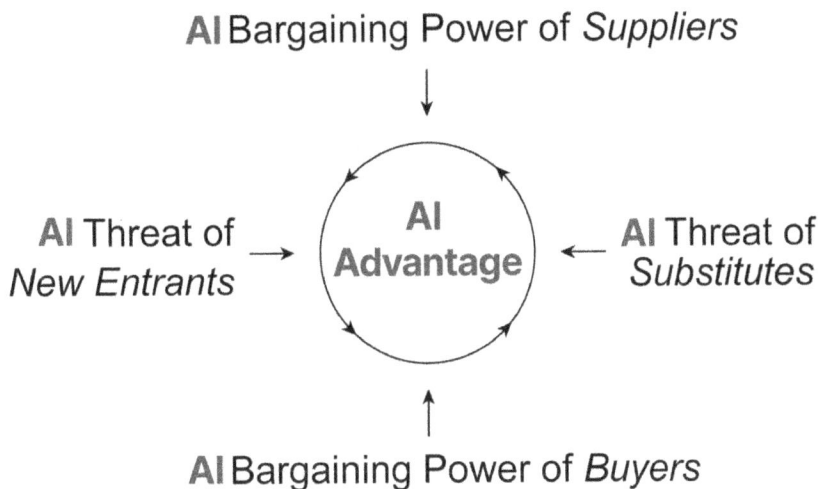

AI Bargaining Power of *Suppliers*

AI Threat of *New Entrants* → AI Advantage ← AI Threat of *Substitutes*

AI Bargaining Power of *Buyers*

Figure 1.2: AI as a new force enabling the AI revolution

Companies must now consider their AI advantage as a core part of their strategic positioning, making sure to remain or regain competitiveness in their respective markets. Instead of waiting for a big bang and big tech to figure it out, this means building the technical and non-technical readiness over time to effectively leverage the opportunities that new AI technology will bring. PwC estimates that AI will add $15 trillion to the world's economy by 2030. To put that into perspective, that's another EU entering the world map of economic output.

AI can improve your bottom line through cost savings, higher quality, faster processes, and new opportunities to scale. It reduces expenses and waste, increases margins and customer loyalty, accelerates decision-making and transactions, and enables growth that was previously out of reach. The real power lies in combining these effects to generate exponential results. We'll explore each in depth and show how to translate them into measurable business impact.

To be crystal clear: this is a transformation. AI is not just another technological advancement; it's a fundamental shift that's reshaping our world.

We've seen transformations before. You might have heard *transformation* so often before that it now sounds like just another buzzword. But it's not.

So far, the world has seen three major industrial transformations, each driven by disruptive technology:

- Steam power in the 1760s.
- Electricity and mass production in the early 1900s.
- Computerization in the late 20th century.

Today, we're in the fourth industrial revolution, driven by AI.

The AI transformation is not just about optimizing processes and cutting costs; it's rewriting the rules of work. And if you're not preparing for it, you're already falling behind. But preparing for AI doesn't mean firing your workforce and replacing them with robots. It doesn't mean investing millions in infrastructure and praying for ROI.

In fact, the key to thriving in the age of AI is to double down on your people, empower them, and put them in the lead.

Use AI to:

- Give your sales team the insights they need to close more deals, faster.
- Equip your marketers with the predictive skills to craft campaigns that convert like crazy.
- Supercharge your customer service with the ability to anticipate needs and exceed expectations.

You can achieve all this without hiring an armada of data scientists and locking them in a room for two years. As we will find out throughout this book, augmenting existing workflows with AI is an ideal strategy to enter this space and build your very own AI advantage, unique to your business.

Summary

The AI revolution is not the sudden, seismic shift that was promised. It's a more gradual, uneven process of technological diffusion and organizational adaptation. And it's less about robotic overlords and flashy demonstrations of tech giants but in the everyday operational trenches of businesses across all industries. As Moderna's CIO Brad Miller says:

> *90% of companies want to do GenAI, but only 10% of them are successful, and the reason they fail is because they haven't built the mechanisms of actually transforming the workforce to adopt new technology and new capabilities.*

The potential of AI is immense, and we've only just begun to scratch the surface. But to realize this potential, we need to move beyond the hype and set realistic expectations. Most importantly, it means recognizing that the AI revolution is not just about technology. It's about people - the people who develop and deploy AI systems, and the people whose lives and work are impacted by them. That's where the real AI revolution is happening-not in the labs of Silicon Valley, but in the everyday decisions and actions of businesses like yours.

Future business success will depend on your ability to understand the AI-driven changes in your industry, develop robust AI strategies, and effectively implement AI solutions, starting with augmenting the right workflows. While the pace of change may vary, the long-term impact of AI on competitive dynamics is profound and far-reaching.

In the next chapter, we'll explore how you can approach this revolution from the right angle.

Unlock this book's exclusive benefits now

UNLOCK NOW

Scan this QR code or go to `https://packtpub.com/unlock`, then search for this book by name.

Note: Keep your purchase invoice ready before you start.

2

Understanding Modern AI

Before we explore modern AI, let's briefly look back in history to a time way before AI was even a topic. It's 1891 and the electrical revolution is in full swing. The Edison General Electric Company was mandated to install the very first electrical power lines in the White House. The wires are buried in plaster, with convenient round switches in each room for turning lights on and off. However, they remain largely unused. As it turned out, then President Benjamin Harrison and his family were too scared to even touch them, fearing a shock from the invisible power in the wires. As a result, they left it to their staff to operate the switches. Irwin "Ike" Hoover, an electrician who later was promoted to White House chief usher, recalls in his book, (https://www.amazon.com/Forty-Two-42-Years-White-House/dp/B001RHWC7Y), *"I would turn on the lights in the halls and parlors in the evening and they would burn until I returned the next morning to extinguish them."*

Today, we can see something very similar happening with AI. While large IT consulting companies report record-breaking profits selling *AI expertise* to hesitant businesses, executives keep AI at arm's length, afraid to truly dive in and understand it. As a result, enterprise AI adoption is left shallow, and its potential is widely untapped.

You don't need to become an AI engineer, similar to how not everyone needs to become an electrician to keep the lights on at night. But if you solely rely on external knowledge without ever diving deeper into some of the fundamentals, you'll never be able to operate the switches alone and thus will have to sit in the dark with kerosene lamps or pay fortunes for white-glove services.

A core goal of this book is to empower you to identify and leverage profitable AI opportunities by yourself without heavy reliance on external consultants. That's why this chapter is so critical because it lays the basis for understanding what AI actually is and what fundamental mechanisms power it, so you can understand its capabilities and limitations.

We'll explore the following topics in this chapter:

- Understanding the building blocks of AI: Terminology
- Working with the AI Skills framework and the five AI modes for business
- Understanding LLMs

Feel free to skim this chapter if you're already familiar with AI concepts. However, I still recommend reading the section on the five AI modes for business, as it lays the foundation for the rest of the content. It will set the basis for the rest of the book to come. Otherwise, let's start with some terminology.

Understanding the building blocks of AI: Terminology

Like the electrical revolution of the 1890s, the AI revolution comes with its own set of terms and concepts that might seem daunting at first. But don't panic - understanding these terms is your first step toward confidently *operating the switches* of AI in your business.

To start off, let's swallow a hard pill of truth: AI terminology is confusing, even for seasoned experts in the field. To be honest, no one has really figured it out and everyone has their own set of vocabulary. This confusion in terminology stems from three main factors:

- The complex and evolving nature of AI technology.
- The multiple perspectives of AI practitioners.
- The use of different terms and jargon across specific industries, fields, and organizations.

The latter one is especially important. You might hear different interpretations of the same term depending on whether you're talking to a researcher, a data scientist, or a business executive. This variability is something we need to accept. Remember, the goal isn't to become a stickler for terminology but to grasp the concepts and ideas these terms represent. Think of it as learning a new language - the nuances may vary, but the core meaning remains.

Now, let's build a framework for understanding AI, starting from the broadest concept and narrowing it down to specific applications.

We'll use the following, widely accepted representation of critical AI terms and their hierarchy (*Figure 2.1*):

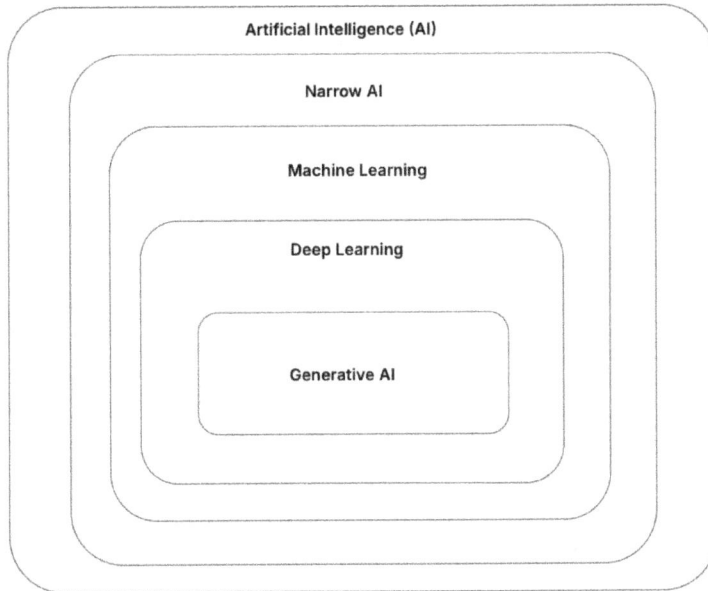

Figure 2.1: AI terminology in a nutshell

At the highest level, we have **Artificial Intelligence (AI)**. This term has become a catch-all for systems or machines that exhibit *intelligent* behavior. When we say *intelligent* in this context, we're referring to the ability to perform cognitively complex tasks such as learning, problem-solving, and decision-making, which is quite a broad field.

The concept of AI isn't new. It dates back to the 1950s, with roots in military research. You might have heard of Alan Turing - his work laid the foundation for what we now call AI. Since then, AI has evolved and expanded, finding applications across numerous industries.

Within the broad field of AI, two main research areas have emerged: Strong AI and Narrow AI.

Strong AI, also known as **Artificial General Intelligence (AGI)**, is the more ambitious of the two. It aims to create systems that can match or even surpass human intelligence in all aspects. Imagine a machine that could solve any problem a human can - and then some. This is the realm of science fiction staples such as sentient robots or omniscient computer systems. However, despite decades of research, Strong AI remains a distant goal. Many researchers debate whether it's even achievable.

On the other hand, **Narrow AI** is what we encounter in our day-to-day lives, and that powers every practical business AI application today. These are task-specific systems designed for particular jobs. When you use a language translation app or your phone recognizes your face to unlock, you're interacting with Narrow AI. Unlike Strong AI, Narrow AI doesn't aim to replicate human intelligence entirely. Instead, it focuses on performing specific tasks efficiently.

In the business world, when we talk about AI applications, we're almost always referring to Narrow AI. These are the systems that are transforming industries today, from finance to healthcare to manufacturing. That's why we will now shift our focus toward Narrow AI approaches - AI technologies that can be applied in the real world, today.

How do these Narrow AI systems actually work? There are two main approaches to creating *intelligent* systems. The first is based on pre-programmed rules for decision-making, often called **rule-based systems.** These systems don't learn from data; they simply follow the rules they've been given. Often, they are also called **expert systems** because experts define the rules.

The second approach, **machine learning (ML),** is what's driving most of the AI advancements we see today.

Let's explore ML a bit more.

Machine learning

ML systems learn from data, identifying patterns and making decisions with minimal human intervention. Think of it as teaching a computer to recognize cats not by telling it, *Cats have pointy ears and whiskers,* but by showing it thousands of cat pictures and letting it figure out the patterns on its own.

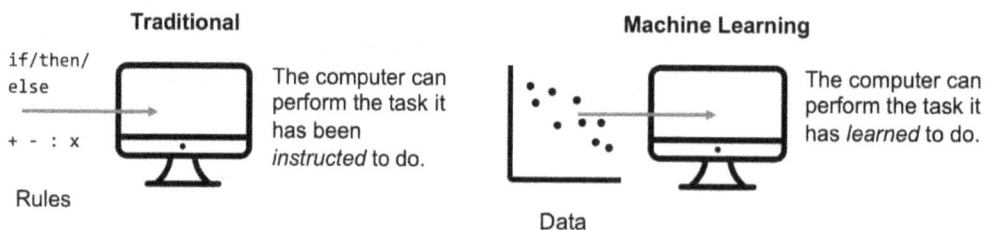

Figure 2.2: Traditional programming versus ML

It's important to note that despite its capabilities, ML doesn't imply self-awareness or emotion. When you hear about ML, don't picture a sentient computer with feelings. Instead, think of it as a highly sophisticated pattern recognition system. It's essentially a statistical approach to automated data analysis.

The core concepts behind ML power most modern AI applications today. For decades, companies have applied ML - especially on structured tabular data - to run predictive algorithms such as linear regression or decision trees at scale. Common use cases include demand forecasting, fraud detection, and customer churn prediction.

However, not all data is tabular - in fact, the majority of data generated today is unstructured or semi-structured, such as text, images, or documents. Traditional ML algorithms often struggle with such data types, as they typically require manual feature extraction and domain-specific engineering.

This is where **deep learning** (DL), a subfield of ML, comes into play.

Deep learning

You can imagine DL as a fancy subset of ML. While *non-deep*, sometimes also called *shallow ML,* it can be applied on relatively small datasets that would even fit into a tabular Excel spreadsheet. True *deep learning* typically requires more complex and larger data structures such as text, images, or audio data.

To give you a rough idea, consider a 5-megapixel colored image, something that you take with your smartphone every day, would be represented as a table. That table would have 5,000,000 rows and 3 columns - a total of 15,000,000 data points for a single image. If you have a dataset of 1,000 images, which is considered quite small in the DL space, you can do the math.

It's a lot of data.

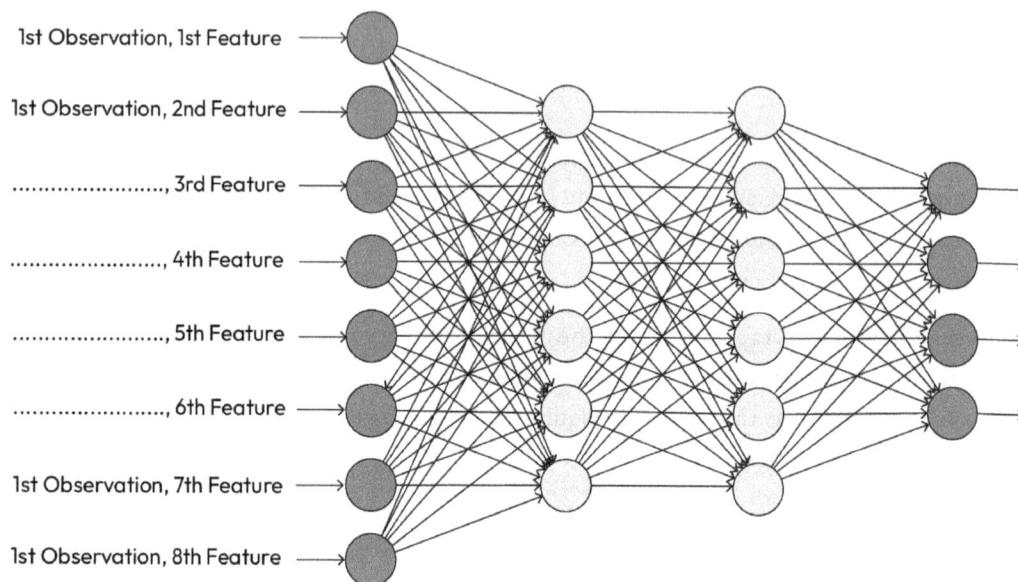

Figure 2.3: Example architecture of an artificial neural network (AI in a Nutshell: A Practical Guide to Key Terminology (`https://blog.tobiaszwingmann.com/p/demystifying-ai-practical-guide-key-terminology`*))*

For these large and complex data structures, an ML architecture called **artificial neural networks (ANNs)** with many layers proved to be quite effective (see *Figure 2.3* for a visual representation). And because these ANNs tend to have many layers (the black dots between the input layer on the left and the output layer on the right), we consider them *deep* - hence the term *deep learning*.

While these neural networks were inspired by the human brain, their actual operation is quite different from biological processes. They're essentially very complex mathematical models designed for pattern recognition.

DL has been behind many of the most impressive AI achievements in recent years, from beating world champions at complex games to generating human-like text and creating realistic images from descriptions.

Next up, we will talk about **generative AI (GenAI)**, which has changed the way an end user uses AI in their day-to-day activities.

Generative AI

GenAI is a subfield of DL - and one you've probably already encountered, whether you realized it or not. If you've ever asked ChatGPT to write an email, played with a tool that turns doodles into photos, or seen an AI-generated image pop up in your feed, you've seen GenAI in action.

The core idea behind GenAI is simple but powerful: instead of just *analyzing* data, these systems *generate* new data. Their narrow task is to generate or modify original content - be it text, images, video, or audio-based on the patterns they've learned from vast datasets. Importantly, they do this *without* truly understanding the content in the way humans do. There is no conscious mind, no common sense, and no real-world grounding. What these systems excel at is spotting statistical patterns and leveraging them to produce output that *looks* smart, creative, or even insightful. But don't let that lack of *understanding* fool you - GenAI is incredibly capable. In fact, the lack of understanding is often what makes these systems so flexible and scalable.

At the center of today's GenAI boom are **Large Language Models (LLMs)**. These are models trained to generate human-like text from prompts. They operate on a staggering number of parameters-GPT-4, for instance, uses hundreds of billions of them - to predict what words (or even entire paragraphs) are likely to come next in a sequence. The result is often coherent, fluent, and contextually appropriate text that feels as though it were written by a human. For curious readers, we have a special technical deep-dive section on how LLMs work toward the end of this chapter.

You've probably heard of ChatGPT - arguably the poster child of modern GenAI. It's brought the power of LLMs to the public in a user-friendly way, allowing anyone to generate emails, brainstorm ideas, write poetry, debug code, or summarize long documents in seconds. But it's far from alone. There are now dozens of LLMs and generative systems on the market, both from commercial providers such as Anthropic or Grok, or open source models such as Meta's Llama series or the models from DeepSeek.

One of the most exciting recent developments in GenAI is the rise of **multimodal models**. Unlike traditional LLMs that only work with text, these new systems are trained on multiple types of input-text, images, audio, and even video. That means they can understand and respond across different media. For instance, you can show a multimodal model a photo and ask it to write a story about what it sees, or give it a chart and have it explain the data in plain English. More impressively, we now have true multimodal systems that can natively generate images from text or from other images-without needing to go through a text-only step.

This kind of direct input-to-output mapping across modalities marks a significant leap in model capabilities and opens up entirely new creative and analytical possibilities.

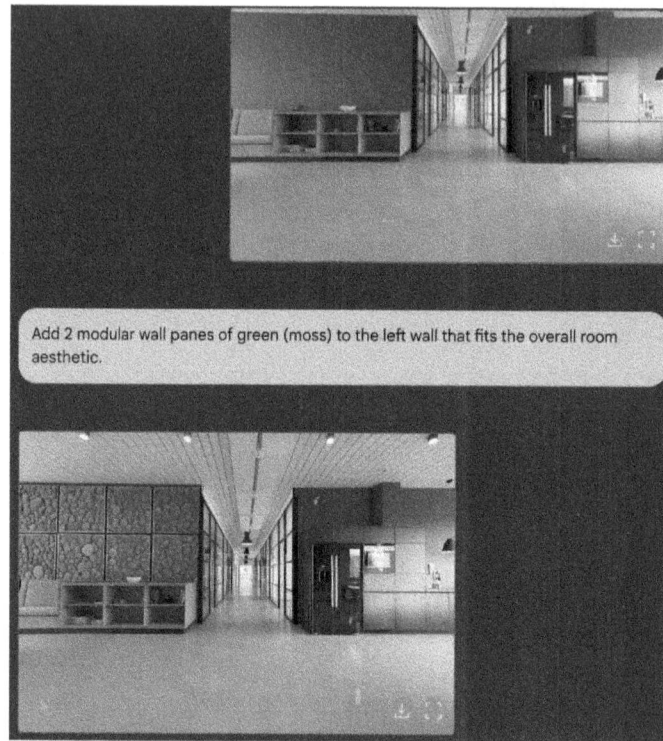

Figure 2.4: Google's Gemini creating a new image based on native image and text input

Just like the early days of electricity, we're still figuring out how best to use these tools. But one thing is clear: GenAI isn't just a trend - it's a foundational shift in how content is created and consumed. And it's only getting started.

But unlike flicking on a light switch, it's easy to get carried away by the sheer novelty and power of GenAI. With so much buzz, so many demos, and a new breakthrough seemingly every week, the harder question often becomes: *How can I actually use this in my business in a meaningful way?*

In my work with clients, I've found that approaching AI from a purely technical perspective rarely leads to actionable outcomes. Instead, the real breakthroughs come when we flip the lens: not *what can the tech do* but *what new business-relevant skills and capabilities does it unlock?* That shift - from tools to capabilities - is where AI starts to make practical sense.

That's why I developed a simple but powerful framework that I call **AI Skills**. It breaks down the noisy, fast-moving world of AI into five practical modes of value creation that every business leader can grasp and act on today.

Let's take a closer look at them.

Working with the AI Skills framework and the five AI modes for business

To cut through the noise and make AI practically usable, we need a new lens. Not a technical one but a *business-relevant* one.

Instead of trying to memorize every algorithm, vendor, or acronym, a better question is: *What can this technology actually do for me?* More specifically, *What capabilities does it unlock for my team, my product, or my operation?*

To make this shift easier, I'm using the **AI Skills framework** with my clients around the world - a simple but powerful way to categorize the business-relevant skills that AI tools can provide.

For this, I've broken down modern AI into five core modes, based on the types of business skills these systems enable. These are practical capabilities that leaders and teams can apply today, regardless of industry or technical background. Each mode reflects a different way that AI adds value in real business contexts.

Here's a quick overview:

- **Prediction mode**: AI that anticipates what's next by using past data to forecast trends, estimate outcomes, model scenarios, and predict what's going to happen next.
- **Perception mode**: AI that senses the world-capable of seeing, hearing, reading, and extracting information from unstructured sources such as images, documents, and audio streams.
- **Creation mode**: AI that produces content - code, designs, text, visuals, or music. It's about speed, scale, and lowering the barrier between an idea and a working output.
- **Thinking mode**: AI that reasons, connects, summarizes, or personalizes based on context. It brings insight and intelligence to complex or ambiguous tasks.
- **Agentic mode**: AI that acts. These systems send messages, trigger workflows, carry out tasks, and adapt dynamically - autonomously pushing things forward.

Each of these modes includes a range of skill types that mirror things people already do at work every day - and that AI can help do things faster, better, cheaper, or at scale.

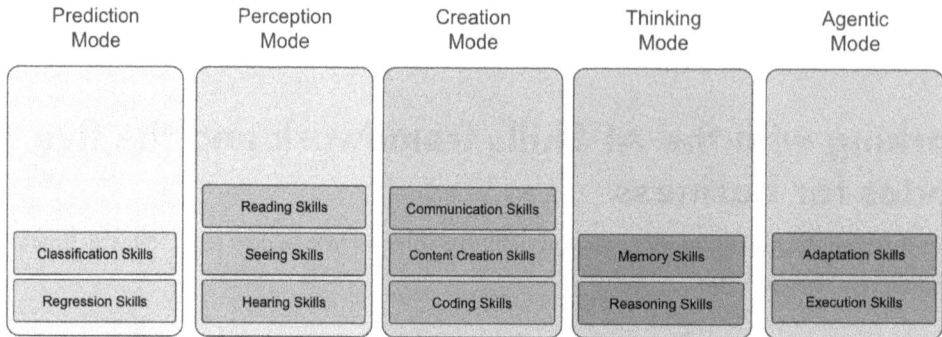

Prediction Mode	Perception Mode	Creation Mode	Thinking Mode	Agentic Mode
	Reading Skills	Communication Skills		
Classification Skills	Seeing Skills	Content Creation Skills	Memory Skills	Adaptation Skills
Regression Skills	Hearing Skills	Coding Skills	Reasoning Skills	Execution Skills

Figure 2.5: Five AI modes for business overview

In the sections that follow, I'll walk you through each of these five modes. I'll highlight the kinds of tasks they can support, the technologies that power them - such as ML, DL, or GenAI - and what kinds of tools or approaches are typically used.

You don't need to learn the math behind a neural network. But by the end of this chapter, you'll be able to recognize the key AI capabilities that align with your business goals and understand how to translate them into practical action.

Let's start with the first mode: *Prediction*.

Prediction mode of AI

Prediction is one of the oldest and most proven use cases in modern AI - and still one of the most valuable. This mode is all about *anticipating, categorizing,* and *making sense of complexity* using data. You've likely seen this in action without realizing it: when Netflix recommends a show, when a bank detects fraud, or when a warehouse restocks inventory just in time. Prediction mode is the quiet engine behind it all. It doesn't always make headlines but it often drives the clearest ROI.

> For the rest of this chapter, we will use the term *skill(s)* to refer to a skill that AI can perform.

Prediction mode includes three key types of AI skill sets:

- **Regression skills**: These systems forecast future values or outcomes based on historical data. Think of them as the AI equivalent of estimating, projecting, or scoring - whether it's next month's sales or the risk profile of a loan applicant.

- **Classification skills:** These skills sort, label, group, and match information. They help structure messy inputs, such as assigning categories to documents or tagging emails by urgency.

Together, these skills help businesses, structure and score reality in ways that scale far beyond manual effort.

What powers these skills?

Most of the prediction mode is powered by traditional machine learning techniques, leveraging statistical algorithms like linear regression, decision trees, or clustering methods for structured, tabular data. Tools like XGBoost, Facebook Prophet, and automated ML platforms such as Azure AutoML are commonly used here.

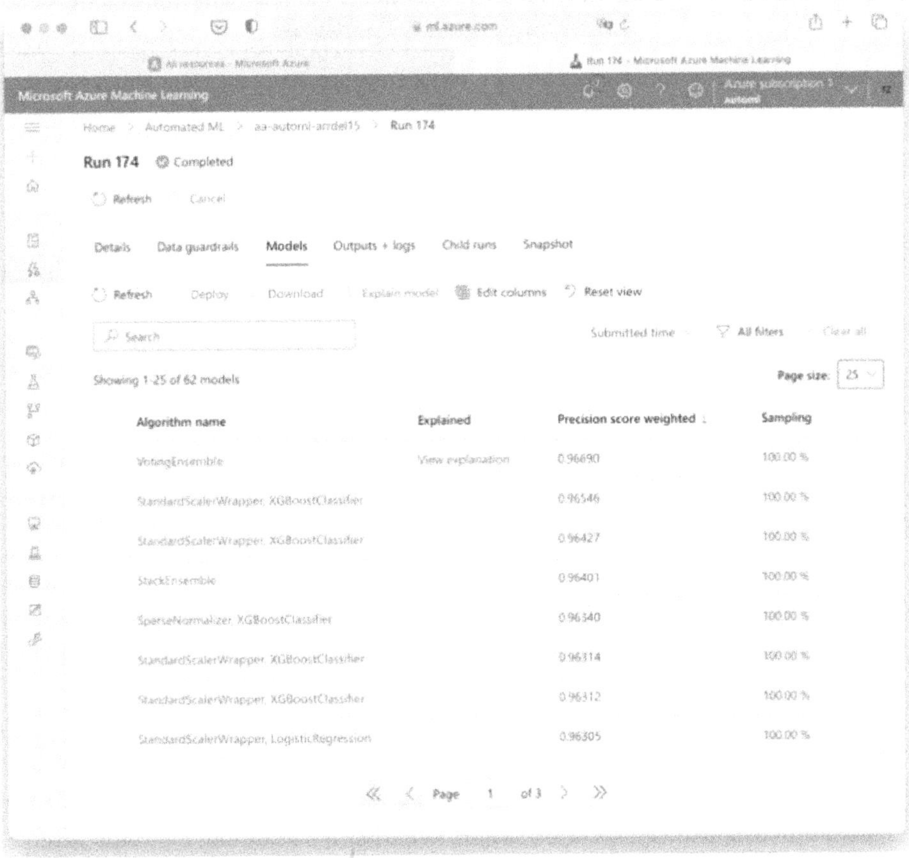

Figure 2.6: Screenshot of Microsoft Azure AutoML comparing 62 machine learning models to identify the best one for a flight delay prediction task

However, GenAI, and particularly LLMs, can also play a role in this mode, especially when dealing with unstructured or text-based inputs. For example, LLMs can classify emails as spam or not, detect sentiment in reviews, or map country codes from messy, open - text address fields. In these scenarios, generative models act more like advanced classifiers, helping structure data rather than generate original content.

Where it shows up in the business?

For these kinds of image or audio analyses, platforms such as Google Cloud Vision, Azure Document AI, or OpenAI Whisper (for speech) come into play. Even ChatGPT could be used for this.

While many modern platforms offer pre-built models or no-code interfaces - allowing business teams to get started with AI without needing an armada of data scientists - many prediction scenarios require you to train your own models from scratch, or at least fine-tune models based on your own data. There are several business use cases for the Prediction mode with it being deeply embedded across business functions. Here are some common use cases you will come across:

- **Marketing** uses it to score leads, forecast campaign performance, and group customers by behavior.
- **Finance** applies it for risk modeling, fraud detection, and demand forecasting.
- **Customer support** teams rely on it to prioritize tickets, match queries to help content, and detect patterns in support volume.
- **Operations** use it to estimate inventory needs, detect anomalies, and automate quality checks.

We will now talk about the world of perception. In this mode, AI moves beyond clean, tabular data.

Perception mode of AI

While Prediction mode helps make sense of structured data, Perception mode allows AI to interpret the *unstructured* world – especially through reading, seeing, and hearing. This mode expands the reach of artificial intelligence to formats that were once accessible only to humans: documents, images, speech, and beyond.

Think of Perception mode as giving AI the ability to understand sensory input. This is where machines start to *perceive* the world in a human-like way - processing real-world signals and turning them into usable business information. Whether it's scanning a receipt, interpreting a voice memo, or extracting data from a PDF, Perception mode is the foundation for unlocking insight from raw inputs.

Core skill categories in Perception mode

Perception mode includes three core categories of AI skills:

- **Reading skills**: These capabilities allow AI to process and interpret written or printed language, especially in unstructured formats like scanned documents, PDFs, handwritten notes, or long - form text. **Optical character recognition (OCR)**, layout detection, and document parsing fall under this category.

- **Seeing skills**: These visual perception skills help AI systems interpret images, videos, diagrams, or even physical environments. From detecting defects in a manufacturing line to classifying products in a photo, recognizing a face or understanding complex layouts in PDFs – these skills give AI visual understanding.

- **Hearing skills**: These systems convert and analyze audio inputs – like transcribing spoken language, identifying speakers, or detecting emotion and tone. Or just recognizing your favorite song. Hearing skills unlock vast potential from audio data.

Together, these skills enable AI to *sense* reality, bringing previously inaccessible formats into the realm of structured processing and decision-making.

What powers these skills?

Perception mode is increasingly powered by deep learning techniques, particularly **convolutional neural networks (CNNs)** for vision and **transformer models** for language and audio. Unlike shallow machine learning, these models excel in handling complex, high-dimensional inputs like pixels or waveforms. But also GenAI has led to huge breakthroughs here. Transformer - based architectures, like those behind OpenAI Whisper or GPT-4o, enable AI to *read*, *see*, or *hear* with contextual awareness across modalities.

Modern AI platforms often abstract this complexity through user-friendly tools and APIs - so even non-technical teams can tap into perception capabilities without needing to train models from scratch.

Where it shows up in the business?

Perception mode is widely used across industries:

- **Operations** use it to inspect product quality, monitor safety via cameras, or extract text from invoices and shipping labels.

- **Customer experience** teams use it to transcribe and analyze support calls, or classify incoming documents automatically.

- **Legal and compliance** use it to read contracts, extract clauses, or detect anomalies in scanned agreements.

- **Healthcare** applies it to analyze X - rays, digitize handwritten notes, or interpret patient voice inputs.

By giving AI the ability to read, see, and hear, Perception mode turns the analog world into digital fuel - enabling deeper insight and greater automation in contexts that were once entirely manual.

Next, let's step into the world of the Creation mode. In this mode, AI stops analyzing and starts building.

Creation mode of AI

If Prediction mode and Perception mode help you understand what *is* or what *might be*, Creation mode is where AI begins to *build*. This is where content is generated, ideas come to life, and execution gets dramatically faster - with machines taking on creative and technical tasks that once required expert human hands. If you've ever asked ChatGPT to write an email, used Copilot to create a social image, or seen a tool turn a prompt into working code, you've touched Creation mode in action.

Creation mode includes three core categories of AI skills:

- **Programming skills**: AI can generate, explain, debug, or convert code based on simple language prompts. These skills bridge the gap between idea and implementation - especially for non-technical users or lean teams.

- **Content creation skills**: These are generative capabilities that produce original outputs - text, images, video, audio, or even interactive designs. The results aren't just templated, often generated completely from scratch or with a light reference direction.

- **Communication skills**: AI can write, reply, translate, explain, or carry on conversations with natural fluency, allowing businesses to streamline internal workflows and customer - facing communication alike.

Together, these skills give individuals and teams the power to create more, faster, with less overhead and often less skill-specific bottlenecking.

What powers these skills?

Most of the Creation mode is powered by GenAI systems designed to produce new original content rather than just regurgitate existing data. This includes models such as the following:

- **LLMs** such as GPT-4 or Claude, which generate human-like text from prompts.
- **Diffusion models** such as Midjourney or Flux, which generate original images from textual input.
- **Multimodal models** that can generate or transform content across text, image, audio, and even video formats such as GPT-4o or Google's Gemini.

On the technical side, Creation mode builds on the architecture of deep neural networks - especially transformer models and convolutional networks. But from the user's perspective, most tools are now *incredibly accessible*. Many use drag-and-drop interfaces or prompt-based inputs, requiring no technical skill at all.

Where it shows up in the business?

Creation mode is rapidly reshaping creative, technical, and communication workflows. Here is how various businesses harness the power of the Creation mode AI:

- **Marketing** teams use it to generate campaign copy, visuals, and video assets.
- **Product and design** teams use it to build mockups, pitch decks, and documentation.
- **Sales** teams use it to write outreach emails, follow-ups, and value propositions at scale.
- **Engineering** teams use it to speed up prototyping, code conversion, and bug resolution.
- **Customer experience** teams use it to draft replies, translate messages, or explain product features in plain language.

AI in Creation mode augments the work of creative professionals, dramatically increasing their speed and reducing the lift of first drafts, repetitive edits, or simple production tasks.

Next, we'll move into a more cognitive space. Let's explore how AI can *think, reason*, and *interpret*.

Thinking mode of AI

Some business problems can't be solved by guessing what token comes next - they require *reasoning*, *interpreting*, and *connecting the dots*. That's what the Thinking mode is for. This mode becomes especially powerful in situations where the answer isn't obvious, or when information needs to be extracted, transformed, or interpreted before any action can be taken.

Think of tasks such as summarizing a 40-page research report, mapping product features to customer pain points, or deciding how to route a support ticket based on multiple variables. These aren't just content problems - they're *thinking* problems.

Thinking mode includes two key skill areas:

- **Reasoning skills:** These systems analyze, connect, interpret, summarize, and make decisions based on data or unstructured input. They're ideal for synthesis, insight generation, and intelligent prioritization.

- **Memory skills:** These capabilities allow AI to access and apply stored information - whether from its own training, a knowledge base, or recent interactions. They improve response accuracy, personalization, and contextual relevance.

These skills let AI operate more as an analytical partner - not just responding to prompts, but allowing them to *think* through them by leveraging internal or external information.

What powers these skills?

Under the hood, Thinking mode is still powered by LLMs, but with an important twist: many of the frontier AI models used here, such as, GPT-5 and later models, Gemini, or Claude - let you spend extra compute at inference time to favor accuracy over speed. This is often marketed as **reasoning** or **thinking** features; the exact mechanisms and ways to influence this process vary by provider.

This slower, more deliberate approach is designed for tasks where simple text completion would fall short. For example, proving a mathematical theorem, interpreting legal language, or maybe even just counting the number of *r*s in *strawberry*. These tasks require stepwise logic, not just fluency.

Because of this, reasoning models may take longer - sometimes several minutes - to generate a response. But they're built to shine in situations where accuracy, depth, or complexity matter more than fast response generation.

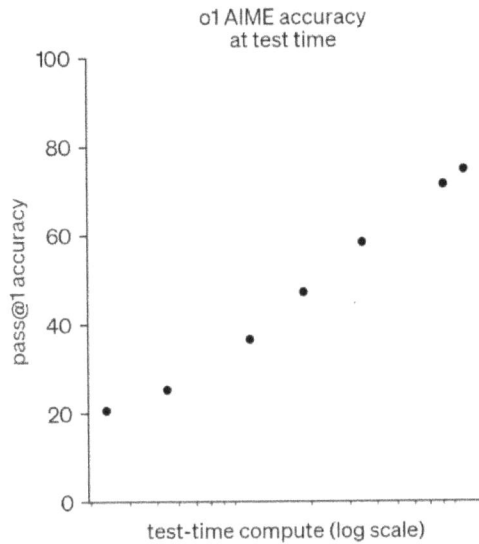

Figure 2.7: Improving accuracy with longer test-time compute ("thinking time"). Source: https:// openai.com/index/learning-to-reason-with-llms

You'll also hear terms such as **retrieval-augmented generation (RAG)** used in this mode, where the model pulls in relevant documents or data at runtime.

🔍**Quick tip**: Need to see a high - resolution version of this image? Open this book in the next - gen Packt Reader or view it in the PDF/ePub copy.

📖**The next - gen Packt Reader** is included for free with the purchase of this book. Scan the QR code OR go to `https://packtpub.com/unlock`, then use the search bar to find this book by name. Double - check the edition shown to make sure you get the right one.

The high-level RAG architecture is shown in *Figure 2.8*:

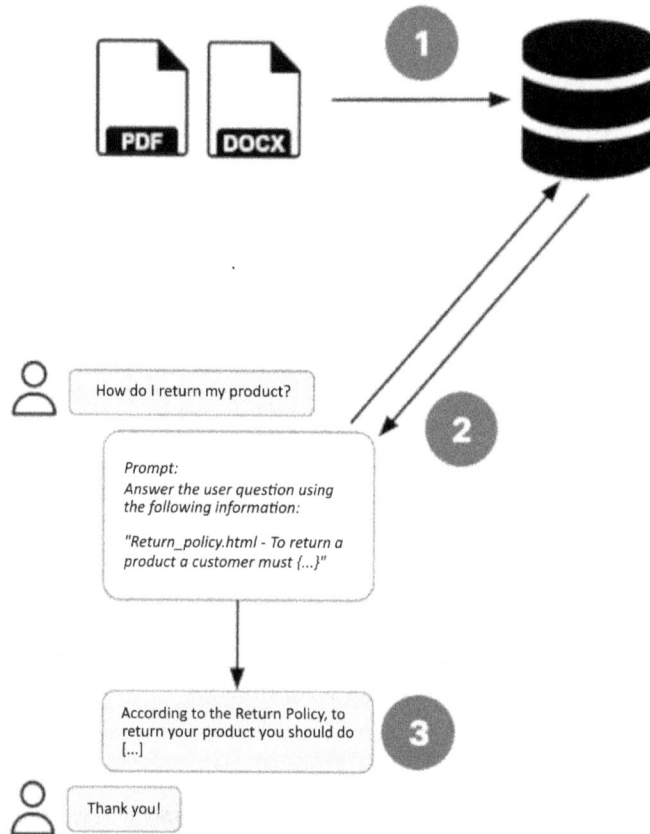

Figure 2.8: High-level RAG architecture

In simple words, RAG works as follows:

1. A collection of documents is stored in a searchable database - typically a vector store that encodes the semantic meaning of the content into numerical representations.

2. When a user asks a question, the system searches this database in real time to identify the most relevant pieces of information and injects them into the prompt alongside the user's query.

3. This augmented prompt is then passed to the language model, enabling it to generate a response that is grounded in the retrieved content.

4. The result is a more accurate, context-aware answer that reflects the most current and domain-specific knowledge.

This way, RAG is able to ground LLM responses. By **grounding** its responses in external data rather than relying solely on pre-trained knowledge, RAG systems can significantly reduce hallucinations and enhance the reliability of AI - generated outputs.

Where it shows up in the business?

Thinking mode has huge potential for knowledge-heavy, insight-driven tasks:

- **Customer experience** teams use it to interpret customer feedback or decide next-best actions.
- **Product and strategy** teams use it to map insights or prioritize features based on complex criteria.
- **Legal, compliance, and HR** teams use it to extract relevant clauses, interpret documents, or align policies across departments.
- **Analysts and researchers** use it to generate structured summaries, draw conclusions, or synthesize open-ended survey responses.

Thinking mode doesn't replace human insight but it accelerates how quickly teams can get to it, especially when navigating complexity.

> **Note**
>
> These modes aren't mutually exclusive - they're often combined in real-world AI solutions. For instance, Thinking mode can be paired with Creation mode to generate high-quality, structured output based on complex reasoning. You might use a non - reasoning model such as GPT-4o-mini to quickly draft documentation for a function, or bring in a reasoning-capable model such as Grok - 3 to refactor an entire codebase intelligently. The combination of depth (Thinking) and output (Creation) is where many advanced business use cases come to life. You'll learn more about how to combine these skills to design your own solution concepts later in this book.

With all these modes combined - Prediction, Perception, Creation, and Thinking - modern AI systems already become incredibly powerful. But modern AI capabilities don't end here.

Let's take a look at the Agentic mode of AI.

Agentic mode of AI

Most AI systems today are reactive - they analyze, generate, or explain but only if they get instructed to do so. But what if AI could act? Agentic mode is where AI shifts from being a passive assistant to an active operator. In this mode, AI systems don't just produce outputs - they take actions, trigger workflows, and coordinate tasks across tools, systems, and environments.

Agentic mode includes two main categories of skills:

- **Execution skills:** These are the operational arms of AI. They send messages, trigger processes, execute tasks, and orchestrate multi-step flows across systems, allowing AI systems to interact with the real world and collect feedback.

- **Adaptation skills:** These skills allow AI to evolve its behavior over time based on feedback, performance data, or environmental changes with just minimal human intervention.

These capabilities move AI from a tool you *ask* to one that proactively *does* - based on derived logic, triggers, or learned behavior.

What powers these skills?

Agentic mode is enabled by a combination of technologies:

- **LLMs** act as the reasoning layer, interpreting intent and making dynamic decisions.

- **Function calling frameworks** (such as OpenAI Functions or LangChain) let AI trigger actions or external tools.

- **Workflow automation platforms** (such as Zapier, N8N, or custom APIs) handle task execution.

- **Autonomous agents and orchestration frameworks** (such as LangGraph or CrewAI) manage longer, multi - step tasks with memory and feedback loops.

- **Reinforcement learning and feedback-based systems** support adaptation, allowing agents to learn from performance and evolve over time.

While execution skills are already accessible via low - code platforms, adaptation skills are more advanced, often requiring deeper integration, monitoring, and guardrails.

A quick reality check

Agentic mode is by far the most complex and technically demanding of all five AI modes. While the idea of a self-running AI agent sounds like the ultimate solution, it's rarely a good starting point. These systems require careful configuration, monitoring, and often deep customization to work reliably in production.

Throughout this book, you'll learn how to scale your AI journey - from low to high automation - in a way that's realistic and sustainable. For now, just remember: Agentic AI might sound like the answer to every problem, but the reality often lands very differently.

Where it shows up in the business?

Agentic mode is still emerging - but it's already changing how work gets done:

- **Sales and marketing** teams use it to send follow-ups, auto-generate reports, and update CRMs without lifting a finger.
- **Support and success** teams use it to resolve customer tickets, escalate issues, and adapt knowledge-based responses over time.
- **Cross-functional teams** use agents to orchestrate multi-system handoffs, coordinate deliverables, or drive end-to-end processes automatically.

Agentic mode is where AI kind of *comes alive* - bridging insight and action to drive real outcomes on autopilot.

These five AI modes - Prediction, Perception, Creation, Thinking, and Agentic - together with the underlying AI skill categories will be your guardrails when mapping AI opportunities and designing AI solution concepts along with this book. To make it easy for you to access these modes, I've created a spreadsheet you can keep close and use any time you want: `https://github.com/PacktPublishing/The-Profitable-AI-Advantage/blob/main/ch02/AI_Skills.xlsx`.

Before we wrap up this chapter, let's dive a little deeper into how LLMs work. LLMs are now an integral part of modern AI, hence it is essential to briefly touch upon how they function. You can skip this section if you know how LLMs function.

Understanding LLMs

I know this isn't supposed to be a super technical book, but since LLMs can be found at so many interaction points with modern AI systems and are often used across all the five AI modes, it's worth understanding how they work at a high level so you don't fall for the most common pitfalls. LLMs can be a lot like those magicians you see on stage. If you don't know how their *trick* works, you might easily overestimate their capabilities. Of course, they can't make a real coffee table fly, but the illusion is perfect. So, let's take a look behind the curtain.

At their core, LLMs, such as the ones used in ChatGPT, perform one primary task: they predict the next word (or more precisely, a token, which can be just a part of one word, but we'll talk about words to keep it simple) in a sequence based on the context they've been given. This seemingly simple mechanism powers everything from casual conversation to deep strategic insights.

Consider this example: you enter the phrase The sky is into an LLM. Behind the scenes, the model assigns probabilities to possible next words: *blue* might be highly probable, while *usually* or *the* would score much lower. You can see this example in *Figure 2.9*:

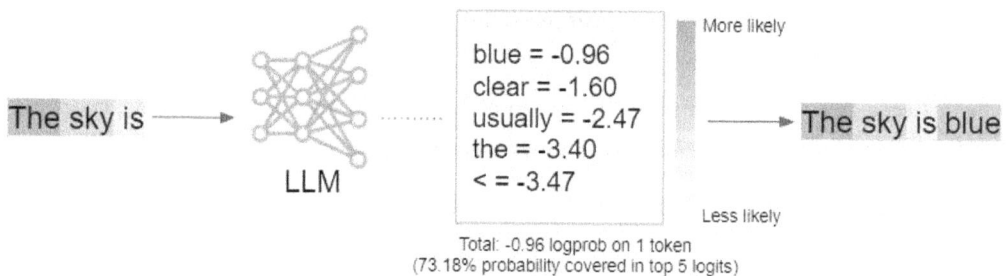

Figure 2.9: Illustration of how an LLM works. Source: Annie Surla/NVIDIA blog at https:// developer.nvidia.com/blog/how-to-get-better-outputs-from-your-large- language-model/

So the LLM doesn't really *know* that the sky is blue - it's simply inferring that based on having seen that phrase frequently in its training data and learned the statistical patterns.

But how exactly does the AI know which word to predict?

A pivotal moment came in 2017 with Google's *Attention is All You Need* paper (`https://en.wikipedia.org/wiki/Attention_Is_All_You_Need`). This introduced the concept of **attention mechanisms** - an approach that helps models decide which parts of a sentence to *focus* on to predict the next word more accurately. This way, the input `The sky is` will likely return `blue`, but the input sequence `The sky is not always` might instead yield `clear` or `predictable`, because the model is now attending to the word *not* as well. In essence, attention enables the model to weigh the importance of each word in context, rather than treating all preceding words equally. This approach, known as attention, is now a core component that still underpins all modern LLMs.

You might wave this off as a technical detail, but understanding the power and limitation of this attention mechanism is crucial when working with LLMs. If you clearly explain what you want to an LLM, you'll get a better response. On the other hand, one tiny misplaced character in the instruction might lead the model to return entirely different outputs. This is why the instructions you give an LLM - called **prompts** - are so important. Crafting strong prompts is not just a technical trick; it's a practical skill that unlocks better results.

A common misconception is that LLMs *get better* the more you use them. In truth, they **start from scratch with each session**, unless fine-tuned or explicitly designed to remember context (e.g., via custom solutions or memory-enabled setups such as personalization in ChatGPT).

So, improving LLM performance ad hoc is less about *training the model* and more about adapting your inputs - a skill known as **prompt engineering**.

To immediately get better outputs, you must adapt to the LLM, not the other way around!

Let's walk through an example to see how the LLM *thinks*.

Suppose you prompt the model with something like this:

```
What are the best practices in digital marketing?
```

Internally, the LLM begins by generating a probability distribution over the next possible words:

Some likely continuations might include words such as *It*, *The*, or *Typically*. The model chooses the next token based on a probability distribution - which means that if you run the same input multiple times, you might get the same response or a different one. It all depends on how probable each option is and how the model samples from that distribution.

This built-in randomness is intentional. It allows for variation and creativity in the output, rather than just repeating the same phrasing or parroting the training data. This is what makes LLMs *generative* - they're not simply retrieving answers, they're creating responses word by word based on probabilities.

Figure 2.10: LLM considering several possible completions

Let's say the model picks the word *The*.

Hence, after sampling one completion, the LLM will add it to the input context, as follows:

```
What are the best practices in digital marketing? The
```

The model then predicts the next word based on this updated context.

And it continues from there, one word at a time. The key point is that once a word is selected, it becomes locked into the sequence. There's no going back. No built-in revision.

The model is now forced to compute the following probability distribution given that the word *The* is observed at the end of the input sequence:

Figure 2.11: LLM adding completion to input prompt and continuing completion process (second word)

This process continues, and the LLM produces the output sentence word by word (or technically, token by token):

```
What are the best practices in digital marketing? The most effective
```

And so on...

```
What are the best practices in digital marketing? The most effective
practice
```

And so forth...

```
What are the best practices in digital marketing? The most effective
practice is
```

Until

```
What are the best practices in digital marketing? The most effective
practice is ads.
```

The model decides whether the prediction is complete or reaches the maximum number of tokens to predict. You see this behavior when ChatGPT *types* its response in real time. That's essentially how LLMs work. **Next word prediction**. You can observe this behavior in ChatGPT.

This is also why tools such as ChatGPT can find their own mistakes when asked to double-check their output.

For instance, you might see in the preceding example that the model *decided* the best digital marketing practice was *ads*. An *unlucky* sampling of the word *practice* instead of *practices* has limited the model to suggest only one *best practice* instead of multiple ones. As LLMs generate their output, they can only look forward, not backward. To *review* their work, you must explicitly ask them, and they'll likely catch their errors (although that's not guaranteed).

There's a secret sauce that makes this whole process work so well, generating astonishing results that stretch the definition of *fancy autocomplete*. To understand it, let's look at an LLM that has just completed training on a large corpus of data (e.g., the internet, a whole library of books, and more). This is what AI people call a **base model** or **foundation model**.

If you gave this base model two questions, it would return a third question, because it's trained to predict/repeat the input sequence pattern.

What are the best practices in digital marketing?

What are the best practices in classical marketing?

What are the best practices in outdoor marketing?

Figure 2.12: Text completion by base model

The first GPT models up to GPT-3 worked this way. But that's not very useful. When we ask an LLM two questions, we want two (ideally correct) answers. So, OpenAI researchers came up with a trick. They took a smaller dataset of question-answer pairs and used it to fine-tune their base model. Instead of giving another question, it would give an answer. On top of that, to improve the answers, they hired people to manually vote on the best response. As a result, OpenAI generated an ***instruction-tuned*** model - an LLM that does not just autocomplete but actually follows instructions. So, if we ask two questions, we get two answers:

What are the best practices in digital marketing?
What are the best practices in classical marketing?

Use data-driven strategies, SEO, and personalized content.
Focus on brand consistency, audience research, and clear messaging.

Figure 2.13: Text completion after instruction fine - tuning

That was the breakthrough moment for ChatGPT. It worked so well that people often forgot they were interacting with an AI doing next-word prediction. This is where the magic happened - and where many people got the wrong idea about AI systems. Because ChatGPT follows instructions so well and behaves confidently, you might think it knows what it's doing. In practice, this can lead to disappointment and pitfalls. ChatGPT or any other LLM-based chatbot doesn't really *know* anything. It has no self-awareness or consciousness. This is super critical to remember. So, instead, you should think of the model as *dumb*, but at the same time incredibly useful when applied to the right things.

The bottom line: LLMs predict the next word in a sequence. Your main control over the output is the prompt. As you can see next, when we provide more context in addition to just asking for marketing best practices, ChatGPT's answer is adjusted to fit that context - which is both a powerful and also tricky concept to master:

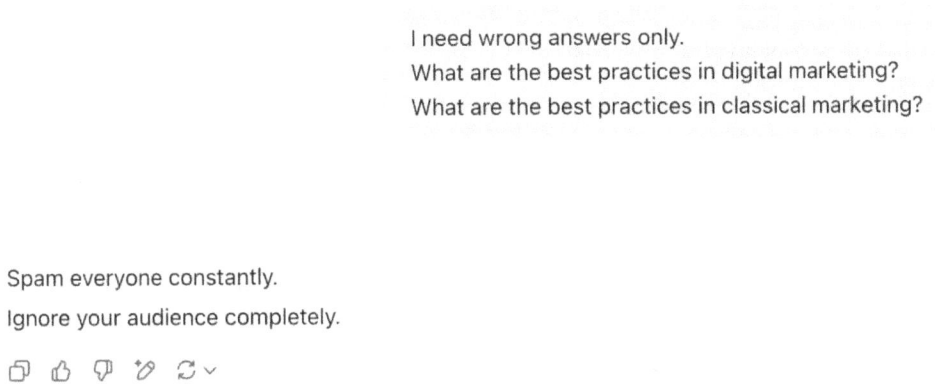

> I need wrong answers only.
> What are the best practices in digital marketing?
> What are the best practices in classical marketing?

Spam everyone constantly.

Ignore your audience completely.

Figure 2.14: Context (prompt) influencing LLM response

That's the essence of prompt engineering. Be very specific about what you want. The way to control the behavior of an LLM is to control the prompt you give it.

Summary

As we wrap up this chapter on understanding modern AI, one thing should be clear: this field is vast, fast-moving, and layered with complexity. From high-level ideas such as AI to practical tools such as GPT-5, each layer introduces new capabilities, and new challenges.

By understanding the five AI modes - Prediction, Perception, Creation, Thinking, and Agentic - you now have a practical framework to navigate this space. These modes reflect not just what the technology *is* but what it can *do* - and how those capabilities can translate into value for your business.

Remember, just as the POTUS once feared touching the light switch, it's normal to feel cautious with something new. But the goal here isn't to become an AI engineer, it's to become confident flipping the right switches inside your own organization.

In the next chapter, we'll shift from understanding to application. You'll learn how to spot and design AI-powered solutions that match your business context-without getting lost in the technical weeds.

Unlock this book's exclusive benefits now

Scan this QR code or go to `https://packtpub.com/unlock`, then search for this book by name.

Note: Keep your purchase invoice ready before you start.

3

Approaches to Successful AI Adoption

Most companies I work with struggle to grasp what successful AI adoption truly looks like. They often fall into one of two camps. First, there are the idealist types who dream of AI robots doing all the work, so they can finally spend their days sipping margaritas on the beach. On the flip side, you have those who view AI as this Matrix-like code that goes over their heads - something to be completely handled by their IT department, hoping that *the experts* know what they are doing. However, both views are flawed and will not bring you closer to your goal of succeeding with AI.

To get answers for successful AI adoption, business leaders and IT professionals alike often turn to the inventors of modern AI, big tech companies from Silicon Valley. *"They invented this tech, so they must know how to use it"* is the general thinking here. But as we will learn, copying the AI playbooks of Silicon Valley is a sure recipe for disaster for most *normal* businesses.

This chapter unpacks why the answer for successful AI adoption does not lie in the Bay Area, and where you need to look instead to find AI strategies that are aligned to your organizational context.

In fact, there are four different methods that I'm going to introduce that I've found work very effectively across many industries and businesses, regardless of size. They are backed up by real-world success. This chapter will give you a solid foundation to kick off your own AI journey successfully.

Let's start!

In this chapter, we will cover the following main topics:

- The pitfall of imitating big tech
- AI divide and conquer approach
- AI moonshot approach
- Product led AI approach
- Opportunistic AI approach
- Finding your AI approach: Where you are, where you want to go, and why it matters

The pitfall of imitating big tech

There's a strange and persistent phenomenon in the business world where companies - especially those with high legacy and low tech - often try to imitate the practices of comparably young, high-tech companies such as Google, Meta, or Amazon. Now, this trend isn't new and also is not constrained to AI. Take **Objectives and Key Results (OKRs)**, for example. OKRs are a goal-setting framework pioneered by Google to help aim for big goals while remaining agile and flexible. Many organizations jumped on the OKR train, assuming that what worked for Google would also work for them. However, they often found that this framework didn't align with their operational realities, so they were left disappointed by what this technique could deliver. Often, the only professionals that really benefited from this were consultants selling OKR training.

AI is now being swamped by the same broken logic. Many companies worldwide are under the impression that if they simply mimic the AI strategies that worked for the companies that are at the forefront of modern AI innovation - big tech - they too will achieve AI success. However, what most fail to realize is that these tech giants are playing an entirely different game.

Think about it: does your company have $40 billion to spend on AI R&D, like Meta? Can you afford to allocate $3 billion to experimental technologies, as Amazon does? Does your organization hold over 24,000 patents and give core technology away free of charge, like Google? The reality is, these are moves that only a tiny fraction of companies - perhaps 0.0001% - can make. But it doesn't mean the rest of us are far away from achieving AI success. The key is to play your own game. Take the tools and technologies developed by these giants and adapt them to suit your specific needs and capabilities.

To find what works for you, you don't have to start from scratch. Over the years, I've identified four distinct *AI approaches* that your company can take - especially if you are a normal business operating outside the tech bubble. These strategies have been successfully adopted by various companies across different industries and sizes, proving that there is more than one way to win with AI.

Let's explore these approaches and discover what success looks like in each category.

AI divide and conquer approach

The **AI divide and conquer** approach is often used by companies seeking to leverage AI on a large scale in industries that are very likely to be disrupted by AI. These are particularly data - and knowledge-intensive industries such as finance, insurance, legal, biotech, and pharma, but also functions such as marketing, sales, and customer service. These fields deal with vast amounts of data and rely heavily on information for decision-making, making them ideal candidates for AI transformation.

Inspired by the ancient Roman military strategy, the business world's AI divide and conquer approach involves managing the AI transformation of a large organization by breaking it down into smaller, more manageable components that exhibit a high degree of self-control under clearly defined guardrails. This strategy allows different units within the organization to pursue their own AI initiatives independently while adhering to a common, overarching goal.

Spreading AI adoption broadly with multiple smaller projects prevents the *boil the ocean* problem, where companies become paralyzed by the sheer size of a monolithic AI initiative. Many enterprises commonly follow this approach in managing their wider digital transformations, typically led by a central hub, often an **AI Center of Excellence (AICoE)**.

Take a look at *Figure 3.1*. The AICoE coordinates efforts but allows flexibility and innovation at the departmental level without wielding ultimate directive authority over the various business units.

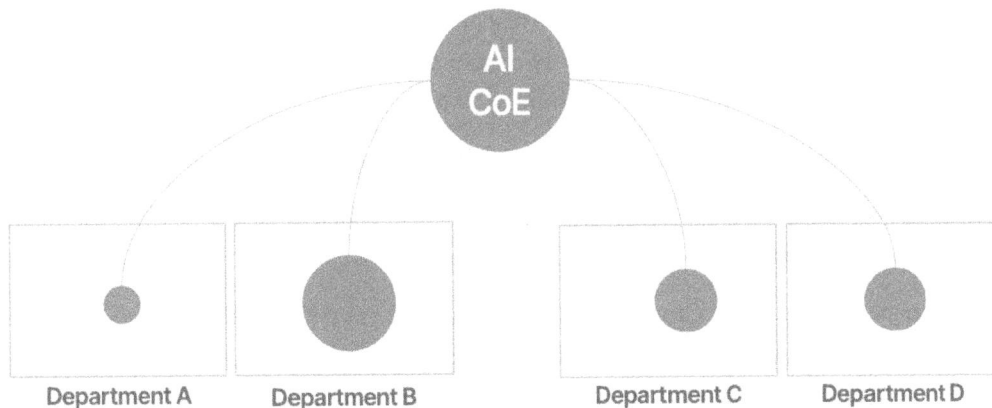

Figure 3.1: AI divide and conquer approach

If you carefully observe this image, the AI projects have different sizes based on the requirements of each department. For instance, Department B may have several use cases for AI while Department A may have fewer use cases that can be driven by AI. This approach thus allows for adopting AI based on requirements as smaller, more manageable projects.

Let's talk about how this approach can be applied in an organization.

In practice, the AI divide and conquer approach requires empowering different departments or units within the organization to operate independently while maintaining alignment with a common AI-driven goal. This often starts with creating a comprehensive backlog of AI use cases - sometimes numbering in the hundreds - that each department can prioritize and pursue according to their specific needs and capabilities. These use cases might range from automating routine administrative tasks in HR to deploying advanced predictive analytics in the marketing department.

The AICoE plays a crucial role in this process. It not only curates and prioritizes these use cases but also provides the necessary support in terms of resources, expertise, and best practices. This ensures that while each department has the freedom to innovate, their efforts remain aligned with the broader organizational strategy. The AICoE might organize regular cross-departmental meetings, workshops, or hackathons to share insights, foster collaboration, and ensure that the AI projects are moving in a direction that benefits the company as a whole.

As these AI projects roll out, their cumulative effect can be transformative. Individually, each project might seem modest, but collectively, they can drive significant improvements in efficiency, innovation, and overall organizational performance. By engaging employees at all levels in these projects, the organization fosters a culture of continuous learning and improvement, upskilling its workforce and preparing them for the future of work.

There are several advantages and disadvantages of this approach. Let's talk about them.

The divide and conquer approach to incorporate AI independently across verticals and teams offers several benefits:

- **Organizational-wide enablement:** Enabling different teams within an organization to experiment with AI can foster innovation from the ground up, finding new cost savings and capabilities that may not be discovered otherwise.
- **Higher employee engagement:** Engaging in AI projects can drive motivation among the workforce by showing them how their work is impacted, and ideally improved, by AI.

- **Scalability and adaptation:** Since each department is working on smaller, manageable projects, there is less risk of large-scale failure, making it easier to pivot or iterate on strategies as needed. Projects can be tackled in parallel, which further accelerates AI adoption.

But this approach comes with some limitations too:

- **Alignment challenges:** Ensuring that all departments are moving toward the same overall AI strategy can be challenging. Without careful coordination, there's a risk of departments working in silos, leading to a fragmented approach that dilutes the impact of AI initiatives.
- **Measuring impact:** Quantifying the overall impact of numerous small projects is tough. While individual projects might yield measurable results, aggregating these to understand the full value of AI adoption can be complex.
- **Budget constraints:** Because there's no overarching business case, the projects generally need to be funded from existing departmental budgets, which may limit their scope. Departments might prioritize short-term gains over long-term innovation if they're restricted by budget constraints.
- **Inconsistent data practices:** As different departments or units work independently on their AI projects, there can be inconsistencies in how data is collected, processed, and analyzed. Without a standardized approach to data management, these inconsistencies can lead to data silos, where valuable information is not shared across the organization. This can hinder the ability to derive comprehensive insights, reduce the overall effectiveness of AI initiatives, and make it difficult to maintain a unified data strategy that could ultimately unlock higher value AI use cases.

Let's move our focus on to how Moderna successfully used the AI divide and conquer approach across its different functions.

Case study: Moderna

Biotech innovator Moderna exemplifies the *AI divide and conquer* approach by strategically integrating AI across various functions within the company. From legal and R&D to manufacturing and commercial operations, AI tools have been embedded into the daily workflows of over 80% of Moderna's workforce.

At the core of this transformation is Moderna's internal AI platform, *mChat*, a proprietary instance of ChatGPT built using OpenAI's API. Initially launched in early 2023, mChat sparked a cultural shift toward AI adoption, leading to the rollout of ChatGPT Enterprise across the organization. This enterprise-grade implementation includes capabilities such as advanced data analytics, image generation, and custom GPTs tailored to department-specific needs.

Moderna reported to have deployed over 750 purpose-built GPTs that act as digital assistants, supporting employees in tasks ranging from summarizing contracts to evaluating clinical trial data. For example, in the R&D department, the Dose ID GPT analyzes thousands of pages of clinical data to recommend optimal vaccine doses. It not only provides rationale and visualizations but also allows researchers to converse with the model to explore findings from multiple angles, which significantly accelerates data-driven decision-making in drug development.

Quite surprisingly, the legal department was the first to fully adopt AI, achieving a 100% usage rate early on. Tools such as Contract Companion GPT allow legal teams to upload contracts, generate summaries, and query specific clauses, freeing up time for higher-impact legal strategy work. This early adoption created internal momentum and trust in AI, which likely contributed to the smooth scaling of these tools across other departments.

In manufacturing, AI enhances precision and efficiency, enabling rapid scaling during high-demand periods, such as the COVID-19 pandemic. Commercial teams also benefit from AI-driven insights and automation that boost productivity.

Moderna's success with AI offers several actionable takeaways:

1. **Start with a strong data foundation**: Moderna was already a digital-first, machine learning-native company, which made AI integration more seamless.

2. **Invest in internal tooling**: Rather than waiting for one-size-fits-all solutions, Moderna built mChat in-house and developed hundreds of tailored GPTs for different functions.

3. **Focus on workforce transformation, not just tools**: Moderna didn't just install software but redesigned workflows and trained employees to work *with* AI, treating it as an extension of their capabilities.

4. **Lead with high-ROI departments**: Early adoption by the legal team demonstrated clear value and helped build organizational momentum for wider rollout.

5. **Use AI to scale without bloating the workforce**: Moderna aims to launch 15 products in 5 years with fewer than 6,000 employees - something that is only feasible through automation and augmentation via AI.

Using this strategic divide and conquer approach, Moderna has not only improved internal productivity but also strengthened its ability to scale impact in healthcare, providing a great case study to learn from.

The next approach we will discuss is the **AI moonshot** approach, which, instead of transforming the organization widely, aims to build a central core AI solution for extremely high business impact.

AI moonshot approach

The AI moonshot strategy is all about honing in on a single, transformative AI project that has the potential to revolutionize not just a company's operations, but also its entire industry. This strategy stands in stark contrast to the *AI divide and conquer* approach, which disperses efforts across multiple smaller projects. Here, the company channels its resources, talent, and focus into one high-impact initiative - a moonshot project that could redefine the company's market position and set new standards within its industry.

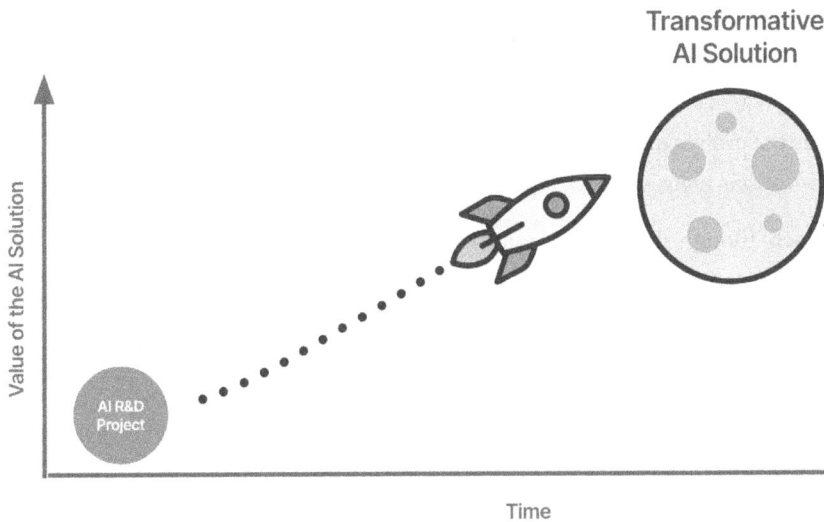

Figure 3.2: AI moonshot approach

Usually, in the moonshot approach, the product keeps on evolving over time to reach complete transformation with AI (see *Figure 3.2*). But what exactly qualifies as an AI moonshot? It's more than just a successful application of AI; it's a project that has the ability to fundamentally change the way the company operates or delivers value to its customers, thereby changing or expanding its core business model. Imagine a call center that builds an autonomous voice bot that answers incoming customer queries in more than 10 languages, 24/7, always with the latest information, and at a fraction of the cost of human-staffed call centers. This would disrupt an entire offshoring industry. Or imagine an online university that provides 1:1 learning experiences in all subjects, tailored to each student for optimal learning performance. These are use cases that, if done right, would not just *improve* business but turn it on its head.

Let's see how this approach can be implemented in practice.

Implementing the AI moonshot strategy requires deep vertical integration within the organization and a level of commitment that goes beyond what is typical in most AI projects. Moonshot projects are typically centrally funded. The company must be prepared to allocate substantial resources - in terms of both capital and human talent - to ensure the success of this single initiative. This often involves significant investments in R&D, acquiring or developing cutting-edge technology, and possibly even bringing in external expertise to supplement internal capabilities.

The chosen AI use case becomes the centerpiece of the company's AI strategy, commanding continuous attention from top management. To ensure success, the organization may need to undergo structural changes, such as creating new roles or departments dedicated to the project or realigning existing teams to better support the initiative. Cross-departmental collaboration is also essential; while the project may be spearheaded by a specific team, it will likely require input and expertise from various areas of the company, including IT, operations, marketing, and legal.

A moonshot approach, though risky, comes with some benefits:

- **Industry leadership:** Successfully executing a killer AI use case can position a company as an unrivaled leader in its sector, and build a massive moat for the company, allowing it to capture much larger market shares.
- **Transformational impact:** The right AI use case can transform the company's operations, potentially opening up entirely new business models or revenue streams, and potentially creating completely new industry categories.

But there are quite a few limitations that you need to be aware of while adopting this approach:

- **High risk of failure:** Focusing on a single project carries inherent risks. If the project fails to deliver as expected, it could leave the company vulnerable, with significant sunk costs and missed opportunities.
- **High upfront investment:** This approach requires considerable investment in terms of capital, talent, and time. Smaller companies, or those with limited resources, might struggle to sustain the required level of commitment.
- **Sunk cost fallacy:** Because of the massive upfront investment needed and the long-term goal, it's always hard to say whether you just need to keep pushing or whether it's time to discontinue the project. The longer the project goes on, the higher the likelihood you will keep pushing, because of all the resources you have already invested in it.

- **Regulatory challenges**: Depending on the industry, the company might face significant regulatory hurdles. For example, in healthcare or finance, strict regulations around data privacy and security can complicate the development and deployment of AI solutions, especially when they touch new business areas.

- **Organizational resistance**: The focus on a single, transformative project can encounter resistance within the organization, especially if it requires significant changes to established workflows or threatens existing power structures.

A quintessential example of the AI moonshot strategy is Tesla's ambitious pursuit of autonomous driving, which we will discuss next.

Case study: Tesla

Tesla's focus on achieving full self-driving capability is not just a side project; it's central to the company's long-term vision of transforming from a traditional car manufacturer into a global leader in shared mobility services.

Tesla has invested heavily in AI research and development, including the creation of custom AI chips, the development of a massive dataset collected from millions of Tesla vehicles, and the hiring of top-tier AI talent. This initiative has required deep integration across the company's engineering, software, and hardware teams, as well as continuous investment in infrastructure to support the AI models that power autonomous driving features.

What makes Tesla's approach distinct is its vertical integration across the entire AI stack - a rare feat even among the most advanced tech companies. On the hardware side, Tesla designed its own *Full Self-Driving (FSD)* computer, equipped with custom neural network inference chips optimized specifically for real-time driving decisions. These chips process vast volumes of visual data directly on the vehicle, reducing latency and increasing safety.

Tesla also controls the data pipeline from end to end. Every Tesla vehicle on the road acts as a sensor hub, contributing to what may be the largest video dataset ever assembled for driving scenarios. With billions of miles driven and petabytes of real-world footage, Tesla has a massive training advantage. The company's auto-labeling systems use AI to annotate video data at scale, enabling rapid iteration on model training.

On the software side, Tesla has built its own AI training infrastructure, including its proprietary Dojo supercomputer, which is purpose-built for video-based neural network training. This allows Tesla to push the boundaries of vision-only autonomy, avoiding reliance on costly LiDAR and instead doubling down on foundational research in computer vision. For this, Tesla entertains an AI team that operates at a world-class level.

The potential rewards of this AI moonshot are enormous. While Tesla hasn't yet achieved full autonomous driving, the progress they've made over the past decade - going from 0 to SAE Level 2 by relying solely on AI to *look* at image data (computer vision) instead of equipping cars with specialized, expensive sensors - is remarkable. Successfully achieving full autonomy could open up new revenue streams for Tesla, such as autonomous ride-hailing services, and could significantly strengthen its market position by offering a feature that few competitors can match. However, the stakes are equally high - failure to achieve full autonomy within a reasonable timeframe could jeopardize Tesla's broader business model, especially as competitors advance their own autonomous driving technologies.

Tesla's journey illustrates the high-risk, high-reward nature of the AI moonshot strategy. It's a bold approach that, if successful, can redefine an industry - but it requires unwavering commitment, substantial resources, and a willingness to face significant challenges head-on.

Other organizations pursuing a breakthrough AI product can learn from Tesla's approach:

1. **Control the full stack:** Tesla didn't just rely on off-the-shelf solutions - it built its own chips, collected its own data, and developed its own training infrastructure. This tight integration gives the company unmatched flexibility and speed of innovation.

2. **Use scale to create data advantage:** With millions of cars on the road acting as data collectors, Tesla created a feedback loop where real-world performance constantly informs model improvements.

3. **Build for your specific use case:** Tesla's Dojo supercomputer and custom AI chips weren't designed for general-purpose AI - they're optimized for real-time, video-based perception, showing the value of bespoke infrastructure in a focused AI use case.

4. **Invest in foundational research:** Tesla has contributed novel computer vision techniques tailored to driving, giving it an edge not just in implementation but in the core science powering its models.

5. **Accept risk as part of the strategy:** Tesla is betting big on a single AI application that could define its future. This requires sustained investment and the resilience to weather delays, technical challenges, and regulatory hurdles.

Tesla's AI strategy underscores that sometimes, the biggest payoffs might not come from spreading AI broadly across every department, but from betting big on a singular, transformative use case and building everything needed to make it real.

Next up, we will talk about the **Product-led AI** approach.

Product-led AI approach

The Product-led AI strategy is centered around enhancing - not necessarily redefining - existing products with AI capabilities, thereby improving functionality, user experience, and overall value. This approach is particularly suited for companies that aim to maintain their core business model while remaining competitive in a crowded market. Instead of AI being the primary selling point, it is subtly integrated into products to augment their features and ensure they continue to meet and exceed customer expectations.

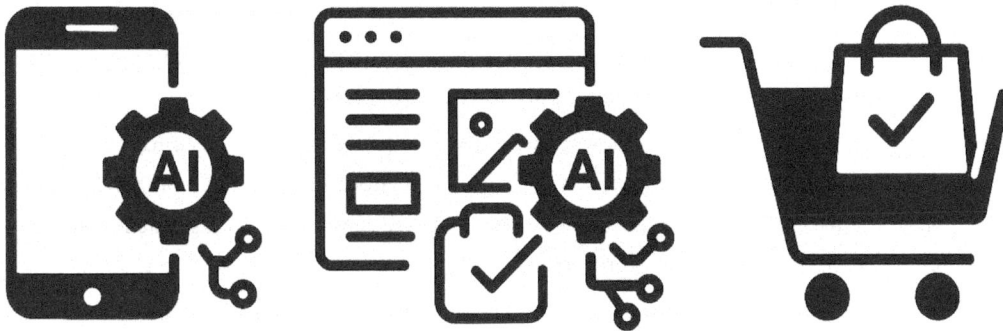

Figure 3.3: Product-led AI illustration

What sets the Product-led AI approach apart is its focus on incremental improvement rather than radical transformation. AI is used to fine-tune products, making them smarter, more intuitive, and more responsive to user needs. This strategy allows companies to leverage AI's potential without having to undergo a complete business model overhaul, which can be risky and resource-intensive.

Here is a primer on how you can bring the Product-led AI approach into practice.

For companies adopting a Product-led AI strategy, the goal is to integrate AI in a way that enhances the product without overshadowing its core value proposition. This typically involves embedding AI technologies into the product to add new features, improve performance, or provide a better user experience. For example, in the technology industry, AI could be used to improve software algorithms, enabling more personalized recommendations or faster processing times. In consumer products, AI could improve product usability through features such as speech recognition or automated adjustments based on user behavior.

A critical aspect of this approach is that AI itself is not the focus of marketing or customer engagement. Instead, the focus remains on the product and the benefits it provides. This requires close collaboration between product development teams, AI engineers, and marketing professionals to ensure that AI capabilities are seamlessly integrated and enhance the overall user experience.

In a Product-led AI strategy, AI ultimately becomes another means to the end of delivering a feature on the product backlog.

Let's take a look at some of the benefits of this approach:

- **Enhanced user experience**: By integrating AI into products, companies can offer new features and improved functionality, leading to a better user experience. This, in turn, can increase customer satisfaction and loyalty, as users find the product more valuable and easier to use.

- **Competitive differentiation**: In crowded markets, AI enhancements can help a product stand out from the competition. Even small improvements, such as faster response times or more accurate predictions, can be significant differentiators.

- **Incremental innovation**: This approach allows companies to innovate continuously without the need for drastic changes to their business model. By focusing on product-level improvements, companies can stay ahead of the curve without taking on the risks associated with large-scale transformations.

- **Low risk**: Since AI capabilities are rolled out as feature enhancements, there's typically less risk of expending massive resources without seeing anything in return. Features are typically scoped to allow for agile delivery, so AI development increments need to be small. This allows you to better control costs and monitor the ongoing process.

The Product-led AI approach comes with its own set of challenges, some of which are listed as follows:

- **Replicability**: Because AI improvements are often incremental, there is a risk that competitors will quickly replicate them, reducing the competitive advantage. Copycats could even deliver a better experience than first movers if they find a way to learn from the user experience of early adopters.

- **Less organizational learning**: Focusing on product-level AI integration may not lead to a broader organizational understanding of AI. This could limit the company's ability to scale AI solutions across the organization or explore more transformative AI opportunities in the future.

- **Missing out on big innovation**: If your product is leading the AI innovation, the scope for innovation is inherently limited by the scope of your product. This can lead to situations where you improve a product to perfection only to miss the bigger trend that makes your product obsolete (see, for example, computer manufacturers who missed the mobile boom).

- **Innovation pressure**: The reliance on continuous product improvement can put pressure on R&D teams to constantly innovate, focusing on short-term improvements and losing sight of long-term innovation.

Let's take a look at how the Product-led AI approach drives success in Apple.

Case study: Apple

Apple's subtle yet powerful integration of AI into its products exemplifies the Product-led AI strategy. While Apple rarely emphasizes AI in its marketing, the technology is deeply embedded in many of its offerings, enhancing both functionality and user experience.

Take *FaceID*, for instance. This facial recognition system, powered by advanced AI algorithms, has revolutionized the way users interact with their devices. It offers a seamless, secure, and highly intuitive method for unlocking phones, authorizing payments, and accessing sensitive information. By integrating this AI-driven feature into its devices, Apple has not only improved security but also enhanced convenience, reinforcing the brand's reputation for innovation and user-centric design.

Another example is the use of machine learning in Apple's camera systems. Thanks to AI, your smartphone can analyze and optimize every pixel in an image, producing photos that are sharper, more detailed, and more true to life. These enhancements are not marketed as AI features per se; instead, they are presented as part of the overall photography experience, which is a key selling point for Apple devices.

What distinguishes Apple's strategy is its *deeply embedded, vertically integrated AI architecture*, recently branded as *Apple Intelligence*. Rather than focusing on a single killer app or a department-wide rollout, Apple has chosen to let AI quietly elevate the core experiences of its flagship products - iPhone, iPad, and Mac - through features users rely on every day.

With the 2025 rollout of Apple Intelligence in iOS 18, iPadOS 18, and macOS Sequoia, Apple introduced a suite of generative AI capabilities designed to enhance language, image creation, personal context, and task automation. This includes tools like:

- Smart text processing, for writing, rewriting, and proofreading across apps.
- Clean Up in Photos, which removes unwanted elements from pictures.
- Notification summarization and mail categorization, using on-device models to streamline communication.
- Visual intelligence, which leverages the camera for object recognition, text translation, and context-aware actions.

Behind the scenes, this capability is powered by a highly integrated AI stack:

- **Apple silicon**: The M-series chips with dedicated Neural Engines are purpose-built to handle AI workloads efficiently and securely on-device.

- **On-device processing**: Most Apple Intelligence features run locally, preserving privacy without sacrificing speed.

- **Private cloud compute**: For more demanding tasks, Apple offloads data to encrypted servers - only when needed and only with user consent - ensuring privacy isn't compromised even at scale.

Apple also tailors AI features to the form factor and strengths of each device. On iPads, for example, new capabilities such as Math Notes and Smart Script in iPadOS 18 make handwriting more interactive and functional. Users can solve equations with Apple Pencil in real time or edit handwritten notes as fluidly as typed text.

Notably, Apple rarely markets these capabilities as *AI*, per se. Instead, they're seamlessly folded into the product narrative: intelligence that just works. This lets Apple focus on delighting users, rather than dazzling them with technical jargon.

Apple's approach offers clear lessons for companies looking to infuse AI into their product lines without overwhelming or alienating users:

1. **Design AI around the user experience, not the buzzword**: Apple doesn't lead with AI; it leads with usability. AI features are surfaced only when they make something faster, simpler, or more delightful.

2. **Control the tech stack**: From chip design (Apple silicon) to privacy-preserving cloud compute (Private Cloud Compute), Apple ensures its AI ecosystem is secure, efficient, and optimized for its products.

3. **Deploy AI invisibly where it matters most**: Features like FaceID, Smart Script, or Clean Up in Photos are AI-powered, but Apple positions them as enhancements to core product functionality - not standalone tools.

4. **Prioritize privacy by default**: Apple's commitment to running models on-device wherever possible, and encrypting any data used in the cloud, builds long-term user trust - especially crucial in consumer tech.

5. **Leverage form-specific intelligence**: Whether it's real-time handwriting enhancements on iPads or photo cleanup on iPhones, Apple ensures each AI application fits the context of the device.

By integrating AI in ways that enhance product value without overshadowing it, Apple has managed to maintain its leadership position in a highly competitive market. This approach allows Apple to continuously improve its products, offering users new and valuable features that keep them loyal to the brand, while also setting the bar for competitors in terms of product quality and innovation.

Approach 4: Opportunistic AI

The **Opportunistic AI** approach is ideal for companies that prefer a cautious, risk-averse strategy for AI adoption. The general attitude here is, *We don't need AI until you prove me wrong*. While this may sound naive, there are many industries where the most pressing challenges have nothing to do with AI. Take the trades, construction, or any other brick-and-mortar business as an example. The Opportunistic AI approach involves integrating AI only when a compelling, well-defined use case emerges - one that provides immediate, tangible benefits for specific business functions or processes. Rather than pursuing AI for innovation's sake across the enterprise, companies using this strategy focus on practical, proven applications that align with their existing operational goals.

This approach works best when companies want to improve a single job within specific functions that have a proven track record of being improved by AI. Think of jobs in customer service or marketing.

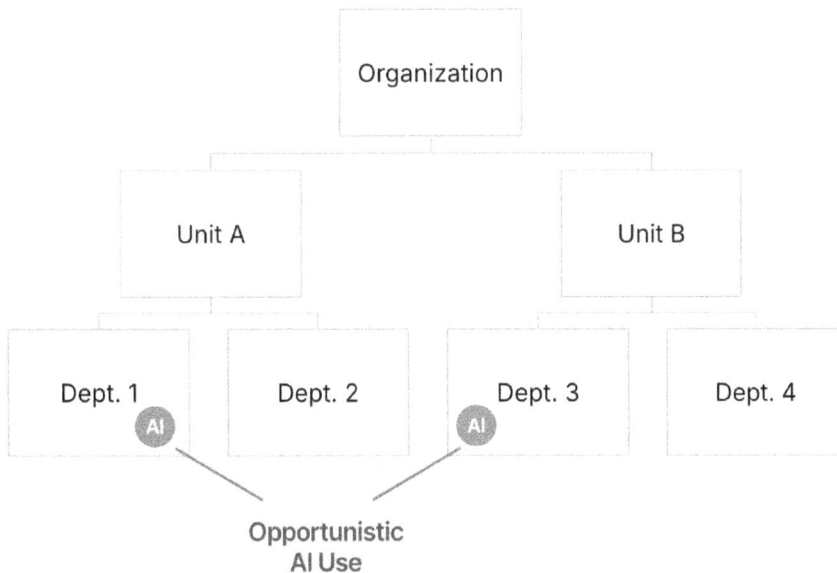

Figure 3.4: Opportunistic AI adoption illustration

By selectively deploying AI in these areas, companies can achieve efficiencies and cost savings without undertaking large-scale transformations or taking on significant risk. Unlike the divide and conquer approach to AI, adoption in these areas isn't a *push* - initiated by the C-suite - but often a *pull* - as business professionals discover that AI can improve their daily work.

Implementing the ***Opportunistic AI*** approach is very often tool-driven. A new software or vendor catches the attention of a business professional or mid-level business leader, and they *fight* to get resources to implement that tool. Since the default decision is *we don't need it*, business users who want to benefit from AI technology must create a clear business case for the tool. This leads to well-defined, well-scoped use cases, but may also result in longer implementation cycles, depending on the cost and complexity of the tool and the size of the organization.

A key aspect of this approach is the emphasis on efficiency and quick wins. The selected AI applications are typically low-risk and have a high probability of delivering immediate benefits, such as reducing operational costs or improving customer satisfaction. This ensures that the company can see tangible results without disrupting existing processes or requiring significant changes to its overall business model.

Here is how your organization can benefit from the Opportunistic AI approach:

- **Risk reduction:** By focusing on AI implementations in specific, proven areas, companies minimize the risks associated with untested or experimental applications. This allows them to leverage AI's benefits without the high costs or potential failures of broader, less targeted initiatives.

- **Immediate returns:** The selective nature of this approach ensures that AI integrations are closely aligned with specific business goals, leading to quick and measurable improvements in efficiency, cost savings, or customer satisfaction.

- **Leveraging proven success:** Companies can adopt AI technologies that have already been validated in similar functions or processes by others, reducing uncertainty and enabling the use of best practices.

There are some limitations to this approach that you need to be aware of before you adopt it:

- **Missed broader opportunities:** By focusing only on specific functions or processes, companies might overlook broader, transformative AI opportunities that could revolutionize other parts of the business. This selective approach might also limit the company's ability to quickly adapt or pivot in response to changing market conditions or competitor advances.

- **Risk of falling behind competitors**: Companies that adopt AI selectively in only a few areas might fall behind more aggressive competitors who implement organization-wide AI strategies. This can lead to losing out on a first-mover advantage, potentially impacting market share and diminishing the company's position as an industry leader.

- **Complacency leading to stagnation**: There's a risk that companies may become too comfortable with their existing processes, leading to stagnation. Over time, this could limit the organization's capacity for innovation or adaptation to future disruptions. Companies need to guard against this by continually monitoring technological advancements and experimenting with new AI opportunities to stay competitive.

- **Integration challenges:** Opportunistic AI adoption will often lead to integration challenges, where AI systems may not seamlessly connect with existing workflows or each other, resulting in inefficiencies or a fragmented approach. This can complicate efforts to scale AI across the organization and reduce the overall effectiveness of AI initiatives.

The Home Depot - exemplifying a classic retailer here - is a good lesson in the *Opportunistic AI* approach of focusing on proven, high-impact AI applications. Let's dig deeper.

Case study: The Home Depot

The Home Depot uses supervised machine learning and computer vision to optimize inventory processes, ensuring products are in the right place at the right time. This targeted use of AI has led to cost savings and improved customer satisfaction, both in-store and online.

It has also selectively enhanced its e-commerce experience with AI-powered search and product recommendation systems. These tools improve engagement and drive conversions - but only where the return on investment is clear and measurable.

Some of the key initiatives that the company undertook are:

- **Sidekick app:** A mobile application developed in-house that uses machine learning and computer vision to assist store associates with real-time inventory management by directing them to restock shelves as needed.

- **Magic Apron:** A suite of generative AI tools designed to provide customers with expert advice and product recommendations online - particularly helpful for DIY projects.

- **Enhanced search functionality**: AI-driven algorithms improve the relevance of on-site search results, leading to increased click-through rates and higher conversion.

While similar applications exist across many modern retailers, The Home Depot stands out for its focus and discipline in deploying AI where it matters most.

Here are some of the key takeaways from this strategy:

- **Identify high-impact areas**: Focus on domains where AI delivers clear, measurable value - such as inventory management or customer service.

- **Leverage existing expertise**: Use internal knowledge and operational data to design relevant, domain-specific applications.

- **Maintain operational simplicity**: Avoid unnecessary complexity. Prioritize technologies that enhance, not disrupt, existing workflows.

- **Monitor and evaluate outcomes**: Continuously measure the impact of AI tools and adjust as needed to ensure long-term effectiveness.

The Home Depot's Opportunistic AI strategy serves as a model for companies - retail or otherwise - that want to embrace AI without overhauling their operations. It shows that AI doesn't have to be flashy to be effective. A focused, thoughtful approach can deliver substantial business results - without the cost or risk of *implementing AI everywhere*.

Now that we have looked into various approaches for AI adoption, we will talk about how to identify which approach suits your organization the best.

Finding your AI approach: Where you are, where you want to go, and why it matters

So, which of these four approaches - AI divide and conquer, AI moonshot, Product-led AI, or Opportunistic AI - should *you* choose for your organization? That's like asking, *What's the best car?*, without any context about who's driving, where you're heading, or why you're traveling in the first place. The right AI strategy, much like the right vehicle, hinges on your *current state*, your *target future state*, and the big reason *why* you need to get there.

We'll walk through the key considerations to help you figure this out.

Assessing your organization's AI readiness

Before you jump headfirst into any of the four approaches, you need a clear-eyed view of where you stand right now. Have you actually worked with data at scale before? Do you have AI talent on board, or will you need to rely on external partners and vendors? Is there a budget set aside for digital transformation initiatives, or are you already squeezed? Is your organization's culture open to the idea of *failing forward* with new technology, or are you dealing with a fortress of skepticism at every department door?

These questions aren't trivial. Your organization's *AI maturity* will guide whether you're ready for a high-octane, R&D-heavy *Moonshot*, or whether a low-risk, incremental *Opportunistic AI* pilot is more realistic. If you don't have a robust data infrastructure or enough internal AI expertise, launching a massive, AI-fueled moonshot (approach 2) might be like handing the car keys to a 14-year-old. It's not going to end well.

The easiest way to pinpoint your AI maturity is to map your current state to the four adoption approaches. What are you doing right now with regard to AI? Are you already wrapped up in a big AI project? You might be carrying out the product-led or moonshot approach. Have you not done anything with AI at all? Well, it seems you're in the opportunistic playing field - no AI unless convinced otherwise.

So - if you had to simplify it - which of the current AI adoption approaches reflects your current business reality best?

Define your future state

Once you've nailed down where you stand, it's time to ask: ***Where do we want to be a year from now? Two years? Five?*** And, more importantly, ***why?*** This is where understanding how AI influences your market dynamics becomes crucial - Recall the ***AI as a new force*** concept we introduced in *Chapter 1*. Each of the approaches we've covered can help you move the needle on at least one of those competitive levers:

- **Threat of new entrants**: If your industry is at high risk of AI disruption from new entrants (think banks facing fintech upstarts or retailers battling e-commerce pure-plays), you might need a bigger AI strategy to stay ahead. *AI divide and conquer* or *AI moonshot* might allow you to build a moat before the competition floods in.

- **Threat of substitutes**: If your products or services face a real risk of AI-driven alternatives, you might need a transformative approach - such as, doubling down on a killer AI use case or layering AI deeply into your product suite - to avoid becoming obsolete.

- **Bargaining power of suppliers**: In data-heavy industries, consider whether an *AI divide and conquer* approach can democratize knowledge and reduce dependency on a single AI supplier.

- **Bargaining power of buyers**: If your customers can easily compare and switch to AI-savvy competitors, maybe a ***product-led AI*** approach is the easiest way to differentiate yourself and keep them loyal.

- **Rivalry among existing competitors**: If your market is cutthroat, do you really have time for incremental changes? If not, you might opt for a bold *moonshot use case* that redefines the entire playing field.

Your future state is essentially the vantage point from which you look back and say, *We got the AI puzzle right - and we did it faster (or smarter) than our competitors*.

Your big reason why

A compelling *why* is the imperative for change that keeps your AI journey going, even when you hit roadblocks (and you will hit roadblocks). If your *why* isn't clear, you'll struggle to justify the costs, resource allocations, and potential risks that come with AI adoption. No matter which approach you choose, tie it back to a clear, business-oriented rationale. For example:

- **Increasing ROI** through cost savings or revenue boosts.
- **Securing a competitive moat** by building superior AI-driven features or experiences.
- **Opening new markets** or product lines that simply aren't possible without AI.
- **Building resilience** against the five forces: for example, by lowering supplier power or reducing buyer churn.

Depending on where you started, it might be that your future state is actually the same as what it is right now (e.g., if competitive dynamics in your industry do not demand instant change with AI, you might as well stick with a very opportunistic AI adoption approach just like now). Or perhaps your future state is a combination of what you're doing (e.g., divide and conquer) plus some additional focus in certain verticals (e.g., product-led AI for a certain business area).

Getting clarity on this end goal will not only help you confidently charter your AI journey and allocate budgets. It'll also help you communicate the vision of how AI fits into your organization and get buy-in from your teams, as well as your executives and shareholders.

Balancing AI ROI and AI R&D: Knowing which game you're playing

One of the biggest pitfalls I see is when companies *think* they're playing an ROI-first game but are actually funding R&D moonshots - *or* vice versa. This mismatch results in disappointment, frustration, and the dreaded *AI is overrated* refrain. Here is how you can differentiate what drives your ROI:

- **ROI-driven AI**: If your industry moves slower, or if you're simply not ready for massive disruption, it could be wise to *start small* and iterate quickly. *Opportunistic AI* or *Product-led AI* can offer immediate returns with minimal risk. But if you try to dress them up as game-changing transformations, you'll only look foolish when the results underwhelm senior management. Going forward in this book, we'll primarily build your AI roadmap using this lens.

- **R&D-driven AI**: If you're in an industry where AI disruption could be existential (such as autonomous mobility or high-end manufacturing), you might need a *moonshot use case* approach to secure a *long-term* advantage, even if the payoff is uncertain and years away. Just don't promise short-term ROI to justify these big bets. Instead, openly communicate that this is a strategic R&D investment for potential category leadership down the road.

The lesson here is to be brutally honest about which game you're playing. Align your budget, your timelines, and your KPIs accordingly. If you're going down the ROI route, measure short-term success in dollars saved or earned. If you're going down the R&D route, set milestones around research breakthroughs, prototypes, or patents, rather than immediate revenue.

Let's put it all together. Here's how you might match your organizational reality (current state), your endgame (future state), and your big *why* (imperative) to the four approaches:

Approach	Best for	Why	RoI versus R&D
AI divide and conquer	Organizations with moderate to high AI readiness, broad data availability, and an industry likely to see widespread AI-driven disruption.	You need to outpace rivals by embedding AI across multiple functions. Think large-scale transformation but tackled in small, manageable bites.	Mixed. Some incremental ROI in each department, with a modest R&D angle from a central AICoE.
AI moonshot	Companies aiming to change the game in an industry with high stakes.	You want to capture a massive first-mover advantage, and you have (or can acquire) the resources and talent to do it.	Heavy R&D. Big risk, big potential reward. Expect a longer timeline before you see returns.

Product-led AI	Firms with established products and loyal customers, looking to stay ahead without radical reinvention.	You want to continuously delight customers and differentiate your product in a crowded space.	Primarily ROI-driven with incremental improvements. Low to moderate risk.
Opportunistic AI	Organizations in low-tech or slow-moving industries (or pockets within bigger industries) that see AI as nice to have rather than existential.	You only commit to AI if there's a clear, well-defined business case. You prefer quick wins and minimal disruption.	Very ROI-focused. Little to no R&D appetite - lowest risk, lowest potential for industry-shaking innovation.

Table 3.1: Comparing the four approaches to AI adoption

Can you mix and match these approaches? Of course, but try not to get stuck in the details. Choose your primary focus and let that be your North Star. Feel free to add other elements here and there, but always keep your main objective clear. As you consider your next steps, ask yourself: Which of these four approaches resonates most with you? Why? Making the right turn at this critical intersection is crucial to your future AI and business success. Whichever approach you pick, remember that *AI is a journey, not a one-off project*. Your market context, capabilities, and strategic objectives should be in constant dialogue. Keep an eye on the shifting five forces. Reevaluate your approach as you gain more AI maturity. Stay laser-focused on that "why," because that's what will guide you when internal politics, budget constraints, or technological hiccups threaten to derail your plans.

Sure, you might need to tweak your strategy mid-journey. Maybe you start with an Opportunistic AI approach, prove out some ROI, and then level up to Product-led AI once your internal teams gain confidence. Or perhaps you'll dabble in Product-led AI for stability and eventually decide to double down on Moonshot because your market is suddenly disrupted by a well-funded competitor.

Whatever path you take, it's better to pick an approach intentionally than to stumble into an *accidental AI strategy* that doesn't fit your organization's needs. AI is too important to leave to chance. So, figure out where you are, be bold about where you want to go, and keep your eyes on the big reason driving you there. The rest is just execution.

Summary

Knowing which AI game you want to play is crucial to your organization's success in adopting and leveraging AI. As this chapter has shown, blindly mimicking the strategies of Silicon Valley giants is a recipe for failure for most companies. Instead, the key to successful AI adoption lies in recognizing your unique context and capabilities and selecting the right approach that aligns with your business goals and operational realities.

In this chapter, you have seen some examples of companies in different industries and of different sizes that have already found their own winning strategies by playing their own game. Don't treat them as a strict blueprint, but rather as inspiration to follow and ultimately build your own customized AI journey that will give you your unique AI advantage.

In the following chapters, I'll give you the resources to do just that. We will explore how *exactly* you can get started on your AI journey, using practical tools and proven frameworks that take the guesswork away and help you confidently take the first steps toward building your very own AI advantage.

Unlock this book's exclusive benefits now **UNLOCK NOW**

Scan this QR code or go to `https://packtpub.com/unlock`, then search for this book by name.

Note: Keep your purchase invoice ready before you start.

Stay tuned

To keep up with the latest developments in the fields of Generative AI and LLMs, subscribe to our weekly newsletter, AI_Distilled, at `https://packt.link/80z6Y`.

Part 2

Charting the Course

With the foundations and a good orientation in place, it's time to chart your own course. In this part, you'll learn how to take ownership of your AI roadmap, identify pain points and bottlenecks, and map them against AI's capabilities. We'll explore practical techniques for spotting opportunities, designing concrete use cases, and sequencing them into a structured AI roadmap. By the end of this part, you'll be equipped to move from vague ambition to a prioritized plan of action.

This part of the book includes the following chapters:

- *Chapter 4, Getting Started on Your AI Journey*
- *Chapter 5, Finding AI Opportunities in Processes and Products*
- *Chapter 6, Designing AI Use Cases*
- *Chapter 7, Building Your AI Roadmap*

4

Getting Started on Your AI Journey

Hot take: Your AI journey has already started. After all, your interest in AI is what brought you to this book. Perhaps you've experimented with tools like ChatGPT or interacted with AI in other forms, sparking your curiosity to learn more. This widespread curiosity and accessibility are what truly distinguish the modern AI revolution from the early days of AI and machine learning back in the 2010s.

Today, AI is nearly everywhere - from your smartphone to the supply chains that power global commerce. So, the real question isn't whether to start your AI journey, but rather, where you currently stand on it.

In this chapter, we'll explore the following topics:

- Why a roadmap matters
- Common pitfalls in AI adoption
- Taking ownership of the AI roadmap
- Overview of the AI roadmap process
- Identifying pain points and bottlenecks: The foundation of your AI roadmap
- Finding the right starting point for profitable AI projects
- Implementing a value filter

Why a roadmap matters

Most organizations I've worked with tend to fall somewhere in the middle of their journey. They're often approached by vendors offering tools that promise sophisticated AI solutions. These tools may seem impressive at first, but they often under-deliver, leading to disappointment and, in many cases, leaving AI projects stuck in the prototyping phase. This is what happens when your goal is divide and conquer AI, but what you are doing is selective (opportunistic) AI. This clash will eventually create a cycle of frustration where AI remains a tantalizing but elusive promise rather than a transformative reality.

That's why it's critical to start with a clear **AI roadmap**. Understanding where you are on this journey - and knowing when to move forward or take a step back - is key to avoiding these common pitfalls. A roadmap will help you be clear about where you start, where you want to go, and which obstacles you need to overcome on your way to get there. Ultimately, your AI roadmap ensures that AI initiatives are tied to your business interests right from the start.

Without a roadmap, it's easy to get lost in the hype, invest in the wrong tools, or set unrealistic expectations. A roadmap provides clarity and direction, helping you stay focused on what truly matters: solving your business challenges and driving business outcomes.

This chapter is designed to help you build that roadmap. It will lay the foundation for approaching AI solutions in a structured way, guiding you through the process of integrating AI into your company's processes. Most importantly, it will help you nail down the starting point, identifying where AI can have the most significant impact on your business. The rest of this book will build on the phases introduced here, so whenever you feel uncertain, you can refer back to this roadmap and reassess where you are and whether you're on the right path.

Common pitfalls in AI adoption

Jumping into AI without a clear plan can lead to some common pitfalls. One of the biggest mistakes is over-reliance on vendors. External vendors can offer valuable tools and expertise, but their solutions are often generic - designed to meet the needs of a broad audience rather than tailored to your specific business challenges. This can leave you with a prototype that never scales into a real implementation ultimately adding more cost than value.

Another challenge is setting unrealistic expectations. AI can be exciting, and it's easy to assume it will deliver quick, easy wins. But in reality, AI projects often require significant time, resources, and even cultural changes within your organization - especially after the prototyping phase. Without understanding these demands, you might become disillusioned when AI doesn't immediately deliver the results you were hoping for.

Integrating AI into existing systems is another major hurdle. AI needs to work seamlessly with your current processes, data flows, and organizational structure. If you don't account for this, you could end up with disruptions, inefficiencies, or even project failures. A company might invest heavily in an AI-driven customer service tool, only to find that it doesn't integrate well with their existing CRM system, leading to frustration and a lack of adoption by the team.

Lastly, there's the pitfall of ignoring the human element. AI can help you to speed up tasks or provide higher-quality outputs, but it's the people in your organization who will ultimately determine its success. If your team isn't on board, or if they don't understand how AI fits into their daily work, your AI initiatives are likely to falter.

All of these pitfalls could be prevented by ensuring proper alignment between business objectives and technical capabilities, embedded in a pragmatic AI governance framework, which are core components of your AI roadmap.

Taking ownership of the AI roadmap

AI is often seen as the domain of data scientists, IT experts, and tech-savvy innovators. While these specialists are essential for the technical side of AI, the real responsibility for driving AI initiatives should rest on the shoulders of business leaders in the entire organization. Here's why: AI isn't just another piece of software that you can install and expect to run smoothly. It's a transformative technology with the potential to revolutionize how your business operates. The use case for this technology must come from you - the business leader.

Think of it like trying to build a skyscraper without a blueprint. You could have the world's best engineers and construction workers, but without a clear plan, the result would be chaotic at best, catastrophic at worst. The same goes for AI. Your organization might have talented data scientists and IT professionals, but without a clear vision and strategic direction, your AI initiatives will easily miss the mark.

Why leadership matters

As a business leader, it's your job to define that vision. You understand your company's goals, market position, and competitive landscape better than anyone else. You know where the business needs to go, and it's up to you to steer AI initiatives in that direction. Yes, you'll rely on experts to navigate the technical aspects, but the roadmap should be driven by what your business needs, not just by what's technically possible.

Introducing AI into your organization often requires a cultural shift, much like how a conductor might introduce a new piece of music to an orchestra. This shift can be met with resistance, as people may be wary of change or uncertain about how AI will impact their roles. As a leader, it's your responsibility to champion this change, address concerns, and foster a culture of experimentation and learning. Remember, your involvement is not just beneficial, it's essential. When AI initiatives are driven by business leaders who understand the company's strategic goals, they are far more likely to succeed. Leaders who actively participate in AI adoption not only guide the strategic direction but also set the tone for the organizational culture around AI.

Now that we've established why taking ownership of the AI roadmap is crucial, let's take a look at what this process actually looks like. The next sections will guide you through building a practical, actionable roadmap that aligns with your business objectives, leverages the strengths of your team, and sets you up for long-term success in your AI journey.

Overview of the AI roadmapping process

The high-level framework for building an AI roadmap below comes from my years of AI consulting experience in the field. It has worked successfully for both small and big companies, and the process is always the same. What's different, though, is the entry point where you start. Depending on your AI adoption strategy and your current situation, it can be one of three entry points:

- **Process-based:** You look at this roadmap from a process perspective, typically driven by a department leader or head of a business unit. This fits nicely with the Opportunistic AI approach.
- **Product-based:** This looks at user journeys instead of process steps. Your goal is to improve an existing product by shipping new (or improved) AI-enhanced features. This maps to the Product-led AI approach.

- **Organizational-based:** When you gather your C-level in a room and start thinking about AI opportunities, then taking this roadmap from an organizational view is a good start. This typically involves looking at your org chart and then collecting opportunity areas on a super high-level. From there, you typically need to either go into process-based or product-based deep dives to flesh out your use cases.

This approach works for approaching AI through a Divide-and-conquer or a Moonshot approach.

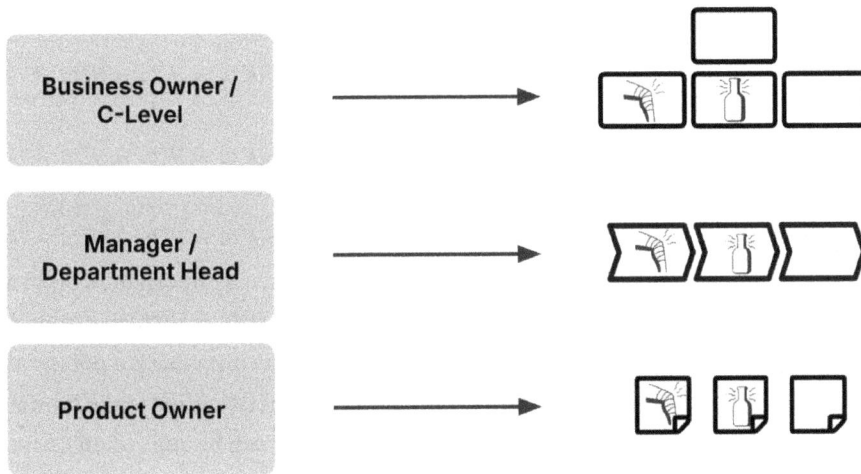

Figure 4.1: Entry points for AI roadmapping process

If this doesn't make total sense to you right now, don't worry. Everything will get clearer once we go through the roadmap framework in detail. Just remember that the key steps and milestones will stay the same, but they might come in different flavors, and the level of details varies depending on your starting point.

So, let's walk through these milestones (*Figure 4.2*) so you can get a sense of what's involved.

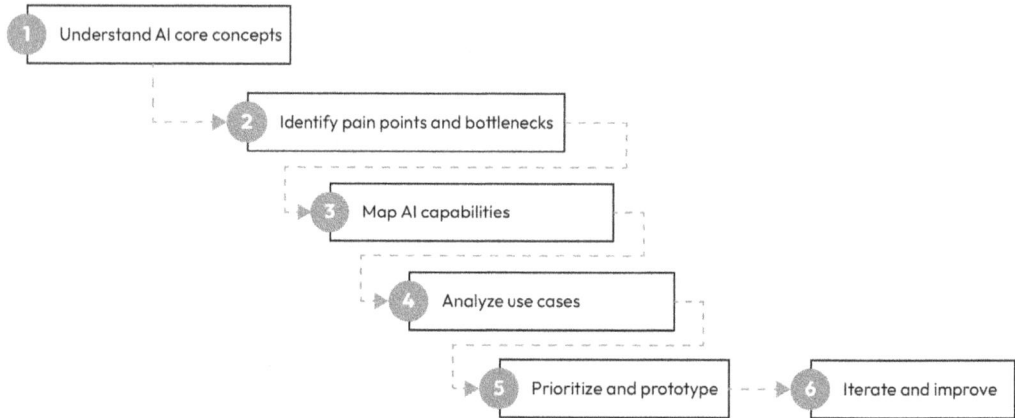

Figure 4.2: AI roadmapping process milestones

- **Milestone 1: Understanding AI core concepts**

Before you can effectively integrate AI into your business, it's important to build a shared knowledge foundation. Otherwise, AI will always be a buzzword, which means different things to different people, and you won't be able to figure out what's a potentially good problem for AI to solve and what isn't. This involves understanding of the fundamentals of AI - what AI is, how it works, and the different ways it can be applied. In *Chapter 2*, we laid out these basics, covering the 5 AI modes and some common terminologies. You can always spend more time learning AI core concepts, but it'll be much easier to do so while your roadmap unfolds.

To get started, make sure everyone involved in AI projects shares this basic understanding. Consider organizing workshops or seminars to get everyone on the same page and ensure that AI discussions are based on a common knowledge base.

If you wish to explore some AI core concepts, here are a few resources that could help:

- Elements of AI Free Online Course (https://www.elementsofai.com/)
- AI For Everyone by Andrew Ng (Free Course) (https://www.deeplearning.ai/courses/ai-for-everyone/)
- AI in a Nutshell: A Practical Guide to Key AI Terminology (Blog article) (https://blog.tobiaszwingmann.com/p/demystifying-ai-practical-guide-key-terminology)

- **Milestone 2: Identifying business pain points and bottlenecks**

  With a solid foundation in place, the next milestone is to look for AI opportunities in your business. This stage involves identifying the specific challenges - both current and future - that are big enough to be even considered as AI enhancements. We'll filter these challenges with the $10K threshold using the concept of pain points and bottlenecks for later in this chapter.

- **Milestone 3: Mapping AI capabilities to business needs**

  Once you've identified your pain points and bottlenecks, the next milestone involves exploring how AI can address these issues. This is where you map your business needs to specific AI capabilities. For example, if processing large volumes of customer feedback is a challenge, AI reading skills, which can be referred to as AI reading skills, might be the right fit. If you want to predict e-commerce sales, **Supervised Machine Learning** (or Prediction mode for simplicity) might be an important capability to explore.

  Achieving this milestone is about finding the intersection where your business challenges and AI's capabilities meet. It's not about chasing the latest AI trends; it's about identifying practical applications that deliver tangible results. We will explore this area further in *Chapter 5*.

- **Milestone 4: Defining and analyzing AI use cases**

  With your business needs and AI capabilities aligned, the next milestone is to work on and conceptualize specific AI use cases. These use case concepts help you pull everything together into a roadmap and ultimately decide which projects to tackle and in what order. At this stage, your ideas begin to take shape, transforming from broad ideas into specific, well-defined initiatives with clear business objectives that will eventually become your first AI projects. *Chapter 6* will be all dedicated to this.

- **Milestone 5: Prioritizing and prototyping AI initiatives**

  The next milestone is to prioritize and prototype your AI initiatives. Not all AI projects will have the same impact or be equally easy to implement. It's crucial to prioritize initiatives based on their potential impact and feasibility as well as their cost of prototyping. Reaching this milestone is where your strategy begins to translate into action. Chapters *7* and *8* will be packed with actionable tips and strategies for this stage.

- **Milestone 6: Iterating and scaling AI initiatives**

  Once you've launched your first AI projects, the final milestone is to make sure you're ready to learn from failure and deliver increments toward a clear goal. Adopting AI is not a one-time effort; it's an iterative process that requires continuous monitoring, refinement, and scaling. Reaching this milestone allows you to adapt to new information, experiment with new ideas, and scale successful projects across the organization. Chapters 9 and 10 take a closer look at this critical phase.

Overall, your AI roadmap is the place where your AI initiatives evolve from ideas to pilot projects to integral components of your business strategy. It's a living and breathing document that guides your process of learning, adapting, and growing, ensuring that your AI efforts continue to deliver value over time.

Your role as a business leader in each step

As a business leader, your role is central at every stage of this roadmap. You're not just overseeing the process - you're actively guiding it. Your involvement ensures that AI initiatives stay aligned with business objectives and that the organization remains focused on driving real value.

In the early stages, your role is to set the vision and identify the areas where AI can have the most impact. As the journey progresses, you'll make strategic decisions about which initiatives to prioritize, how to allocate resources, and when to scale successful projects.

Throughout the process, your leadership will be crucial in fostering a culture of experimentation, learning, and continuous improvement.

Be a visible champion for AI within your organization. Clearly communicate the vision, involve key stakeholders early, and ensure that everyone understands how AI fits into the broader business strategy.

Now that you have a clear picture of the overall roadmap, it's time to dive deeper into the foundation of your AI strategy: identifying your business's pain points and bottlenecks.

This is where your AI journey truly begins.

Identifying pain points and bottlenecks: The foundation of your AI roadmap

To make sure AI will deliver value by solving real problems, you need to think about your AI roadmap business first, not technology first. When there's no problem to solve, there's no need for AI. If your customer support can handle every incoming query easily, you don't need a chatbot. If you're selling an evergreen product, you probably don't need a good demand forecast. So, understanding AI opportunities means understanding your business needs.

This is where a concept called pain points and bottlenecks comes into play. In simple terms, these are problems that your businesses are either unfolding right now or in the future.

Pain points are the current issues that are causing friction within your business. These could be anything from inefficiencies in your processes to rising costs to customer dissatisfaction. Pain points are often things that are actively hurting your business right now, and they're usually quite visible - they show up in financial reports, customer feedback, or operational metrics.

Figure 4.3: Pain points: Business problems that are hurting right now

For example, imagine you're running a customer service department. If you're seeing a high volume of customer complaints about slow response times, that's a pain point. It's something that's negatively impacting your customer experience, and by extension, your business.

Bottlenecks, on the other hand, are constraints or limitations that could prevent your business from thriving in the future. They might not be a significant issue right now, but if left unaddressed, they could become serious roadblocks to scaling, innovating, or maintaining a competitive edge. Bottlenecks often represent potential risks or missed opportunities - they're the obstacles that prevent future growth.

Figure 4.4: Bottlenecks: problems that limit your growth or competitiveness in the future

Consider a straightforward, non-AI example: If your company plans to expand into new markets, but your current production line can't handle the increased demand, that's a bottleneck. It's not a problem today, but it needs to be removed so you can grow. While bottlenecks like this are often obvious in traditional, non-technical workflows, they become more obscure and difficult to identify in digital and AI-driven environments. In the context of AI and digital processes, bottlenecks often lurk in places that aren't immediately visible. They can include outdated IT infrastructure that can't support the integration of AI tools, data silos that prevent the efficient flow of information, or even a lack of skilled personnel capable of leveraging new technologies. These digital bottlenecks can silently undermine your company's ability to innovate, respond to market changes, or scale effectively.

Finding the right starting point for profitable AI projects

Pain points and bottlenecks can be analyzed from a process-, product-, or organizational-level. But before diving into the specific processes and methodologies for identifying pain points and bottlenecks, it's critical to recognize that the starting point for this journey will vary depending on your role within the organization. Whether you're a C-level executive overseeing the entire organization or a department leader focused on a specific business unit, the approach you take to uncover these challenges will differ. Understanding your position and the scope of your responsibility is key to effectively navigating the AI roadmap.

So, there are typically two scenarios that can happen. Let's explore each in turn.

Scenario 1: Organizational-level approach for C-level leaders

If you're an executive, your perspective naturally extends to the entire organization. At this stage, you need to get a helicopter-level view, which typically means mapping the major pain points and bottlenecks on an organizational chart, as shown in the following figure:

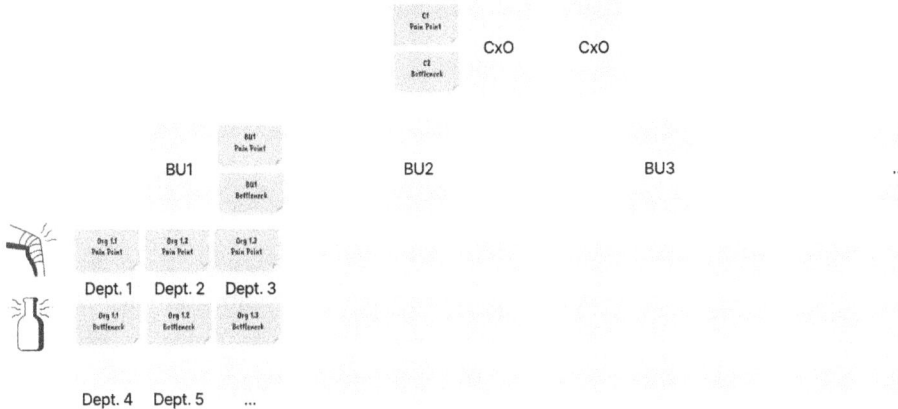

Figure 4.5: Mapping pain points and bottlenecks to an org chart

This organizational overview serves as the foundation for identifying where AI can create real impact - but it needs a clear north star to guide it. Before scanning departments, pinpoint your top-level business goal: What is the most pressing challenge right now? Do you need to cut costs, accelerate growth, or launch a new line of business? Having this north star helps narrow the analysis to pain points and bottlenecks that matter in direct relation to that goal.

Examples of north stars I've seen include: doubling output without doubling desks, achieving cost leadership, or launching a new business line in the next six months. Once the goal is clear, assemble your leadership team and systematically evaluate the organization, unit by unit, to identify where inefficiencies, delays, or customer dissatisfaction are blocking progress toward that north star.

But the organizational view is just the beginning of the journey. It gives you the context you need and informs the approach you should take: Opportunistic AI, Product-led, Divide and conquer, or Moonshot. Depending on this, your AI initiatives will be driven by different people:

- **Opportunistic AI approach:** Departmental leaders take responsibility for AI initiatives within their areas of control, focusing on specific process improvements.

- **AI divide-and-conquer approach**: An AI **Center of Excellence (CoE)** coordinates AI efforts across the organization, working closely with business units to ensure alignment and resource efficiency.

- **AI Moonshot approach:** The moonshot is typically directly overseen by a member of the C-level executive team and implemented as a separate project.
- **Product-led AI approach**: The head of product is ultimately responsible for driving AI innovation in the products they oversee.

Scenario 2: Business unit or department leaders - focusing on specific areas

If you're a leader of a business unit or department, your approach to identifying pain points and bottlenecks will be more focused and specific to your area of responsibility. Unlike C-level leaders who must consider the organization as a whole, your task is to dive deep into the processes or product journeys that directly impact your department's performance - ideally as part of a team of experts that are deeply involved in the daily operations.

Depending on your role, function, and AI adoption approach, you can run this exploration as process- or product-based.

Process-based analysis

For department managers, the easiest place to start is often a process-based analysis. This approach involves breaking down the key processes within your department into a series of key steps. Breaking down a process into 5-6 key steps that transform a given process input into a desired process output has proven to be an effective abstraction.

Don't try to stay too high-level, but don't get bogged down in the details.

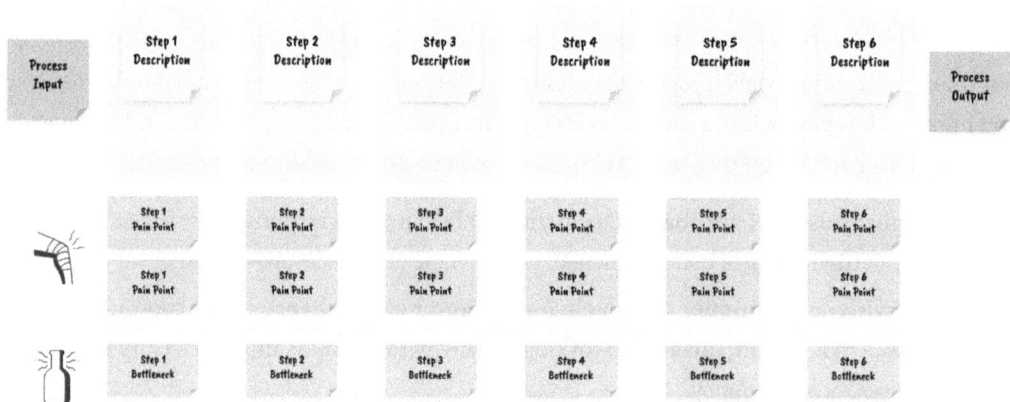

Figure 4.6: Mapping pain points and bottlenecks to a business process

For example, if you manage a sales department, you might break down the sales process into stages such as lead generation, qualification, nurturing, and closing. By examining each stage, you can pinpoint where leads might be falling through the cracks, where sales cycles are getting too long, or where communication with potential customers could be improved. For each step, ask yourself:

- Where do we spend most resources?
- Where do we experience the most delays?
- Where are errors or inconsistencies most common?
- Which steps generate the most customer complaints or dissatisfaction?

We will explore some more methods to source pain points and bottlenecks below. But first, let's see how this analysis would look if we were looking at products, not processes.

Product-based analysis

If your department is product-focused, such as in product management or development, a product-based analysis may be more appropriate. This approach involves examining the entire user journey associated with your product, from initial awareness to post-purchase support. By mapping out the customer experience, you can identify pain points that are causing friction or dissatisfaction.

The setup looks very similar compared to the process-based analysis, with the only difference that, instead of process steps, you're looking at steps in the user journey - often described with user stories that are required to move the user from a given starting state to a desired end state.

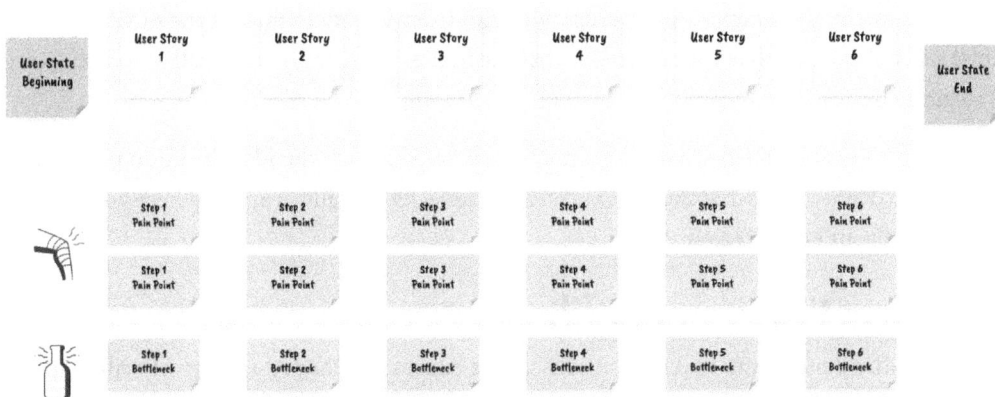

Figure 4.7: Mapping pain points and bottlenecks across a user journey

For example, if your product is an e-commerce platform, you might look at the user journey from the moment a customer lands on the site, through browsing and selection, to checkout and delivery. Are customers dropping off during the checkout process? Is there confusion about product descriptions? Are delivery times inconsistent? These are all potential problem areas that, if addressed, can significantly enhance the customer experience and increase satisfaction and loyalty.

In both process-based and product-based analyses, the key is to be thorough and specific. The more detailed your understanding of where the pain points and bottlenecks exist, the more targeted and effective your AI solutions will be.

What's important at this stage is that we're not talking about AI solutions yet; just collecting problems, waiting to be solved (whether AI is a good fit for that will be the next step to decide).

Coordinating with organizational strategy

While your focus is on your department or product, it's important to ensure that your efforts are aligned with the broader organizational AI strategy. If your organization has adopted an Opportunistic AI approach, your initiatives should be coordinated with other departments to ensure consistency and resource sharing. If a divide-and-conquer approach is in place, work closely with the **AI CoE** to leverage their expertise and align your projects with organizational goals.

For product-led AI initiatives, your role is crucial in driving innovation and ensuring that AI is integrated seamlessly into the products under your purview. Collaboration with other departments, such as marketing, engineering, and customer support, is essential to ensure that AI solutions are effective and enhance the overall product offering.

In all cases, maintaining open communication with C-level leadership and the AI CoE (if applicable) will help ensure that your efforts contribute to the organization's overall AI roadmap and strategic goals.

Now that we've established where to start and how to approach the identification process, it's time to dive deeper into what pain points and bottlenecks actually are, and where you can find them within your organization.

Implementing a value filter

Identifying the pain points and bottlenecks to the success of your AI initiatives will help you deliver the meaningful impact of AI adoption in your organization.

How do you identify pain points effectively? Below is a series of techniques that you can use, no matter if you're looking for pain points on an organizational, process, or product level:

1. **Identify internal frustrations**: One of the most straightforward ways to identify pain points is to ask your employees. Conduct surveys or interviews to gather insights about where they encounter frustrations or inefficiencies in their daily work. Often, your team is keenly aware of the obstacles that prevent them from being as effective as they could be. For example, an internal survey might reveal that your sales team spends an inordinate amount of time manually entering data into the CRM system, which prevents them from spending time with customers.

2. **Customer service feedback**: Your customers can also be a valuable source of information about your pain points. Analyze customer complaints, inquiries, and feedback to understand what aspects of your product or service are causing dissatisfaction - both qualitatively and quantitatively. This external perspective can highlight issues that may not be as visible internally. Some customer feedback can be measured, such as your email marketing open and click-through rates as a proxy for customer engagement, while others require more explicit surveys and interviews.

3. **Workflow analysis**: Take a close look at your existing workflows. Where are the tasks repetitive, time-consuming, or prone to errors? Map out the steps in your processes and identify where delays or mistakes commonly occur. A good example of this is missing or wrong information provided in manual customer support. Both your customer service reps and your customers probably wouldn't even bother because *they don't know what they don't know*. But the fact that customer insights need to be pulled manually by support reps is a huge hidden pain point.

4. **Competitive analysis**: Look at how your competitors are addressing similar issues. If they're outperforming you on a given task with regards to quality, speed, or cost of delivery, it could be a sign that you're facing a severe pain point. For example, if you see that your competitor has successfully rolled out personalized marketing campaigns, while you're still using generic outreach, this might highlight a pain point in your marketing strategy. Conduct regular competitor benchmarking to stay informed about industry best practices and innovations.

But it's not just about addressing the problems you have today. You also need to think about the challenges that could arise tomorrow. That's where bottlenecks come in.

Looking for things that limit future growth is typically harder than looking for specific pain points, for the same reason that more people buy aspirin than vitamins. We're usually so busy solving today's most pressing problems that we forget to anticipate tomorrow's. That's why it's so important to think strategically about this area. Here are some ways to get started:

1. **Capacity limitations**: Identify areas where your operations hit a ceiling - whether it's data processing capabilities, production throughput, or the ability to serve more customers. These limitations can become significant bottlenecks as your business grows. For example, a financial institution might find that its manual fraud detection processes are effective today but would struggle to scale as transaction volumes increase.

2. **Skill gaps**: Find out where your team lacks the skills needed to support future growth. As digital tools become more integrated into business operations, the demand for certain skills, such as data literacy or AI-specific knowledge - will increase. Identifying and addressing these gaps now can prevent them from becoming bottlenecks later. For example, if nobody in your operations understands AI, how would they be able to control and monitor AI-driven systems effectively?

3. **Scalability issues**: Assess processes that work well today but might not scale efficiently as your business expands. This could be anything from manual data entry to customer service processes that rely heavily on human agents. For instance, a B2B e-commerce platform could rely on manually curated recommendations for now, but this approach won't scale as their product catalog grows.

4. **Innovation blockers**: Sometimes, the desire to innovate is there, but existing technological or organizational limitations stand in the way. These blockers can prevent you from delivering new products, services, or business models that could drive growth.

By identifying these bottlenecks, you can proactively address the challenges that might slow down your business in the future. In many cases, AI can play a key role in overcoming these limitations, helping you to stay agile and competitive as you grow.

Filtering business problems worth solving: The $10K threshold framework

After identifying pain points and bottlenecks across your organization, processes, or product journeys, you'll likely end up with a substantial list of problems. Not all of these issues are worth the investment of your time and attention, especially not when AI gets involved. This is where the **$10K threshold framework** comes in - a simple yet powerful framework I've developed through my years of consulting work.

Why do we need a value filter?

Before diving into specific solutions, you need to determine which problems are significant enough to warrant your attention. Many business leaders make the mistake of looking at problems that look *most interesting* or that they personally find most *annoying*. However, while making them great candidates, this isn't necessarily a sufficient reason. So, what do you do?

Of course, you could try to exactly measure or quantify impact of every problem in meticulous detail. But this approach doesn't just cost a lot of time; it's also very hard, as not every problem can be exactly quantified. What I find much easier, instead of prioritizing or measuring problems, is **filtering** them. Quickly get rid of problems that are *too small* and prioritize all the remaining ones later once you get closer to the solution space.

For this, you need one single number to start with: Your **value threshold**.

Your value threshold defines the minimal reward you want to see in order to get started on a new journey.

For example, if I told you *Solving this problem will save you $35K per year*, would you do it? Your answer depends on your situation. If you're a small business, then probably yes - you'd take this opportunity. However, if you're working for a large enterprise, a $35K per year impact might not even be worth the meeting time you'd spend with your colleagues discussing this idea.

A value threshold will also help you to keep everyone aligned. Some people need *moonshots* in order to change anything in an existing process, while others are happy if a little improvement just pays for itself.

You'd better find out what the minimum hurdle is for everyone to jump over before you work on any solution, otherwise, you'll realize it when it's too late.

How the $10K threshold works?

How do you set this threshold? I've learned that using a recurring multiple of $10K works great for this. $10K isn't an arbitrary number. It represents a reasonable proxy for human labor costs in many contexts - roughly what it might cost to employ someone for a month, including salary, benefits, and overhead. Breaking it down further, that's about $500 per business day, $60 per hour, or $1 per minute.

Now you can adjust this number to a timeframe to adjust it to the size of your business and your risk appetite.

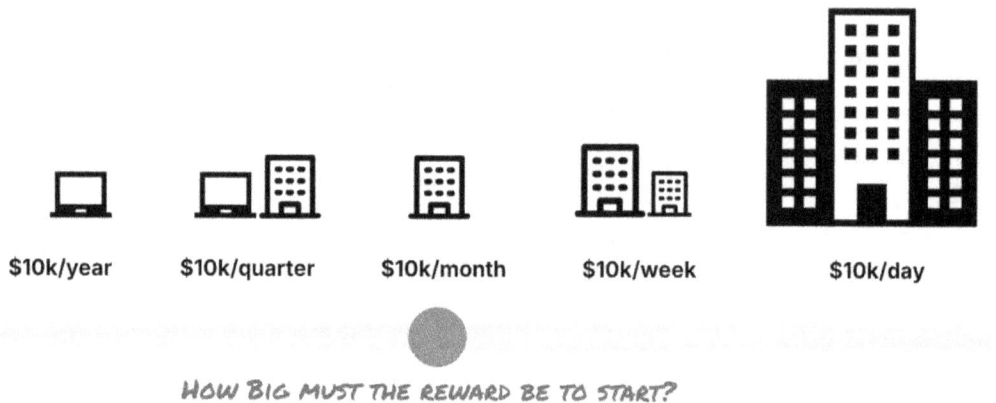

$10k/year $10k/quarter $10k/month $10k/week $10k/day

HOW BIG MUST THE REWARD BE TO START?

Figure 4.8: $10K threshold depending on business size

Choosing a minimal impact of $10K per year will work great for small businesses or for larger businesses that don't want to engage in complex AI projects and just want to see quick ROI by implementing low-hanging fruit solutions that pay for themselves within a short time.

The other extreme - $10K per day - roughly translates into a $3.6 million impact per year, which would even be noticeable for larger corporations. At the same time, this typically results in more complex solutions (because you're looking at bigger, more complex problems) and ROI becomes harder to achieve.

Whatever threshold you pick, make sure that the team working on the AI roadmapping process has the same understanding of their minimal reward to move.

Applying the $10K threshold

Once you set the $10K threshold for yourself, you can go through all your listed pain points and bottlenecks, and ask yourself:

1. **Will solving this problem generate at least $10K in recurring value (year/quarter/ month/day)?**

This could come through:

- **Revenue increases**: Will it create new customers or boost sales worth at least $10K?
- **Cost reductions**: Will it eliminate wasted labor, reduce outsourcing, or prevent inefficiencies worth $10K+?
- **Opportunity unlock**: Will removing this problem allow you to pursue new opportunities worth $10K+?
- **Risk mitigation**: Would failing to address this issue cost at least $10K in compliance penalties, lost opportunities, or competitive disadvantage?

2. **Is the value truly recurring?** One-time benefits, no matter how large, may not justify the continuous resources needed for ongoing solutions, especially with AI systems that require ongoing maintenance.

3. **Does the solution scale?** As your business grows, will the value generated by this AI solution grow proportionally, or will it hit a ceiling? For instance, time savings only hit your P&L if they translate into higher throughput or margin.

By applying this filter early in your process, you can quickly eliminate problems that, while intriguing, simply won't deliver sufficient value to justify the investment. This allows you to concentrate your resources on high-impact areas that will truly move the needle for your business.

For example, a custom AI tool that helps a sales team respond to inquiries 20% faster might sound impressive. But if that only translates to $30K per year in additional revenue, it falls below the $10K per quarter and wouldn't be prioritized. Conversely, an AI solution that reduces customer churn by just 2% might easily exceed the $10K quarterly threshold if that 2% represents significant recurring revenue.

Whatever threshold you set, the key is maintaining discipline in applying it. This prevents the all-too-common pitfall of pursuing AI for its own sake rather than for genuine business value.

As we move forward in the roadmapping process, this initial filtering step ensures you're focused on problems worth solving, setting the stage for matching them with appropriate capabilities - including AI where relevant, and avoiding bringing in AI for AI's sake - in the next milestone.

Summary

Analyzing pain points and bottlenecks allows you to tackle your AI strategy head-on. It's the definitive foundation for aligning everything else down the road. In combination with the $10K threshold, you make sure that the problems you're investigating are actually worth solving with AI, and rally team members around the same goal.

In the next chapter, we'll explore how to map AI capabilities to these pain points and bottlenecks so we can begin developing specific use cases.

Before you move forward, take a moment to reflect on where you are today and which pain points and bottlenecks you see.

Remember, this is a collaborative exercise - gather your team, discuss, and identify the most critical challenges. If you get this right, you'll be well on your way to successfully using AI to deliver meaningful business value.

In the next chapter, we'll look at some real-world examples and practical methods for uncovering AI opportunities within your organization. We'll begin by mapping AI capabilities to your existing processes to pinpoint where AI can resolve pain points and eliminate bottlenecks, helping you to do your work faster, better, or cheaper.

5

Finding AI Opportunities in Processes and Products

You've already taken some important steps on your AI journey. You've built a foundational understanding of AI, mapped out your business's pain points and bottlenecks, and started thinking about how AI might fit into your overall strategy. But now comes a crucial part of the process – identifying the specific opportunities where AI can actually make a difference. This is where the rubber meets the road.

The truth is, not every problem in your business is a good fit for AI. In fact, trying to force AI into a situation where it doesn't belong can lead to wasted resources, frustration, and, ultimately, failure. So, how do you find those sweet spots, those places where AI can really shine and provide tangible value? The answer lies in mapping AI capabilities to your business processes and products.

In this chapter, we'll walk through how to systematically identify AI opportunities. We'll start by exploring how to map AI capabilities to your existing processes, highlighting areas where AI can solve specific pain points or remove bottlenecks. But we won't stop there. We'll also look at how this approach can be applied to your products by enhancing user journeys and improving customer experiences.

By the end of this chapter, you'll not only have a better grasp of where AI can be implemented in your organization, but you'll also understand how to approach this process with a strategic mindset. We'll dive into examples that illustrate these concepts in action, helping you to see the practical steps you can take to identify AI opportunities that are the right fit for your business.

This chapter will cover the following topics:

- Understanding the process of mapping AI capabilities
- Example 1: Finding AI opportunities in the RFP response process
- Example 2: AI opportunities in lead generation and qualification
- Example 3: Enhancing a product user journey with AI
- Practical tips for identifying AI opportunities
- Effective workflow augmentation

Let's roll up our sleeves and start identifying those AI opportunities that can take your business to the next level.

Understanding the process of mapping AI capabilities

When it comes to identifying AI opportunities, one of the most effective methods is to map AI capabilities directly to your business processes and products. This might sound a bit abstract at first, but it's really about taking a step-by-step approach to understanding where AI can add value. Whether you're looking at internal processes or customer-facing products, the goal is the same: find those areas where AI can solve problems, enhance efficiency, or improve the customer experience.

Let's break this down.

Mapping AI to business processes

First, let's talk about business processes. Every organization has them – whether it's how you handle customer inquiries, how your sales team qualifies leads, or how you manage supply chain logistics. These processes often involve multiple steps, and within each step there might be inefficiencies, bottlenecks, or opportunities for improvement. This is where AI can come in.

So, how do you find a good place to start? It depends on your approach.

In an opportunistic scenario, you can start with anything that's currently relevant - like a process you're responsible for. In a divide-and-conquer approach, the entry point ties back to a north star, with processes chosen deliberately because they block progress toward it. From there, source problems without worrying about scoping yet - just surface anything painful, inefficient, or limiting using the pain points and bottlenecks method from the last chapter.

Next, apply your $10K threshold. To recap: this is the minimum recurring value (per month, quarter, etc.) that a problem must offer to justify further exploration. Problems that don't meet that bar are filtered out. Problems that clearly exceed it are kept – and that's when you zoom in.

If a problem seems large – multiple times above your threshold – you don't want to treat it as a single monolith. Instead, break it down into a sub-process with 5–6 meaningful steps. Then, map problems at this more detailed level and reapply the $10K filter. You repeat this loop – map → filter → zoom → repeat – until you reach a level where either of the following applies:

- The $10K problems are *reasonably distributed* across the 5 - 6 steps.
- Breaking it down further would dilute the value below your threshold.

This method keeps your AI exploration focused, actionable, and grounded in business impact. It ensures you're always working on something that's genuinely worth solving.

Let's walk through a quick example.

We assume that our $10K threshold was defined as an impact of at least $10K per quarter. If solving a problem would not potentially bring in that amount, it is not worth our attention right now.

Suppose you've selected the customer support ticket process. You break it down into key steps like this:

1. **Ticket submission**: Customers submit a support request.
2. **Categorization**: The ticket is categorized based on the issue type.
3. **Assignment**: The ticket is assigned to the appropriate team member.
4. **Resolution**: The issue is addressed, and the ticket is closed.
5. **Follow up**: The customer is contacted to ensure satisfaction.

With your $10K threshold set, you now look for problems in each step that – if solved – would meet or exceed that value.

Let's say you find that human agents typically spend a lot of time on categorizing tickets and figuring out the right contact person to assign a ticket to. Looking deeper into this process, you estimate that every agent spends about 2 hours per week on average assigning tickets manually. There are 15 agents all facing the same challenge, so that's 30 hours per week. If a working hour costs us $30, then that's about $900 per week on the table, which translates into $3,600 impact per month and about $10,000 impact per quarter. So, this problem has a good chance of sitting right above our threshold and getting prioritized. However, remember that the $10K threshold isn't meant to measure the size of the problem, but the impact that the resolution of this problem would have. In simple words: if we were able to give human agents these 2 hours per day back, what would they do with them?

If those 2 hours are immediately absorbed by the existing backlog of tickets, the impact will be felt directly through faster response times, higher customer satisfaction, and potentially lower churn or higher revenue retention. If operations are scaling and ticket volume is growing, then the freed-up capacity prevents the need to hire additional agents, which represents a very tangible cost avoidance. On the other hand, if the workload is stable and agents simply end up with more idle time, then the business will not realize the financial gains we calculated, because those hours are not being reinvested into productive work. In other words, the value of solving this problem is only as strong as the downstream use of the recovered time – whether that's reducing backlog, handling growth without new hires, or reallocating capacity to higher-value activities.

Once you've gone through the preceding high-level customer support process and identified a few of these $10K+ problems, that's your signal to bring in AI.

Now revisit the **five AI modes with core skills** (see *Figure 5.1*). Ask yourself: *Which skill areas might apply to the problem?*

For example:

- "AI can help categorize tickets by learning from past cases".
- "AI can draft first responses, saving support reps time".

These draw from skills such as classification, reading, communication, or even reasoning, depending on the context. (This is now also a great time to open the AI skills map (`https://github.com/PacktPublishing/The-Profitable-AI-Advantage/blob/main/ch02/AI_Skills.xlsx`) to quickly look for signal verbs.)

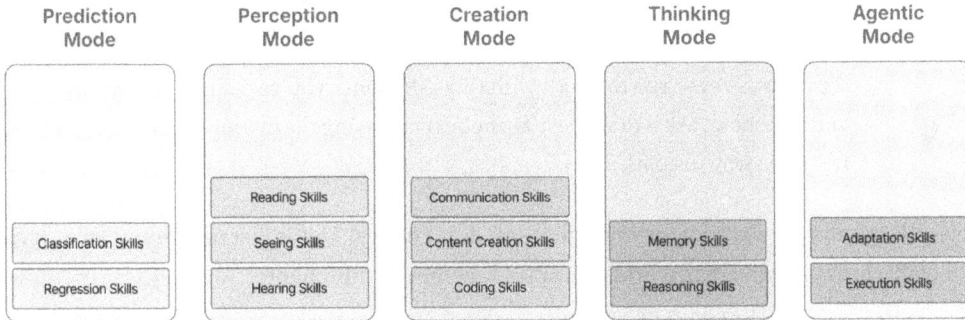

Prediction Mode	Perception Mode	Creation Mode	Thinking Mode	Agentic Mode
	Reading Skills	Communication Skills		
Classification Skills	Seeing Skills	Content Creation Skills	Memory Skills	Adaptation Skills
Regression Skills	Hearing Skills	Coding Skills	Reasoning Skills	Execution Skills

Figure 5.1: AI modes with core skills

🔍 **Quick tip**: Need to see a high-resolution version of this image? Open this book in the next-gen Packt Reader or view it in the PDF/ePub copy.

📖 **The next-gen Packt Reader** is included for free with the purchase of this book. Scan the QR code OR go to packtpub.com/unlock, then use the search bar to find this book by name. Double-check the edition shown to make sure you get the right one.

If you identify a matching skill, make sure it also ties back to one or more **AI value levers** (see *Figure 5.2*):

- Can AI help solve the task **cheaper**? (Cost)
- Can AI help do it **better**? (Quality)
- Can AI help do it **faster**? (Speed)
- Can AI help do it at a **larger scale**? (Scalability)

If it pulls at least one of these levers for a $10K+ problem, it's a strong candidate for a prototype.

> **Tip:** You can even run this part with ChatGPT. Once you've defined your pain points and threshold, ask it to suggest AI applications using the five modes and value levers. It's a fast way to spark ideas.

If this still sounds too abstract for you right now, don't worry! This is just to give you an overview. We'll walk through some real-world examples together in this chapter.

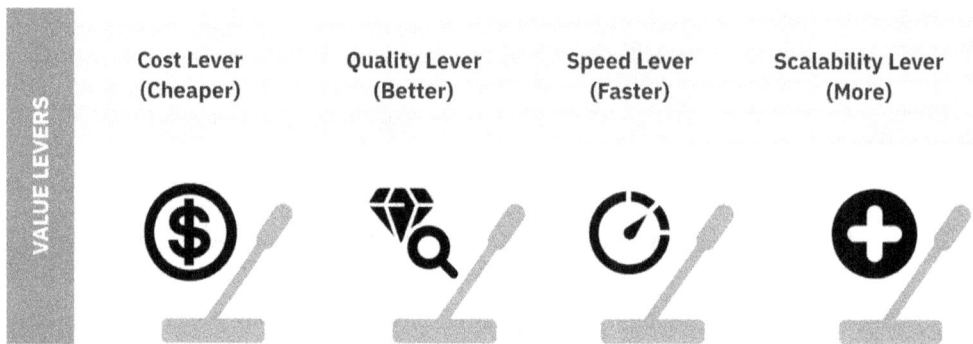

Figure 5.2: AI value levers

While internal processes are often a good entry point, they're not the only one. Sometimes the better lens is your product itself - viewed from the customer's perspective. Let's take a look.

Mapping AI to products

Mapping AI capabilities to products works essentially the same way as mapping to processes. But instead of looking at process steps, you're looking at steps in the user journey, that is, the user's interaction with your product. Each of these steps represents an opportunity to either delight your customers or, if not handled well, frustrate them. The pain points and bottlenecks in this journey define where you need to put your attention with AI. Remember – if there's no pain point or bottleneck, there's no need for AI. This applies both to product- and process-based mappings.

For example, let's say you're developing a mobile app. The user journey might include the following:

1. **Onboarding**: The user signs up and starts using the app.
2. **Daily use**: The user interacts with the app regularly, utilizing its core features.
3. **Feature discovery**: The user explores additional features.

4. **Customer support:** The user encounters an issue and seeks help.

5. **Feedback loop:** The user provides feedback on their experience.

By mapping AI capabilities to the pain points and bottlenecks at these stages, you can uncover ways to improve the user experience - like personalized onboarding or faster support. However, unlike internal workflows, it's harder to prove the value of a better experience in dollars. Be clear about your objective: if ROI is the goal, apply the $10K filter and link improvements to conversion or retention. If you're pursuing product-led AI adoption and differentiation is the main goal, you may need to rely on softer product signals such as higher NPS or engagement. Either way, be explicit about how you define and measure success.

Remember, this isn't a one-off exercise. As your business evolves, your products and processes change, and new AI technologies emerge, you'll need to revisit and refine your mappings. This process is iterative, which means you should be prepared to make adjustments as you gather more insights and data.

In the following sections, we'll dive into three specific examples to show you how this mapping process works in practice. When you carefully map AI capabilities to your processes and products, you're setting the stage for significant improvements – not only in efficiency and cost savings, but also in customer satisfaction and business growth.

Let's map this discussion into a framework that you could follow in practice. This would include four steps:

1. Map the business process(es).

2. Identify the pain points and bottlenecks.

3. Apply the $10K threshold.

4. Map the AI skills to the relevant processes.

The best way to understand this is to look at some examples.

So, let's start with them.

Example 1: Finding AI opportunities in the RFP response process

Let's start with a concrete example of how to identify AI opportunities within a specific business process. Let's say we're the head of sales and, together with our AICoE, we're going to look at the process of responding to requests for proposals (RFPs) because we've identified this as a big opportunity for future growth with multiple $10K opportunities.

Responding to RFPs is a common and often complex task in many industries, where organizations must prepare detailed proposals to win new business.

Step 1: Mapping the business process

The first step is to break down the RFP response process into its key stages. For many businesses, this process might look something like this:

1. **Analyzing the RFP**: Understanding the client's needs and requirements, and deciding whether to pursue the opportunity to add an AI capability.

2. **Assembling the team**: Gathering the right people to contribute to the RFP proposal, including subject matter experts, writers, and reviewers.

3. **Developing a proposal outline and plan**: Creating a roadmap for the proposal, outlining the key sections, and setting deadlines for each part.

4. **Drafting, customizing, and reviewing content**: Writing the proposal content, tailoring it to the client's specific needs, and reviewing it for accuracy and effectiveness.

5. **Finalizing formatting, gaining approvals, and submitting**: Ensuring the proposal is well formatted, obtaining necessary approvals, and submitting the proposal on time.

6. **Following up with the client and internal debriefing**: Contacting the client after submission to address any questions and conducting an internal review to learn from the experience.

By mapping out these stages, we can see where the process might be slowing down, where errors could occur, or where there's an opportunity to improve efficiency. This lays the groundwork for identifying specific pain points.

Step 2: Identifying pain points and bottlenecks

Next, we identify the pain points at each stage of the process. These are the challenges that make the RFP response process time-consuming, costly, or prone to errors. Here are some common pain points:

*   **Analyzing the RFP**: Difficulty quickly digesting complex RFPs, leading to delays in decision-making.

*   **Assembling the team**: Challenges in identifying the right experts quickly, resulting in bottlenecks.

*   **Developing a proposal outline and plan**: Inconsistent planning processes, leading to gaps in the proposal or missed deadlines.

- **Drafting, customizing, and reviewing content**: Struggling to write persuasive, customized content that stands out, while also ensuring compliance with all requirements.

- **Finalizing formatting, gaining approvals, and submitting**: Formatting issues and delays in gaining necessary approvals can lead to rushed submissions.

- **Following up with the client and internal debriefing**: Lack of systematic follow-up with clients and ineffective internal debriefs can result in missed opportunities for learning and improvement.

These pain points represent opportunities where AI could potentially step in to optimize the process.

Step 3: Applying the $10K threshold

For the sake of this exercise and to keep it simple, let's assume all of the above represent a minimal $10K opportunity of $10K per year.

For example, this would include the following:

1. **Analyzing the RFP:** Faster understanding would avoid $10K+ per year wasted on unqualified or misread bids.

2. **Assembling the team:** Quicker access to experts would save $10K+ per year in bottlenecks and lost proposal quality.

3. **Developing a proposal outline and plan:** Clearer planning would prevent $10K+ annual losses due to rewrites and missed deadlines.

4. **Drafting, customizing, and reviewing content:** Stronger content would win $10K+ per year in additional awarded revenue.

5. **Finalizing formatting, gaining approvals, and submitting:** Smoother submission would protect $10K+ per year from avoidable rejections.

6. **Following up with the client and internal debriefing**: Consistent follow-up would increase the chances by $10K+ per year in upsells and future wins.

Step 4: Mapping AI skills to optimize the process

Now comes the exciting part - mapping AI capabilities to the specific stages of the RFP response process to address the prioritized pain points. Here's how AI could be applied:

1. **Analyzing the RFP** would require the perception mode of AI to quickly read and extract key requirements from lengthy RFP documents, helping your team make faster and more informed go/no-go decisions.

2. **Assembling the team** would require classification skills, (the prediction mode), to classify and match the most suitable experts within your organization based on the specific needs of the RFP, ensuring that the right people are involved from the start.

3. **Developing a proposal outline and plan** will require the creation model with the content creation skills to generate proposal outlines after analyzing similar past proposals and suggesting a structure that's both comprehensive and aligned with the client's expectations.

4. **Drafting, customizing, and reviewing content** will utilize the creation and thinking modes:

   - **Creation mode (content creation skills)** can draft initial proposal content, which can then be customized by human writers.

   - **Thinking mode (reasoning skills)** can analyze and interpret requirements to ensure that all mandatory elements are addressed, reducing the risk of non-compliance.

5. Finalizing formatting, gaining approvals, and submitting will require the creation and agentic modes:

   - **Creation mode (content creation skills)** can format the proposal to meet all guidelines quickly and accurately.

   - **Agentic mode (execution skills)** can automate the approval process by routing the document to the right people and sending reminders for approvals.

6. **Following up with the client and internal debriefing** will use the creation and thinking modes of AI:

   - **Creation mode (communication skills)** can draft follow-up emails.

   - **Thinking mode (reasoning skills)** can summarize client interactions post-submission.

As you can see, finding an AI solution does not mean applying a single AI mode or capability to your whole process, but instead, it's often multiple AI modes working together to handle different parts or tasks. Each mode brings specific skills that address particular pain points in your workflow.

Here's a simple table that visualizes this mapping:

RFP Process Stage	Pain Points	AI Skills
Analyzing the RFP	Difficulty digesting complex RFPs	Reasoning skills for quick analysis and key requirement extraction
Assembling the team	Challenges in identifying the right experts	Classification skills for matching and recommending experts
Developing a proposal outline and plan	Inconsistent planning processes	Content creation skills for drafting; reasoning skills for compliance analysis
Drafting, customizing, and reviewing content	Writing persuasive, customized content; compliance	Content creation skills for drafting content; reasoning skills for analyzing and interpreting requirements
Finalizing formatting, gaining approvals	Formatting issues, approval delays	Content creation skills for formatting; agentic mode execution skills for approval automation
Following up and internal debriefing	Ineffective follow-up and debriefs	Communication skills for follow-up emails; reasoning skills for interaction summaries

Table 5.1: AI capability mapping table for the RFP process

Once you map the AI skills to the stages of the RFP response process, we can see where AI can add value, streamline tasks, and improve overall efficiency. This example also demonstrates how AI can pull both the speed and quality levers in your RFP responses, giving your business a competitive edge.

In the next example, we'll apply this same approach to the process of lead generation and qualification, another area ripe for AI-driven improvement.

Example 2: AI opportunities in lead generation and qualification

Now that we've explored how to identify AI opportunities within the RFP response process, let's turn our attention to another critical business process: lead generation and qualification. For many businesses, this process is the lifeblood of their sales funnel, driving new opportunities and potential revenue. However, it's also an area that can be fraught with inefficiencies, missed opportunities, and challenges in scaling effectively. Let's see how AI can help.

Step 1: Mapping the business process

First, let's outline the key stages in the lead generation and qualification process. This process typically involves several steps, which might look something like this:

1. **Lead generation**: Collecting contact information and other relevant data on potential customers through various channels (e.g., website forms, social media, or events).

2. **Lead segmentation**: Categorizing leads based on certain criteria, such as industry, company size, or potential interest in your product or service.

3. **Lead scoring**: Assigning a score to each lead based on their likelihood to convert, which helps prioritize sales efforts.

4. **Lead nurturing**: Engaging with leads through targeted content, emails, or calls to move them further down the sales funnel.

5. **Lead qualification**: Determining whether a lead is ready to be passed on to the sales team based on their level of engagement and fit with your target customer profile.

Each of these stages presents an opportunity for AI to enhance the process by automating repetitive tasks, making better decisions, and providing insights that might be missed by human analysis alone.

Step 2: Identifying pain points and bottlenecks

Next, we need to identify the common pain points in the lead generation and qualification process. These are the challenges that often slow down the process, lead to missed opportunities, or cause inefficiencies. Some typical pain points include the following:

*   **Lead generation**: Outdated or incomplete contact data, leading to high bounce rates and poor-quality leads.

*   **Lead segmentation**: Inefficient or manual segmentation that fails to accurately group leads, resulting in poorly targeted marketing efforts.

- **Lead scoring**: Difficulty in predicting which leads are most likely to convert, leading to wasted effort on low-quality leads.

- **Lead nurturing**: Time-consuming follow-up processes that are not personalized enough to effectively engage leads.

- **Lead qualification**: Inconsistent criteria for determining when a lead is sales-ready, leading to misaligned efforts between marketing and sales teams.

These pain points indicate where AI can potentially step in to optimize the process and improve outcomes.

Step 3: Applying the $10K threshold

Let's assume again that all the steps here would fit a $10K per year scope, so we prioritize all problems for further exploration:

- **Lead generation:** Improved data quality would save $10K+ per year in time saved on not approaching bad contacts.

- **Lead segmentation:** Better grouping of leads could unlock $10K+ per year in additional campaign revenue.

- **Lead scoring:** Focusing effort on the right leads could generate $10K+ per year in higher conversion value.

- **Lead nurturing:** Stronger engagement would prevent drop-offs worth $10K+ per year in lost opportunities.

- **Lead qualification:** Clearer criteria would avoid $10K+ per year in wasted sales and marketing effort.

Step 4: Mapping AI skills to optimize the process

With the pain points prioritized, we can now map AI capabilities to the specific stages of the lead generation and qualification process to address these challenges. Here's how AI might be applied:

1. **Lead generation** can utilize the prediction mode of AI:

   - **Prediction mode with classification skills** can *classify* and *flag* potentially low-quality lead data.

   - **Prediction mode with regression skills** helps *estimate* the expected customer lifetime value (CLV) of a new lead.

2. **Lead segmentation** can employ the **perception mode with reading skills** to read and analyze lead interactions, such as email content or social media activity. This will enable automatically categorizing leads into more precise groups based on behavior, interests, or engagement levels.

3. **Lead scoring** can be best achieved with the **prediction mode with regression skills** that can score and estimate each lead's likelihood to convert, helping to prioritize leads that are most worth pursuing.

4. **Lead nurturing** will require the **creation mode with content creation skills**. This mode can generate and draft personalized content for nurturing campaigns, such as tailored emails or relevant content suggestions based on the lead's interaction history.

5. **Lead qualification** will utilize the prediction mode and the thinking mode:

   - **Prediction mode with classification skills** can classify lead engagement levels and automatically determine when a lead meets the criteria to be passed to the sales team, ensuring that only the most qualified leads are handed off.

   - **Thinking mode with reasoning skills** can analyze and interpret communication patterns to identify leads that show signs of readiness to buy, allowing sales teams to focus on the most promising opportunities.

Here's how this mapping might look in a table:

Lead Process Stage	Pain Points	AI Skills
Lead generation	Outdated/incomplete contact data	Classification skills for data quality flagging; regression skills for missing value estimation
Lead segmentation	Inefficient or manual segmentation	Reading skills for behavior-based segmentation analysis
Lead scoring	Difficulty predicting conversion likelihood	Regression skills for predictive scoring
Lead nurturing	Time-consuming, non-personalized follow-up	Content creation skills for personalized automated follow-ups
Lead qualification	Inconsistent criteria for sales-readiness	Classification skills and reasoning skills for readiness detection

Table 5.2: AI capability mapping table for the lead process

By mapping AI capabilities to these stages, you can see how AI could streamline lead generation and qualification, making these processes more efficient, scalable, and effective. This approach not only helps in generating higher-quality leads but also ensures that your sales team focuses their efforts on the most promising opportunities, ultimately driving better conversion rates.

Example 3: Enhancing a product user journey with AI

Thus far, we've focused on identifying AI opportunities within internal business processes. Now, let's shift our attention to the external side – how AI can enhance your products by improving the user journey and overall customer experience. This approach is particularly valuable for businesses that offer digital products or services, where the user experience can make or break the product's success.

Let's explore how AI can enhance a specific aspect of the customer journey in an e-commerce set-ting – namely, the product search process. This is a critical touchpoint in the customer experience, as it often determines whether a visitor becomes a paying customer or leaves your site frustrated.

Step 1: Mapping the product search process

The product search process in an e-commerce store typically involves several key stages that a customer goes through when trying to find the right product. These stages might include the following:

1. **Search query input**: The customer enters a search term into the search bar or uploads an image of the product they're looking for.
2. **Search results display**: The system returns a list of products that match the search query or the uploaded image.
3. **Filtering and sorting**: The customer refines the search results using filters (e.g., price, brand, or ratings) and sorting options (e.g., relevance or popularity).
4. **Product evaluation**: The customer reviews product details, images, and customer reviews to assess suitability.
5. **Product selection**: The customer adds a product to the cart or decides to continue search-ing.

These steps are crucial in guiding the customer to find exactly what they're looking for, and each one presents opportunities for AI to enhance the experience, making it more personalized, efficient, and satisfying.

Step 2: Identifying user pain points and bottlenecks

To identify where AI can make a difference, we first need to understand the common pain points customers face during the product search process. Here are some typical issues:

- **Search query input:** Customers may struggle to articulate exactly what they're looking for, leading to vague or inaccurate search queries that return irrelevant results. Some may even prefer to search by uploading an image rather than typing out their query.

- **Search results display:** The search engine might return too many results, overwhelming the customer, or too few, frustrating them by not showing relevant options.

- **Filtering and sorting:** Applying filters can be cumbersome, and customers may have difficulty finding the exact products they need without extensive manual sorting.

- **Product evaluation:** Customers often find it challenging to compare similar products based on detailed specifications, reviews, and images.

- **Product selection:** Indecision can arise if the customer isn't confident that they've found the best option, leading to cart abandonment or continued searching.

These pain points highlight the areas where the product search experience can be improved with AI.

Step 3: Applying the $10K threshold

Here's how the $10K prioritization could look:

- **Search query input:** Clearer queries would prevent $10K+ per year in lost sales from irrelevant results.

- **Search results display:** More relevant results would capture $10K+ per year in revenue otherwise lost to frustration.

- **Filtering and sorting:** Easier navigation would unlock $10K+ per year in sales by helping customers find products faster.

- **Product evaluation:** Better comparison would drive $10K+ per year in higher conversions from confident purchase decisions.

- **Product selection:** Reducing indecision would recover $10K+ per year otherwise lost to cart abandonment.

Step 4: Mapping AI skills to enhance the product search process

Let's explore how specific AI skills can be applied to each stage of the product search process to address these pain points and create a more seamless customer experience:

1. **Search query input** will utilize the perception mode:

   - **Perception mode (reading skills)**: AI can interpret and understand customer queries, even if they're vague or complex. For example, if a customer types "comfortable shoes for running," AI can interpret the intent and prioritize showing running shoes with high comfort ratings.

   - **Perception mode (seeing skills):** AI can allow customers to scan and recognize products by uploading an image instead of typing a query. For instance, if a customer sees a jacket they like in a photo, they can upload that image, and AI will identify similar jackets available in the store (in combination with **classification skills from prediction mode**).

   - **Prediction mode (classification skills)**: AI can suggest and recommend smart auto-suggestions as the customer types or immediately after an image is uploaded, offering popular or related search terms to guide the user more effectively. This reduces the likelihood of entering a query that yields poor results.

2. **Search results display** can use the **prediction mode (regression skills).** AI can rank search results based on customer preferences using data such as their browsing history and past purchases to tailor the search results to each individual. For instance, if a customer frequently buys eco-friendly products, the search engine can prioritize sustainable options in the results.

3. **Filtering and sorting** would employ the thinking mode and the prediction mode:

   - **Thinking mode (reasoning skills):** AI can contextualize customer behavior and recommend the most relevant filters based on the customer's query, behavior, or uploaded image. For example, if a customer searches for "summer dresses" or uploads a picture of one, the system might automatically suggest filters such as "lightweight fabrics" or "sleeveless."

   - **Prediction mode (classification or regression skills):** Instead of relying on basic sorting options, AI can rank and prioritize products based on a combination of factors such as relevance.

4. **Product evaluation** would benefit from the thinking and creation modes:

   - **Thinking mode (reasoning skills):** AI can summarize and synthesize customer reviews, extracting key themes and sentiments to provide a quick overview. This saves the customer time by reducing the need to read through dozens of reviews.

   - **Creation mode (content creation skills):** AI can write a summary based on the synthesized insights, which is personalized to the criteria that the user really cares about.

5. **Product selection** can be achieved with the **prediction mode (classification skills)**: Based on the customer's search behavior, uploaded image, and preferences, AI recommends alternative or complementary products based on shopping behavior from similar clients.

Here's how this mapping might look in a table:

Product Search Stage	Pain Points	AI Skills
Search query input	Vague/inaccurate search queries; preference for visual search	Reading skills for better query interpretation; seeing skills for image upload; classification skills for auto-suggestions
Search results display	Too many/too few results; irrelevant options	Regression skills for improved search result ranking
Filtering and sorting	Cumbersome filtering; difficulty finding exact matches	Reasoning skills to suggest relevant filters; classification skills to dynamically re-rank products based on user preferences
Product evaluation	Difficulty comparing products	Reasoning skills for review analysis; content creation skills for personalized summaries
Product selection	Indecision and cart abandonment	Classification skills for cross-promotion and upselling recommendations

Table 5.3: AI capability mapping table for the product search process

By mapping AI capabilities to the stages of the product search process, you can significantly enhance the customer experience on your e-commerce platform. AI doesn't just make the search faster – it also makes it better by making it more intuitive and aligned with what the customer is actually looking for. This leads to higher satisfaction, increased conversion rates, and, ultimately, a more successful e-commerce business.

Now that you've seen the mapping process in action, let's zoom out and review some best practices that apply across all use cases, ensuring you can effectively apply these strategies across both processes and products.

Practical tips for identifying AI opportunities

By now, you've seen how AI can be mapped to both business processes and product journeys to create significant improvements in efficiency, customer satisfaction, and overall business value. But to effectively identify and capitalize on AI opportunities within your own organization, it's essential to follow some best practices. These practices will help ensure that your AI initiatives are not only well conceived but also aligned with your broader business goals:

1. **Keep your business interests first.**

   The first and most crucial step is to align AI initiatives with your overarching business objectives. AI should never be implemented just for the sake of it; it should serve a clear purpose that drives your business forward. Whether your goal is to increase revenue, improve customer satisfaction, streamline operations, or innovate your product offerings, AI should be a means to achieve these ends.

   Tip: Begin by clearly defining the business problems you want to solve or the opportunities you want to explore. For example, if your goal is to reduce customer churn, AI might be used not only to predict at-risk customers but also trigger targeted retention strategies. Always tie your AI projects back to these concrete business objectives to ensure they deliver real value.

2. **Collaborate across departments.**

   AI initiatives are most successful when they are cross-functional. The impact of AI often spans multiple departments, so it's essential to involve stakeholders from different parts of the organization. Create cross-functional teams that include both technical members (such as IT, data science, and data analytics) and less-technical business units (such as marketing, sales, product management, etc.) that are relevant for the given use case. These teams can provide diverse perspectives and ensure that AI initiatives are grounded in both technical feasibility and business needs.

For example, if you're looking to implement AI in your customer support operations, involve people from service, IT, and marketing. Support can surface the most common pain points, IT ensures the chatbot integrates securely with your systems, and marketing makes sure the chatbot connects seamlessly to your website so customers are directed to the right resources.

3. **Iterate and refine**.

Treat this phase as a brainstorming exercise. Move quickly through the mapping process, jotting down where AI might fit and how it could address identified pain points. Don't worry about getting everything perfect for now; the purpose is to create a broad map of possibilities that you'll dive deeper into later. This approach ensures that you're not paralyzed by analysis and can move on to scoping and prioritizing use cases more effectively.

4. **Leverage external expertise**.

This stage is a good opportunity for bringing in external expertise that has worked on similar challenges already, providing specialized knowledge or tools that you might not have in-house.

> **Tip:** Consider working with AI consultants, attending AI-focused workshops, or using AI concept sessions to kickstart your initiatives. External experts can offer fresh perspectives, introduce new methodologies, and help avoid common pitfalls.

5. **Ensure ethical AI use**.

As AI becomes more integrated into business processes and products, it's critical to consider the ethical implications of using AI. While we'll explore the ethical dimension of AI use cases in more detail later, it's best practice to think about ethics from the start. This includes ensuring data privacy and being transparent with customers and stakeholders about how AI is being used. Establish clear ethical guidelines for the use of AI within your organization.

By now, you've identified high-value problems and mapped them to AI capabilities and value levers. But what happens next? Let's talk about it.

Effective workflow augmentation

A common instinct is to ask, *Can AI fully automate this?* but that's not always the best question. A more useful mindset at this stage is: ***How can we bring AI into this workflow to pull at least one of the value levers so we cross our value threshold?***

This is the difference between automation and **augmentation** – a concept we'll explore even further in the next chapter. Instead of handing over full control to AI, effective augmentation means weaving AI into an existing process in a way that helps people work faster, better, and with less effort – or to achieve scale that would otherwise be blocked by manual labor constraints.

Take Apple's Math Notes (`https://support.apple.com/en-gb/guide/iphone/iph46efa613a/ios`) feature, for example. It lets users handwrite equations on an iPad, instantly recognizes the input, and provides real-time results or visualizations – without interrupting the flow. There's no *AI mode* to switch on. It just works.

This kind of experience doesn't happen by accident. It reflects a set of principles known as **TRICUS** (`https://www.oreilly.com/library/view/augmented-analytics/9781098151713/ch05.html`), which define what effective AI augmentation looks like:

- **Timely**: AI offers help at just the right moment.
- **Relevant**: It aligns with the user's intent or goal.
- **Insightful**: It provides meaningful, actionable support.
- **Credible**: The output can be trusted.
- **Unobtrusive**: It doesn't interrupt the user's flow.
- **Specific**: It's tailored to the precise need at hand.

You don't need to redesign your entire process to benefit from AI. In fact, some of the best results come from small, targeted enhancements that remove friction without adding complexity. Of course, once you bring AI into a process, it's worth stepping back to ask whether a more fundamental redesign could unlock even greater value.

This mindset will serve you well as you move into testing and prototyping. In the next chapter, we'll dive deeper into how to scope your AI use cases, build smart prototypes, and ensure your AI solutions aren't just technically sound but truly improve the way people work – and drive business impact.

Summary

Identifying AI opportunities within your business is a strategic process that involves mapping AI modes and skills to your business objectives, involving the right people, and continuously refining your approach. By following these best practices, you can maximize the impact of AI in your organization, turning AI from a buzzword into a powerful driver of business success.

The key is understanding how the five AI modes – prediction, perception, creation, thinking, and agentic – can address specific problems in your processes and products that are worth solving. Whether you're using classification skills to improve lead scoring, reading skills to process customer feedback, or reasoning skills to synthesize complex information, the key is to match these skills to problems that are actually worth solving with AI.

Use your $10K threshold to focus on high-value opportunities, and your value levers – cost, quality, speed, and scalability – to frame how AI will drive impact.

And remember: AI's power often comes not from full automation, but from thoughtful workflow augmentation. Bringing AI into an existing process at the right moment can improve outcomes without adding complexity.

As you move forward, keep these principles in mind: start with clear goals, involve cross-functional teams, iterate on your initiatives, seek external expertise when needed, focus on quick wins, and always consider the ethical implications of your AI use.

In the next chapter, we'll explore how to scope, prioritize, and plan AI use cases effectively – so you can invest in the right projects that deliver real ROI.

6

Designing AI Use Cases

You're now in a crucial phase of your AI journey. In the previous chapter, you explored how you can utilize your newly gained AI knowledge to map high-level AI opportunities within your organization. But getting from this high-level mapping to a profitable AI roadmap is still quite a way. That's why this chapter will dive deeper into the elements it takes to design actionable use cases that not only tell you exactly what to do, but also pave the way for further prioritization and driving ROI along your AI implementation journey. The goal here is not just to identify potential applications of AI (as we did in the last chapter), but to deeply understand each use case's anatomy and implications, and ensure that your AI initiatives are aligned with your business objectives and are primed for success. By the end of this chapter, you will have a detailed blueprint for evaluating potential AI projects, helping you make informed decisions about where to focus your efforts and how to achieve meaningful results.

In this chapter, we will cover the following main topics:

- Why design use cases?
- Use case fact sheets
- The Integration-Automation framework for AI solutions
- Dimensions of Use case fact sheets

Why design use cases?

You might be eager to dive straight into AI implementation based on your high-level mapping. But be careful - the detailed analysis of each use case is essential to avoid costly mistakes.

In fact, designing and conceptualizing your use cases is the bedrock of effective AI implementation. It serves as a safeguard against common pitfalls, such as overextending resources or misaligning AI projects with your strategic goals.

The first reason is that despite its impressive capabilities, AI is not a one-size-fits-all solution. Sometimes, even slight changes in the design of a use case require a completely different approach. For example, consider a manufacturing company that wants to build a support chatbot to make it easier for field service workers to troubleshoot problems. Your mind might say *chatbot*, but is that really what they want? In fact, most service workers probably don't want to chat with a bot; they just want to ask a specific question (or upload a specific image) and get the answer they want right away, without going back and forth with the AI service too much. This requirement would move your use case away from the *AI chatbot* and more into the realm of *augmented search*, which has some very different implications for the technological solution dimension and also the user experience. Instead of a chat interface, the UI would be a simple search prompt. Considering your specific needs, challenges, and goals, along with a thorough analysis, will ensure that you clearly understand the scope, requirements, and potential hurdles before committing resources to a given use case.

Besides getting clarity on what you actually want to build, a detailed use case concept will also allow you to gauge the impact and feasibility of the project better. Not all AI projects will deliver equal value. By analyzing use cases in detail, you can identify which ones align most closely with your business goals and have the potential to offer the greatest return on investment.

But let's get a little more concrete here.

In our previous chapter, we identified various elements in the RFP process as a high-level AI opportunity. Now, we'll break this down into specific use cases and learn how we can analyze each one thoroughly to understand its potential impact and feasibility.

Use case fact sheets

To structure your analysis, we'll use a framework called the **Use case fact sheet**. This tool is designed to capture all the critical dimensions of a use case, enabling you to compare, prioritize, and ultimately decide which projects to pursue. The goal is to give you a single-page overview of what the use case is trying to achieve and what's needed for it.

The following figure shows an example Use case fact sheet:

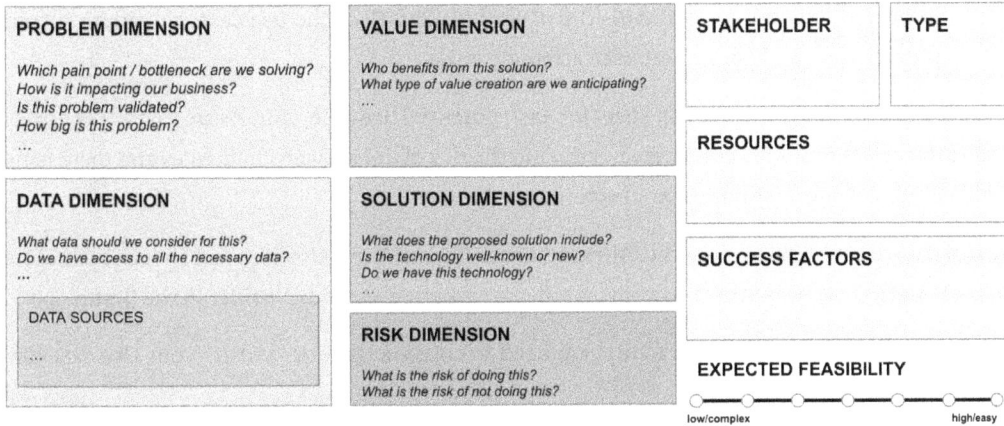

Figure 6.1: Use case fact sheet template

You can find a template version of this fact sheet under this link (`https://github.com/PacktPublishing/The-Profitable-AI-Advantage/blob/main/ch06/Use_Case_Fact_Sheet_Template.pptx`). On a high level, here's what a Use case fact sheet involves:

1. **Problem dimension**: Summarizes the specific pain point or bottleneck that the AI use case aims to address.

2. **Value dimension**: Articulates the intended $10K impact as well as the value lever (speed, cost, quality, and scale).

3. **Data dimension**: Lists the high-level data requirements for the use case.

4. **Solution dimension:** Describes the proposed AI solution, including the relevant AI modes.

5. **Risk dimension:** Identifies potential risks associated with the use case and proposes mitigation strategies.

6. **Stakeholders' involvement dimension:** Lists the key stakeholders involved and their roles in the project.

7. **Type:** Which use case type is this project according to its degree of automation and integration (we'll learn more about this in a bit).

8. **Resources:** Outlines the resources required, including human, technological, and financial.

9. **Success factors:** Defines the **key performance indicators** (**KPIs**) that will determine the success of the use case.

10. **Expected feasibility:** Evaluates the overall feasibility of the use case, considering complexity, cost, and alignment with strategic goals.

By methodically filling out this fact sheet for each potential use case, you ensure that every aspect of the project is thoroughly considered, reducing the risk of unforeseen challenges and increasing the likelihood of successful implementation.

Most of this chapter will explore the different dimensions of these Use case fact sheets, but before we come to that, it's important to know what use cases you should consider in the first place.

Let's briefly discuss two critical factors you need to consider before creating your Use case fact sheets.

- **How many Use case fact sheets should you create?**

  The obvious answer here, of course, is, *it depends*. The size of your organization and the ambition of your AI roadmap really define what's possible here. If you're a mid-sized organization going with a divide-and-conquer approach for AI adoption (*Chapter 3*), it's not uncommon to end up with a list of 100+ potential use cases, perhaps even in a single department. On the other hand, if you're just starting out, you shouldn't try to spend too much time thinking and planning use cases, but get to a position from which you can start moving quickly.

  For most organizations that start somewhere at the beginning, let's say identifying the first AI opportunities in a given process or product, I typically recommend looking for something like 8–10 use cases. Why this number? Because this gives you enough bandwidth to experiment and iterate over different projects, but at the same time, you're not getting overwhelmed by *analysis paralysis*, leaving you with more confusion than when you started.

From here, feel free to take more use cases in as you continue along your AI journey. But don't stretch yourself too thin. Having a **backlog** of 10 AI use cases per process, department, or product is a solid start!

- **What kind of use cases should you consider?**

  When moving from the high-level idea of *AI can help me predict the likelihood of winning a proposal* to a more concrete and actionable form, people often *substitute* complexity with *automation* (usually when they can't fully describe the solution yet). For example, AI will *automatically* analyze incoming proposals and *automatically* recommend the right contact person. But the truth is, the more *automatic* use cases you find in your initial use case descriptions, the more likely it is that those use cases will never work. This is because, for most AI use cases, you need to tell the AI exactly what to do before it can actually do it for you at scale.

To emphasize this point, let's look at two ways that use cases can grow in complexity and how to manage this complexity intentionally.

The Integration-Automation framework for AI solutions

The **Integration-Automation framework for AI (IA-AI framework)** is based on a simple principle: We classify AI solutions based on two criteria - how integrated and automated they are.

Integration refers to how well the AI solution blends or works in synergy with your existing system landscape or business workflows.

Automation refers to how much the AI solution can perform tasks with minimal human intervention.

Think about this for a second. Most people would assume that integration drives automation, and vice versa. But this isn't necessarily true. For instance, you can create a use case that includes some automation but is not fully integrated into your system environment.

Following the IA-AI framework, you'll find four high-level types of AI use cases – different ways an AI solution can be delivered. In practice, of course, the transitions between these can be fluid, but having a strong conceptual understanding of those four types will help you make more intentional, better-informed design decisions.

Figure 6.2 depicts these four types in the four quadrants of the IA-AI framework in the form of a matrix and some of the example tools that belong to each quadrant based on the level of integration and automation.

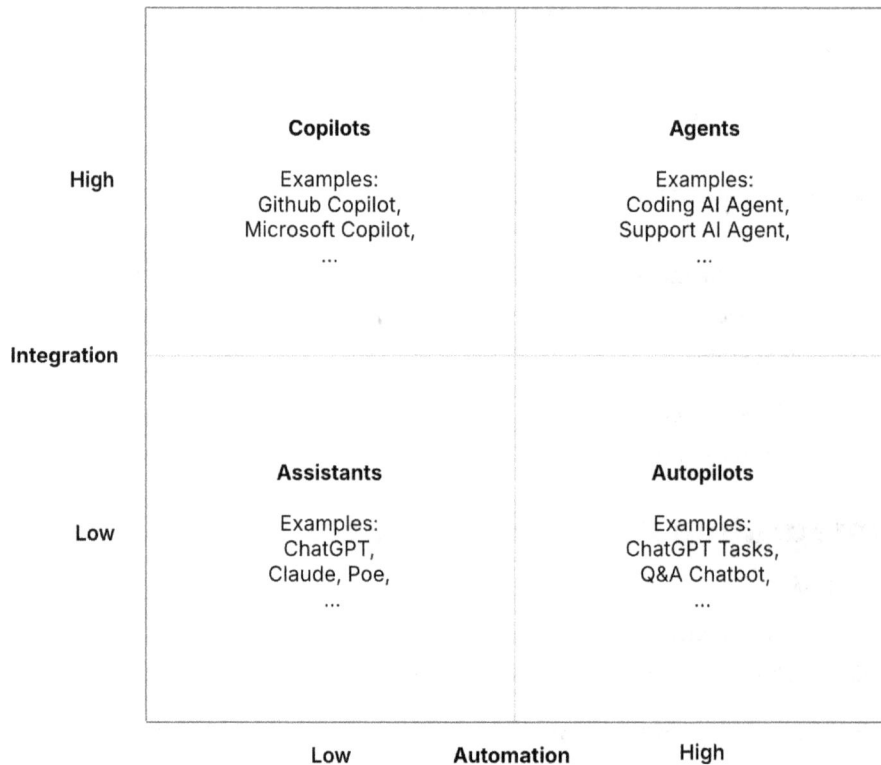

Copilots

Examples:
Github Copilot,
Microsoft Copilot,
...

Agents

Examples:
Coding AI Agent,
Support AI Agent,
...

Assistants

Examples:
ChatGPT,
Claude, Poe,
...

Autopilots

Examples:
ChatGPT Tasks,
Q&A Chatbot,
...

High / Low — Integration

Low / High — Automation

Figure 6.2: IA-AI matrix with some example tools

Let me show you how by walking through the different quadrants of the IA-AI matrix.

Solution type 1: Assistants

The first type of use cases is what I call **assistants**.

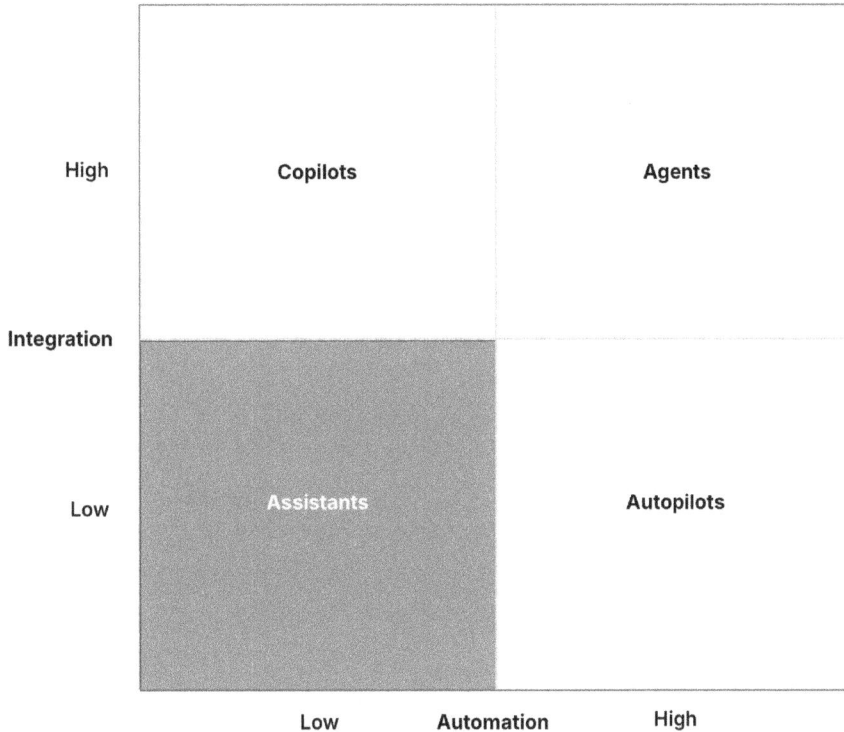

Figure 6.3: Quadrant 1 of the IA-AI framework, the AI assistants

In these solutions, you typically work with an external AI application that requires you to handle inputs and outputs manually (such as copying/pasting text or uploading/downloading a file). The typical degree of integration is low, and so is the automation. ChatGPT is the classic example of this.

Make no mistake - these apps can be increasingly powerful. ChatGPT is probably the most capable external AI assistant you'll likely encounter. Other examples include: Poe.com, Google's Gemini App, and Microsoft's AI-powered Bing search.

Assistants are great for general-purpose, ad-hoc productivity tasks such as writing marketing copy, translating business texts, or just helping AI guide you through a process verbally.

Solution type 2: Copilots

Similar to assistants, **copilots** require you to do the heavy lifting (i.e., their degree of automation is low), but they are more tightly integrated into your system landscape or business workflow.

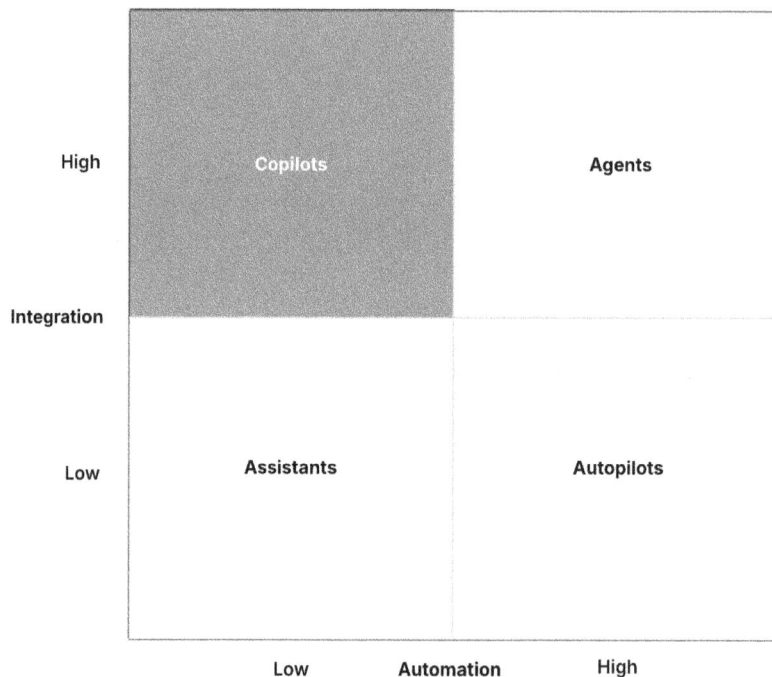

Figure 6.4: Quadrant 2 of the IA-AI framework, the copilots

This is currently the hottest field in AI, and every software company you can think of is looking to include these *copilot* features in their product. Some examples are GitHub Copilot, Microsoft 365 Copilot, Gemini AI in Google Workspace, AI features in Slack, Notion, and so on.

Copilots are great because they know what you're doing at the moment. For instance, if you use Outlook Copilot to reply to an email, it will already know the previous conversation history from that email thread. No copy/paste necessary. It also eliminates the friction of signing up for a new app. However - and that's the biggest difference compared to the next use case type - the AI suggestions cannot be implemented without your approval. So, you have the ability (and responsibility) to review and correct the AI outputs as needed. That's why this use case type is so popular right now. It offers great value, even if the AI models aren't 100% perfect (which they might never be).

Solution type 3: Autopilots

Autopilots show a high degree of automation, but a rather low degree of integration.

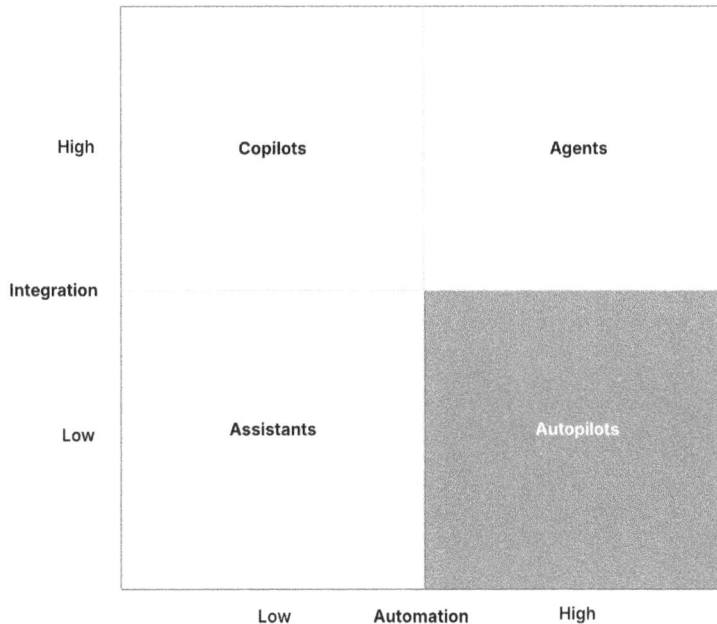

Figure 6.5: Quadrant 3 of the IA-AI framework, the autopilots

So, what's that? Imagine you trained an AI-powered chatbot on your documents to answer first-level customer support queries. Once deployed, this chatbot runs fully automatically, answering customer questions 24/7 without manual intervention. At the same time, this chatbot isn't fully integrated. It usually boils down to putting a small HTML or JavaScript snippet on your website, and this chatbot is not integrated with things like your CRM system. For example, if you tell this chatbot something like *I need to reset my password*, it would be able to guide you through the process verbally, telling you where to click and what to do, but it won't be able to reset the password for you itself. If you want to do that (which is technically feasible), you'd need to increase the degree of integration. This would move the project up to an **agent** use case.

But before we discuss agents in more detail, let's review some more examples of *autopilot* use cases, which can be found across many different domains. For instance, many companies use social media monitoring tools that automatically scan for negative sentiment and then alert a human moderator when a critical event occurs - without taking direct action inside the social platform itself. Another case is the *Task* feature in ChatGPT, where the AI can run a predefined prompt, such as conducting competitor research, on a regular schedule. While the system reliably executes the task, the results are usually just delivered back to the user rather than being connected to downstream workflows. Similarly, automated surveillance systems can analyze video streams in real time and trigger email alerts when specific objects or movements are detected, but they don't automatically take the next steps, such as locking doors or dispatching security staff. Even in the physical world, robotic vacuum cleaners operate as autopilots: they can autonomously navigate a home and clean according to a schedule, but they are not integrated with broader smart-home systems that could, for example, adjust cleaning patterns based on household activity or coordinate with other devices.

Solution type 4: Agents

Agents are the holy grail of AI projects. Everyone wants them.

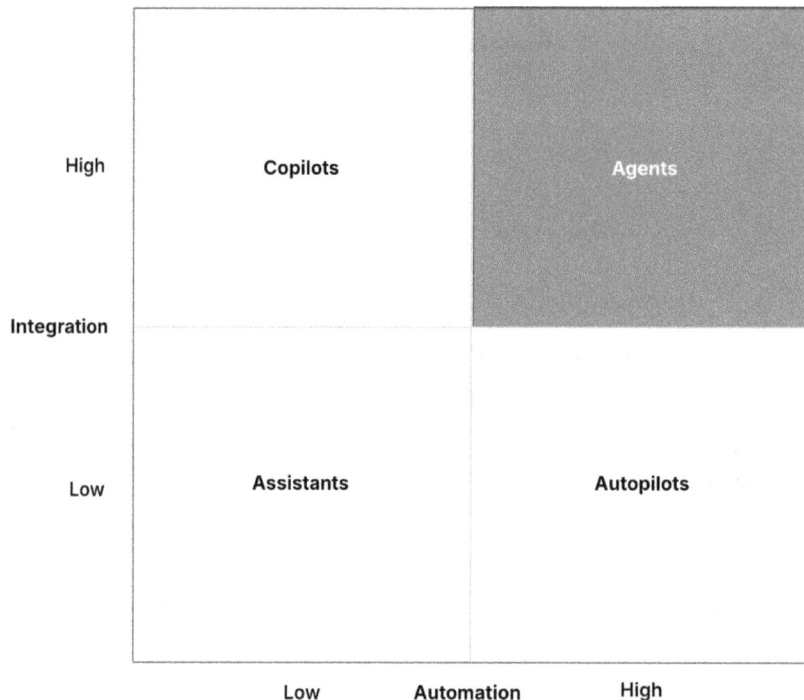

Figure 6.6: Quadrant 4 of the IA-AI framework, the agents

Imagine having a customer support chatbot that can answer common questions but also perform certain tasks, such as sending out a password reset email when a user can't access their account, or even more.

For example, the payment provider Paddle (`https://www.paddle.com/billing/billing-support`) offers an AI support chatbot that automatically handles and resolves typical customer queries related to their clients **Software-as-a-service (SaaS)** offerings, such as processing refunds without human supervision or cancelling subscriptions, cutting support costs, and speeding up ticket resolution to real-time. To be clear, these use cases do exist, but they are the hardest nuts to crack. Because at this stage, you're not only dealing with the challenges inherent in AI (inaccuracies, hallucinations, performance issues, to name a few), but also good old-fashioned IT integration issues involving a bunch of legacy applications – and of course, security.

Other examples of *agent* use cases show just how transformative this level of integration can be. Imagine an AI system that doesn't just scan incoming contracts but actually extracts key terms, files them into your document management system, and kicks off the right approval workflow automatically. Or picture a shopping assistant on your website that doesn't just suggest products but actively bundles personalized offers, applies discounts, and even completes the checkout process on behalf of the customer. In manufacturing, agents can go beyond flagging potential defects: they could halt a machine in real time, adjust parameters to prevent future errors, and notify engineers with a full diagnostic report - all without waiting for human intervention.

While your goal as an organization should be to eventually get to this point, they are by no means the best way to get started. This is where companies new to AI get lost in years of overdue projects and millions in sunk costs. So, where should you start your AI journey?

Working your way through the IA-AI framework

Figure 6.7 shows the two driving forces in the IA-AI framework.

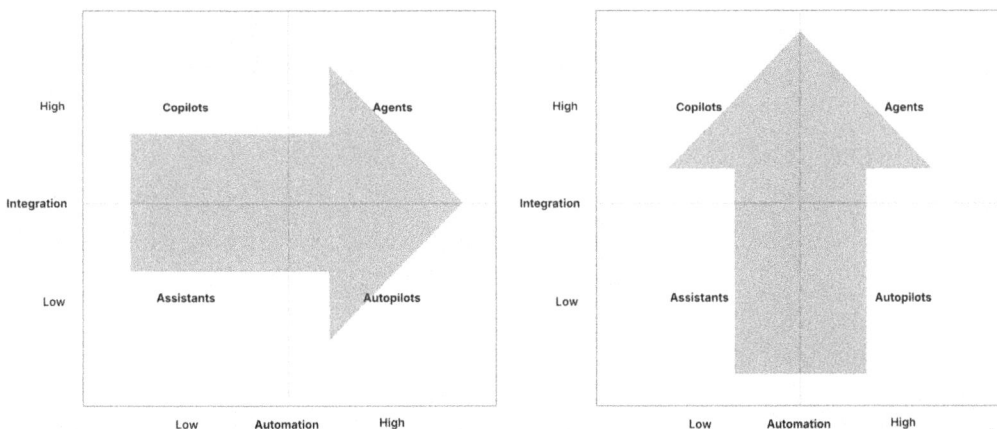

Figure 6.7: Transitioning paths across the IA-AI matrix

In the IA-AI framework, you either proceed from **left to right** (low automation to high automation) and increase the complexity of use cases by automating them more, or you go from **bottom to top** (low integration to high integration), where the main challenge is to integrate what you have even further into your systems or workflows.

It's generally **not a good idea to do both at the same time** (i.e., moving diagonally and increasing the level of integration and automation at once - so don't jump from Assistants to Agents.)

From my experience working with different AI projects across multiple domains, the best approach is to typically tackle use cases in the order I introduced them in this chapter:

Assistants → *Copilots* → *Autopilots* → *Agents*

The key is really to start with so-called *augmented* use cases (assistants and copilots) first, because they always keep a human in the loop.

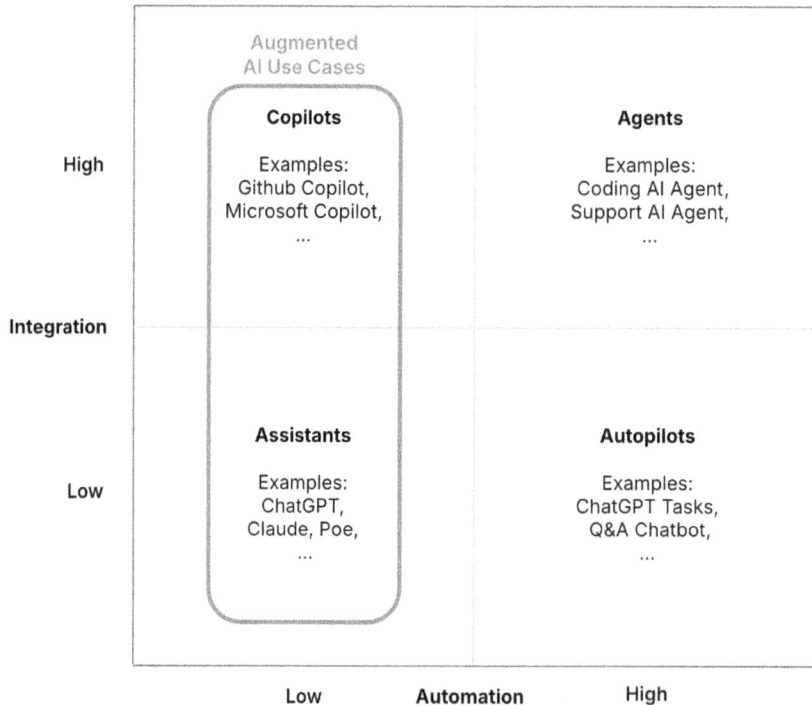

Figure 6.8: Augmented AI use cases in the IA-AI framework

This gives you two major advantages:

- You can control the AI output and ensure quality results
- You learn more and more about how AI works for your organizational use case over time

These two factors are critical components for ensuring long-lasting AI success. They will increase your AI fluency over time. And the beauty of these augmented use cases is that they are typically the least complex, which makes them great candidates for fast prototyping and quick iterations.

Augmented AI use cases also let you apply the TRICUS principles of effective workflow augmentation we touched upon in *Chapter 5*. Building more advanced AI solutions will allow you to integrate them even more seamlessly into your business workflows step by step, instead of spending months (or years) trying to build the perfect integration.

This framework comes in handy while creating your Use case fact sheets. When filling in your Use case fact sheets, make sure to stick to the assistants and copilot use cases at the beginning. If you're finding yourself in an autopilot or agent scenario, then do think twice. Is this really what you want, and are you capable of getting these use cases off the ground? What could be a good intermediary step?

With that in mind, let's get to work on our Use case fact sheets.

Dimensions of Use case fact sheets

As we discussed at the beginning of the chapter, there are ten dimensions that will help you create your Use case fact sheets. We'll cover each of these dimensions step by step.

Problem dimension

The *problem dimension* is the cornerstone of your use case analysis. It defines the specific business problem that the AI solution aims to address. Since you've already thought about that dimension in the previous step, filling this in should come easily. Ask yourself:

- **Which pain point or bottleneck are we solving?** Identify the specific issue that the AI solution is designed to address and whether it's a current problem (pain point) or future issue (bottleneck) that could hinder growth.
- **How is it impacting our business?** Try to describe the effect of the problem. For example, not being able to serve more customers in first-level support could be a pain point. The impact would be that customer satisfaction drops and customer churn goes up. Other impacts might be increased cost or lower sales, for example.

- **Is this problem validated?** How sure are you that this problem really exists? Have you experienced the problem yourself, or is there other evidence that this problem is real? Validation might come from data analysis, customer feedback, or benchmarking against industry standards.

- **How big is this problem?** Evaluate the impact on core business metrics - such as revenue, customer satisfaction, or operational efficiency - using your $10K threshold as a reference point. Ask yourself: does solving this consistently deliver value above the threshold, occasionally cross it, or exceed it by several multiples? Framing the impact this way helps you quickly classify problems into high, medium, or low priority categories.

Let's return to the RFP example from the previous chapter and define the problem dimension (*Figure 6.9*).

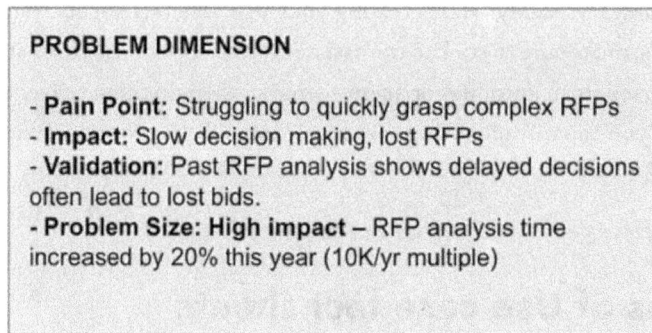

PROBLEM DIMENSION

- **Pain Point:** Struggling to quickly grasp complex RFPs
- **Impact:** Slow decision making, lost RFPs
- **Validation:** Past RFP analysis shows delayed decisions often lead to lost bids.
- **Problem Size: High impact** – RFP analysis time increased by 20% this year (10K/yr multiple)

Figure 6.9: The problem dimension of the RFP use case fact sheet

In the *Analyzing the RFP* process step, we identified that quickly digesting complex RFPs is difficult and leads to delays in decision-making. Our problem dimension could look as follows:

Our proposal team now spends significantly more time on upfront RFP analysis, an increase of 20% this year alone. This extended effort slows the go/no-go decision, leaving less time to prepare the actual proposal. As a result, bids are either rushed and incomplete or abandoned altogether. The pattern is visible in past pursuits, where delayed decisions directly contributed to lost RFPs. With analysis consuming more time while success rates decline, the financial impact easily exceeds the $10K/year threshold and qualifies as a high-impact bottleneck.

Value dimension

The *value dimension* explores the potential benefits of solving the problem (with the help of AI). This can be answered using the **value levers** from *Chapter 5* – how will value be created? Will your process run faster (speed lever), cheaper (cost lever), with higher fidelity (quality lever), or will you be able to do more of something (scalability lever)? Sometimes, a solution pulls multiple of these levers, sometimes just one. However, if you can't identify any of these, it's a strong indicator that the value dimension isn't clear. For example, if your problem is customer churn and you build a customer churn predictor, the predictor alone does not generate much value. Using this information to trigger better (more effective) retention campaigns, does indeed pull a quality lever.

When analyzing the value dimension, consider the following:

- **Who benefits from this solution?** Identify the stakeholders who will directly or indirectly benefit from the AI solution, whether they are customers, employees, or specific business units.

- **How is this value realized?** This applies especially to analytics solutions. How are better insights or predictions realized into business value? Who would make better decisions, and what must happen for this to take place?

- **How does this value align with our business objectives?** Ensure that the value created supports your broader strategic goals. For example, if your business isn't looking for further client expansion, a use case that drives customer growth isn't that attractive.

In the RFP analysis example, an AI-powered RFP chatbot (let's call it **RFP Chatbot Analyzer**) could bring several advantages. Here is the value dimension factsheet for this use case:

> **VALUE DIMENSION**
>
> - **Speed:** Accelerating analysis leads to quicker responses and better chances of winning business.
> - **Beneficiaries**: Sales and proposal teams, enabling faster go/no-go decisions and a higher win rate.
> - **Value Realization:** Increased proposal processing boosts team throughput.
> - **Relevancy:** Aligns with the goal of increasing bid success and securing more client deals.

Figure 6.10: Example of the value dimension for the RFP use case

By accelerating the time it takes to analyze RFPs, the sales and proposal teams can make faster go/no-go decisions, reducing bottlenecks and ensuring more time is available for crafting strong proposals. The direct beneficiaries are the teams themselves, who not only gain efficiency but also improve their chances of winning by submitting higher-quality, timely responses. The real value is realized in throughput: instead of spending days on analysis, teams can process more proposals with the same resources, effectively scaling their capacity without additional headcount. Just as important, this improvement is strategically aligned with the broader business objective of increasing bid success rates and capturing more client deals, thus making the impact both tangible and highly relevant.

Data dimension

Analyzing the *data dimension* is often the toughest of all. Why? Because very often, you don't really know much about your data. And even if you do, there's always some uncertainty involved as to how your data might look in the future. So instead of only describing which data you have, you should also formulate which data your use case needs. Some AI systems have extremely heavy data requirements, especially if you want to train your own models. For others, data requirements are comparably low because you can leverage pretrained off-the-shelf models.

When analyzing the data dimension, consider the following:

- **What data should we consider for this?** Identify the types and sources of data required for the AI solution. This could include structured data, such as transaction records, or unstructured data, such as customer feedback. Keep a separate list of data requirements for more extensive projects.

- **Do we have access to all the necessary data?** Assess whether the organization currently has access to the required data. If yes, who is responsible for these data assets? If not, determine how this data can be obtained or generated.

- **What is the quality of this data?** Evaluate the quality of the available data, considering its accuracy, completeness, and relevance to the problem at hand.

In the RFP analysis example, the data dimension might look as shown in *Figure 6.11*:

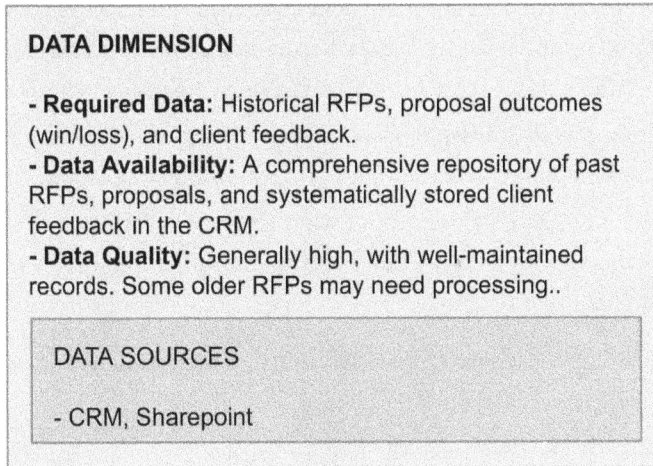

Figure 6.11: Example of the data dimension for the RFP use case

The data requirements for improving RFP analysis are relatively clear. At the core, the solution depends on access to historical RFP documents, past proposals, and the corresponding win/loss outcomes that provide ground truth for what worked and what didn't. Client feedback, where available, adds an additional layer of insight by highlighting gaps or strengths in past submissions. Much of this data could already be available through internal repositories such as the CRM and SharePoint, where proposals and client records are systematically stored. The overall quality might therefore be quite strong if recent records are well maintained, while some older RFPs may require preprocessing or normalization before they can be reliably used. By combining these data sources, the organization would have a solid starting point for developing this use case.

Solution dimension

The *solution dimension* describes the proposed AI solution in detail, including its components, whether the technology is well-known or new, and whether your organization is ready to implement it. Here are some key points to consider:

- **How does the solution work?** Describe in simple, non-technical language what the solution is doing and how it is going to work.

    Tip: Use the action verbs from the AI modes to describe on a high level how the AI solution works.

- **What does the proposed solution include?** Describe the high-level components of the AI solution, including any software, hardware, or integration with existing systems. If these components aren't clear yet, mention that the software needs to be evaluated.

- **Is the technology well-known or new?** Assess whether the AI technology is established and proven or whether it is cutting-edge and potentially more risky.

- **Do we have this technology?** Determine whether your organization already possesses the necessary technology or whether new investments will be required. Is this a commodity AI service or not?

For the AI-powered RFP analysis solution, the solution dimension might be described as follows:

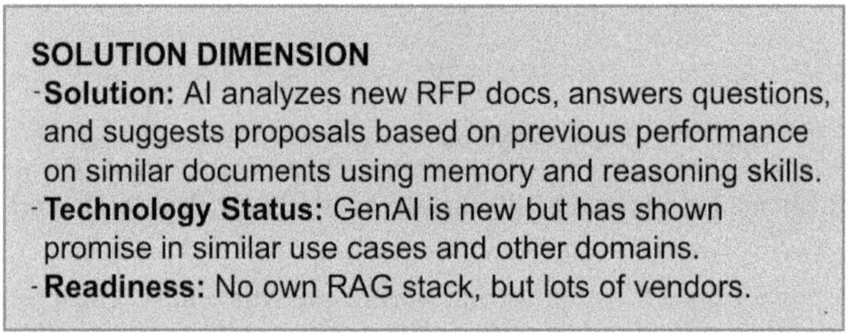

> **SOLUTION DIMENSION**
> - **Solution:** AI analyzes new RFP docs, answers questions, and suggests proposals based on previous performance on similar documents using memory and reasoning skills.
> - **Technology Status:** GenAI is new but has shown promise in similar use cases and other domains.
> - **Readiness:** No own RAG stack, but lots of vendors.

Figure 6.12: Example of the solution dimension for the RFP use case

The AI would take on the task of analyzing new RFP documents by reading and understanding proposal requirements, then applying memory and reasoning skills to surface insights from past proposals and outcomes. On top of this, the system would use communication skills to summarize key points and answer clarifying questions, enabling proposal teams to make faster and more confident go/no-go decisions. The underlying technology is based on generative AI (GenAI) and **retrieval-augmented generation** (**RAG**), which, while still relatively new, have already demonstrated strong performance in document analysis and question-answering tasks across other domains. At present, the organization does not operate its own RAG stack, but given the wide availability of vendor offerings and commodity AI services, adoption would not require building the capability entirely in-house.

Type dimension

Using the *type dimension*, you can classify whether your use case falls into the assistants, copilots, autopilots, or agents category from the IA-AI framework we discussed in the previous section. To define the use case type, look at the required **minimal** degree of automation and integration for this use case to cross the $10K threshold:

- **Degree of integration:** How is this use case integrated into your system landscape? Does it require deep integration at all?

- **Degree of automation:** How is human involvement necessary in this use case? Does the use case run if there's no human involved?

- **Type:** How would you classify this use case accordingly?

Our AI-Powered RFP Chatbot Analyzer could show the following characteristics:

```
TYPE
[ ] Assistant
[X] Copilot
[ ] Autopilot
[ ] Agent
```

Figure 6.13: Example of the type dimension of the RFP use case

Integration-wise, the use case would at least need access to existing CRM data as well as historic proposals and new incoming proposal data, such as data access via SharePoint. Apart from this, the automation needs are rather low since the process would be triggered manually when someone needs ad-hoc insights or answers from a set of proposal documents. Without human intervention, no value would be created. This could make this use case work well as a copilot type. For example, it delivered through a custom chatbot inside SharePoint or Microsoft Teams or basically, any application that proposal teams already interact with every day to keep the workflow augmentation aligned to *TRICUS* principles.

Risk dimension

The *risk dimension* looks at potential risks associated with the AI use case and outlines strategies for mitigating them. Understanding the risks involves both reasoning about doing and not doing the AI solutions, as both could be risky:

- **What is the risk of doing this?** Identify the risks associated with implementing the AI solution, such as technical challenges, data privacy concerns, potential disruptions to existing processes, regulatory compliance (e.g., GDPR, EU AI act, etc.), change management, or internal resistance.

- **What is the risk of not doing this?** Consider the risks of not implementing the solution, such as missed opportunities, competitive disadvantage, or continued inefficiencies. For example, if all your competitors were to write their RFPs with the help of AI and you were the only one sticking to conventional methods, how would this impact your business?

- **How can we mitigate these risks?** What strategies would you apply to manage the identified risks? Are risks manageable at all?

Here is the risk dimension Use case fact sheet for our RFP example:

> **RISK DIMENSION**
> - **Implementation Risk:** Inaccuracies, user adoption
> - **Non-Implementation Risk**: Competitive disadvantage
> - **Mitigation Strategies:** Sources and sampling for accuracy, pilot user group for adoption.

Figure 6.14: Example of the risk dimension for the RFP use case

In the context of the AI solution for RFP analysis, the key risks of implementing an AI-driven RFP analysis tool are inaccuracies in interpreting requirements and resistance from users who may be hesitant to trust automated insights. The bigger risk of not implementing lies in falling behind competitors who adopt such tools and continue to outperform in speed and win rates. These risks can be mitigated through careful data sampling to ensure accuracy and by starting with a pilot group to build user trust and validate feasibility before scaling.

Stakeholder involvement dimension

Many AI projects die, not because the technology doesn't work, but because people don't want the solution to work and build internal resistance. Imagine implementing a customer support chatbot system with the goal of replacing customer support staff, and at the same time, asking the same people to rate the accuracy of that chatbot. The metrics probably won't look good, because who wants to implement technology that takes away their job? What might sound trivial in this simple scenario is actually very hard to detect in large-scale use cases. Often, there are many different perspectives involved, each with its unique interests. While it's not always possible to cater to all, you should at least get an understanding of who's involved and what their role is on this project, with regard to their contributions to the project's success.

Start with these questions:

- **Who are the key stakeholders?** Identify the individuals or groups who have a vested interest in the AI project, such as business unit leaders, IT teams, and end-users. Consider both internal and external stakeholders, depending on the use case.

- **What are their roles?** Define the specific roles and responsibilities of each stakeholder in the project.

- **How will they be involved?** Outline how each stakeholder will be involved in the project, including their level of influence and decision-making authority, for example, using structured tools such as a Responsible, Accountable, Consulted, Informed RACI matrix (`https://www.cio.com/article/287088/project-management-how-to-designa-successful-raci-project-plan.html`).

The Use case fact sheet for this dimension may look as shown in *Figure 6.15*.

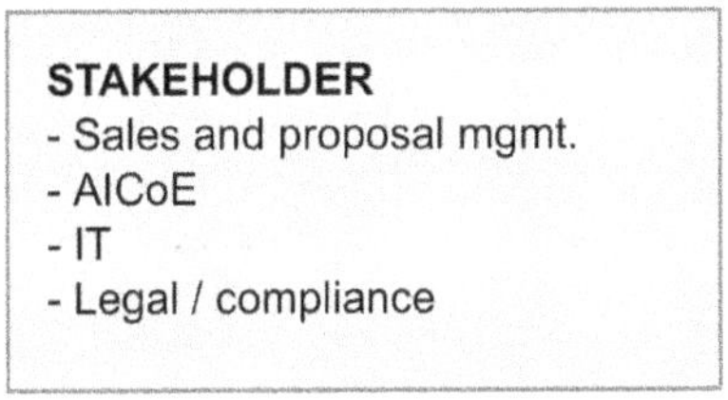

STAKEHOLDER
- Sales and proposal mgmt.
- AICoE
- IT
- Legal / compliance

Figure 6.15: Example of the stakeholder dimension for the RFP use case

For the AI RFP solution, several stakeholder groups play a critical role. Sales and proposal team leads are the primary users; they define requirements, validate outputs, and provide feedback during testing. The IT department ensures smooth technical implementation and integration into existing workflows, while the **AI Center of Excellence (AICoE)** oversees the deployment of models and aligns the use case with broader AI strategy. Legal and compliance teams safeguard data privacy and regulatory adherence, given the sensitivity of client information contained in RFPs. These groups will need to be engaged through structured involvement - workshops to capture requirements, testing phases to validate functionality, and review meetings to resolve concerns. Yet involvement alone is not enough. To secure real buy-in, stakeholders must see the solution as an enabler, not a threat. For example, proposal teams should experience firsthand how the tool saves them time and improves win rates, rather than fearing replacement. Transparent communication of project goals, early inclusion of feedback loops, and visible quick wins are essential strategies to ensure stakeholders are not only consulted but also fully onboard with the adoption.

Resources dimension

The *resources dimension* helps you get a sense of what investments you need to plan for to get this use case off the ground. This is not so much about creating a detailed business plan, but rather getting an idea of what the main resource drivers of this use case will be, such as internal labor hours, external contractors, software licenses, and so on. Since this is often difficult to estimate in advance, it's a good idea to consult either internal or external AI experts.

When analyzing the resources dimension, consider the following:

- **What human resources are needed?** Identify the skills and expertise required to implement the AI solution, such as data scientists, AI specialists, and project managers. Which of these do you have? Which do you need to get from the market?

- **What technology resources are needed?** Determine the technological infrastructure required, such as hardware, software, and integration capabilities.

- **What financial resources are needed?** Estimate the budget required for the project, including costs for technology, personnel, and ongoing maintenance.

For the AI RFP analysis solution, the resources dimension might include the following resources:

```
RESOURCES
- HR: AI architect (AICoE), IT architect (IT), data
engineer (IT), product owner (sales and proposal
team), testers (sales and proposal team)
- Tech: third-party software, data access
- Financials: $10k initial, $10k annual recurring (est.)
```

Figure 6.16: Example of the resources dimension for the RFP use case

The RFP analysis solution will require cross-functional resources, including people from AI, IT, and other departments, as well as someone from the affected proposal team to guide and test the system. Technology needs to center on third-party AI software and integration with CRM and SharePoint. Financially, the project must not cost more than $10K in upfront costs and $10K annually to be profitable, given the defined $10K per year threshold, not factoring in internal labor hours to support ongoing collaboration. To keep the use case viable, resources must either be very lean and cost-effective, or the value threshold must be corrected to a more ambitious target, such as $10K per quarter impact, to justify higher running costs.

Success factors dimension

The *success factors dimension* defines the KPIs that will determine the success of the AI use case. At the end of the day, you need to have clear acceptance criteria to determine whether or not your use case was successful. A lot of use cases die because you can never tell if they actually met their goals as those goals never being defined. So it's a good idea to be clear about them up front. Ask yourself:

- **What are the KPIs?** Identify the specific metrics that will be used to measure the success of the AI project, such as customer satisfaction scores, response times, or cost savings.

> Note: These KPIs can be derived using both quantitative (direct measurement) and qualitative methods (surveys, observations, etc.).

- **How will success be measured?** Determine how these KPIs will be measured, including the data sources and tools that will be used to track them.

- **What is the timeline for achieving success?** Define the timeline for achieving the desired outcomes, including any milestones or checkpoints.

Figure 6.17 highlights some success factors for the RFP use case.

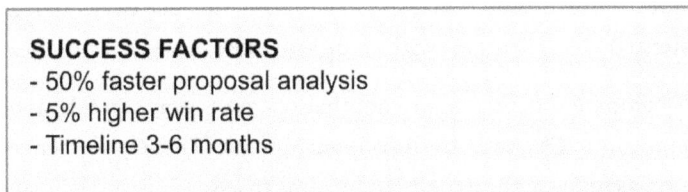

SUCCESS FACTORS
- 50% faster proposal analysis
- 5% higher win rate
- Timeline 3-6 months

Figure 6.17: Example of the success factors dimension for the RFP use case

For the AI RFP analysis solution, the success factors could be:

- **KPIs:** Reduction in time taken to analyze RFPs by 50% (primary) and, increase in win rate by 5% (secondary).

- **Measurement tools:** A/B testing of users with and without the solution.

- **Timeline:** Initial results within the first three months, with full deployment and achievement of KPIs within six months.

Expected feasibility dimension

Last but not least, the *expected feasibility dimension* is your summarized assessment of how likely you think it is to pull this use case off the ground. If you have no idea how to come up with a number right now, don't worry! The next chapter will provide you with some simple heuristics. For now it's best to approach the expected feasibility from a ranking perspective instead of trying to figure out a perfect score. This involves developing one-pagers for all your candidate use cases and then ranking them by feasibility after reviewing each one.

The best way to achieve this ranking is through a head-to-head comparison. Compare two use cases side by side and determine which one seems more likely to succeed based on ease of implementation. Continue this comparison across all your use cases. By the end, you'll have a ranked list from most to least feasible.

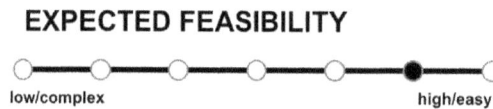

EXPECTED FEASIBILITY

low/complex   high/easy

Figure 6.18: Example of the expected feasibility dimension for the RFP use case

Given everything we know from the previous dimensions, our RFP Chatbot Analyzer ranks highly in feasibility. This is because it has relatively low technological requirements, and we anticipate minimal organizational or cultural challenges in adopting this use case - especially when compared to other potential AI applications within the same RFP process.

For example, let's compare this use case to another use case, which might evolve from our AI opportunity screening from *Chapter 5*, the RFP Team Matcher. The requirements of the RFP team Matcher use case are as follows: the Expert Finder aims to assemble the right **subject matter experts (SMEs)** more rapidly through an integrated Outlook plugin that suggests people to include in an email (CC) for RFP inputs. Looking at the data sources and stakeholders, it's clear that this use case would involve more people and process even more sensitive data, so we would definitely rank it less feasible (more complex) than the RFP Chatbot Analyzer.

Here is the Use case fact sheet for this use case:

Use Case Fact Sheet: Team Matcher

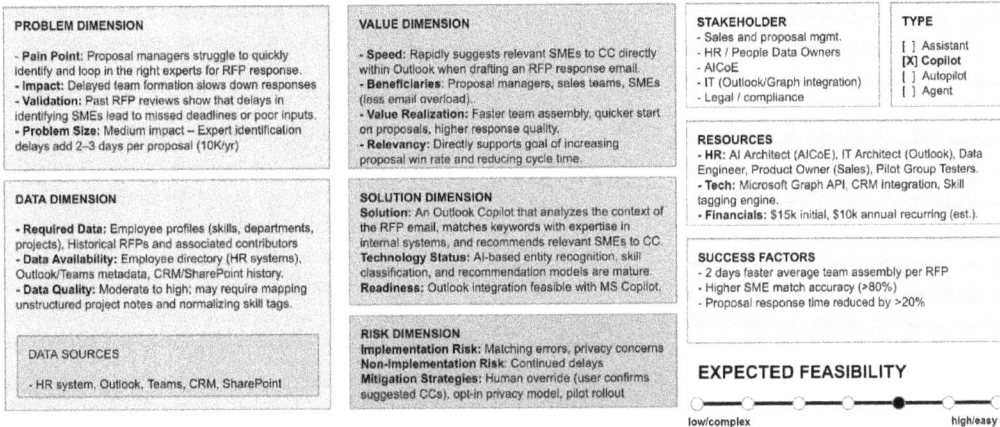

PROBLEM DIMENSION

- **Pain Point:** Proposal managers struggle to quickly identify and loop in the right experts for RFP response.
- **Impact:** Delayed team formation slows down responses
- **Validation:** Past RFP reviews show that delays in identifying SMEs lead to missed deadlines or poor inputs.
- **Problem Size:** Medium impact – Expert identification delays add 2–3 days per proposal (10K/yr)

DATA DIMENSION

- **Required Data:** Employee profiles (skills, departments, projects), Historical RFPs and associated contributors
- **Data Availability:** Employee directory (HR systems), Outlook/Teams metadata, CRM/SharePoint history.
- **Data Quality:** Moderate to high; may require mapping unstructured project notes and normalizing skill tags.

DATA SOURCES

- HR system, Outlook, Teams, CRM, SharePoint

VALUE DIMENSION

- **Speed:** Rapidly suggests relevant SMEs to CC directly within Outlook when drafting an RFP response email.
- **Beneficiaries:** Proposal managers, sales teams, SMEs (less email overload).
- **Value Realization:** Faster team assembly, quicker start on proposals, higher response quality.
- **Relevancy:** Directly supports goal of increasing proposal win rate and reducing cycle time.

SOLUTION DIMENSION

Solution: An Outlook Copilot that analyzes the context of the RFP email, matches keywords with expertise in internal systems, and recommends relevant SMEs to CC.
Technology Status: AI-based entity recognition, skill classification, and recommendation models are mature.
Readiness: Outlook integration feasible with MS Copilot.

RISK DIMENSION

Implementation Risk: Matching errors, privacy concerns
Non-Implementation Risk: Continued delays
Mitigation Strategies: Human override (user confirms suggested CCs), opt-in privacy model, pilot rollout

STAKEHOLDER
- Sales and proposal mgmt.
- HR / People Data Owners
- AICoE
- IT (Outlook/Graph integration)
- Legal / compliance

TYPE

[ ] Assistant
[X] Copilot
[ ] Autopilot
[ ] Agent

RESOURCES
- **HR:** AI Architect (AICoE), IT Architect (Outlook), Data Engineer, Product Owner (Sales), Pilot Group Testers.
- **Tech:** Microsoft Graph API, CRM integration, Skill tagging engine.
- **Financials:** $15k initial, $10k annual recurring (est.).

SUCCESS FACTORS
- 2 days faster average team assembly per RFP
- Higher SME match accuracy (>80%)
- Proposal response time reduced by >20%

EXPECTED FEASIBILITY

low/complex ———————————————————— high/easy

Figure 6.19: Complete Use case fact sheet for the RFP Team Matcher use case

For comparison, here's how the complete Use case fact sheet could look for our RFP Chatbot Analyzer:

Use Case Fact Sheet: RFP Chatbot Analyzer

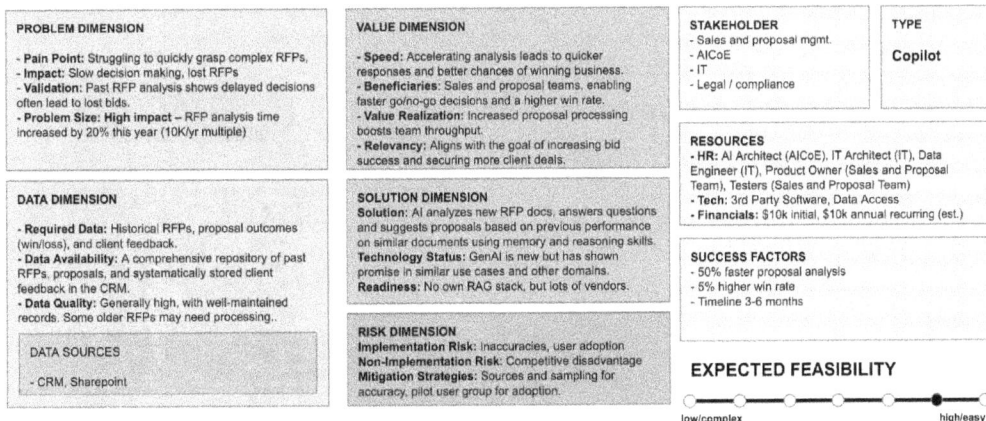

PROBLEM DIMENSION

- **Pain Point:** Struggling to quickly grasp complex RFPs,
- **Impact:** Slow decision making, lost RFPs
- **Validation:** Past RFP analysis shows delayed decisions often lead to lost bids.
- **Problem Size:** High impact – RFP analysis time increased by 20% this year (10K/yr multiple)

DATA DIMENSION

- **Required Data:** Historical RFPs, proposal outcomes (win/loss), and client feedback.
- **Data Availability:** A comprehensive repository of past RFPs, proposals, and systematically stored client feedback in the CRM.
- **Data Quality:** Generally high, with well-maintained records. Some older RFPs may need processing..

DATA SOURCES

- CRM, Sharepoint

VALUE DIMENSION

- **Speed:** Accelerating analysis leads to quicker responses and better chances of winning business.
- **Beneficiaries:** Sales and proposal teams, enabling faster go/no-go decisions and a higher win rate.
- **Value Realization:** Increased proposal processing boosts team throughput.
- **Relevancy:** Aligns with the goal of increasing bid success and securing more client deals.

SOLUTION DIMENSION

Solution: AI analyzes new RFP docs, answers questions and suggests proposals based on previous performance on similar documents using memory and reasoning skills.
Technology Status: GenAI is new but has shown promise in similar use cases and other domains.
Readiness: No own RAG stack, but lots of vendors.

RISK DIMENSION

Implementation Risk: Inaccuracies, user adoption
Non-Implementation Risk: Competitive disadvantage
Mitigation Strategies: Sources and sampling for accuracy, pilot user group for adoption.

STAKEHOLDER
- Sales and proposal mgmt.
- AICoE
- IT
- Legal / compliance

TYPE

Copilot

RESOURCES
- **HR:** AI Architect (AICoE), IT Architect (IT), Data Engineer (IT), Product Owner (Sales and Proposal Team), Testers (Sales and Proposal Team)
- **Tech:** 3rd Party Software, Data Access
- **Financials:** $10k initial, $10k annual recurring (est.)

SUCCESS FACTORS
- 50% faster proposal analysis
- 5% higher win rate
- Timeline 3-6 months

EXPECTED FEASIBILITY

low/complex ———————————————————— high/easy

Figure 6.20: Complete Use case fact sheet for the RFP Chatbot Analyzer use case

When you look at these Use case fact sheets, the ten dimensions – problem, data, value, solution, risk, stakeholders, resources, success factors, type, and expected feasibility – give you a bird's-eye overview and make it easy to scan use cases at a glance. This isn't just useful for yourself or anyone managing the use case pipeline, but also for clearly communicating the big-picture idea and the *why* behind each use case. The format is flexible: it can be condensed to just the solution dimension when you need a quick explanation, or expanded with additional fields such as **Status** when more detail is required. Personally, I like to use it as a one-slide summary for each use case – something I can pull up any time we need to zoom out and align on what we're actually trying to achieve, even well into the implementation phase.

Summary

In this chapter, we explored a practical approach that effectively balances the need for thorough use case analysis with the practical realities of decision-making at a very early stage in your AI roadmap. Focusing on the most achievable projects that can deliver quick wins and build momentum for your AI initiatives is critical, especially in the beginning.

By applying the Use case fact sheet template, you can ensure that each potential AI project is thoroughly understood, from the problem it solves to the resources it requires to the value it creates. Be sure to start with augmented use cases at the beginning and move on to advanced autopilot and agentic use cases as you gain experience and confidence.

In the next chapter, we will focus on prioritizing the analyzed use cases and integrating them into a strategic AI roadmap. This roadmap will guide your AI journey, ensuring that each step is deliberate, aligned with your business goals, and positioned for success.

7

Building Your AI Roadmap

Now that you've created your **Use case fact sheet or fact sheet** – and ideally many of them – the next step is to put them on an AI roadmap. Or better: AI roadmaps. The title of this chapter might suggest we're building one **AI roadmap**, but in reality, most organizations need to build multiple AI roadmaps. Each department or business unit will have its own unique set of AI use cases, strategies, and goals. These various roadmaps must work together, creating a cohesive strategy that aligns with broader business objectives and ensures long-term success.

An AI roadmap in the sense I'm using it for this book is a rather tactical element. While your overall AI adoption approach (see *Chapter 3*) tells you how your organization should tackle the AI age in general, an AI roadmap tells you how to realize a given set of business goals with AI in a shorter period of time. While there's no definite number to what *a shorter period of time* means, I found planning intervals of six months to be very helpful. Six months gives you enough runway to plan AI initiatives upfront, but it is also short enough to embrace changes in the overall AI landscape.

The basis of your roadmap is the Use case fact sheets that you learned about in the last chapter. To turn a loose collection of Use case fact sheets into a cohesive roadmap, we must do the following: organize fact sheets by common denominators; prioritizing fact sheets, to know what to tackle and identify the connections between fact sheets to know which synergies exist.

Based on this information, you can put your use cases onto a project plan that gets executed in a structured way while allowing you to maintain flexibility, and to cycle through options as you gather more feedback, priorities shift or as new opportunities arise.

In this chapter, we'll explore how to build multiple AI roadmaps across an organization that work together towards a larger business goal. While the focus here is on the technical and tactical elements, remember that true success also depends on fostering an AI-ready culture, which we'll address further in *Chapter 10*.

We will cover the following topics:

- Organizing AI use cases
- Prioritizing AI use cases
- Connecting the dots: Finding synergies across use cases
- Sequencing use cases for maximum impact
- Aligning roadmaps across the organization

Organizing AI use cases

There are three main ways to organize your use cases that enable decentralized ownership while allowing strategic decision-making: by department, by product team, or by business goal. Each grouping method offers unique advantages depending on the structure of your organization and the focus of your AI initiatives.

Approach A: Group by department

You can group your use cases by the department or team that generated them. This method typically categorizes use cases by business function, aligning AI projects with specific departmental goals. For example:

- The marketing team may focus on customer segmentation, personalized outreach, and campaign optimization, using AI to better understand customer behavior and improve targeting.
- The operations team might prioritize process automation, predictive maintenance, or improving customer support efficiency through AI-driven solutions.

By grouping use cases this way, you ensure that each department has a clear view of its AI opportunities, and these opportunities are directly tied back to ***core business processes***. This approach works well in opportunistic AI adoption and organizations where departments operate with relative independence, and where AI is seen as a tool to improve department-specific efficiency and performance.

Approach B: Group by product team

If your organization is product-centric, you might prefer grouping your use case fact sheet by how AI supports each product, acknowledging nuances in each product lifecycle as well as the underlying customer journeys.

For example, if your organization runs multiple e-commerce outlets, such as B2B and B2C stores, AI use cases can be grouped by each type:

- **B2C store**: AI use cases might focus on personalized recommendations, dynamic pricing, and AI-driven marketing automation to enhance the customer experience and drive conversions.

- **B2B store**: AI initiatives may include bulk order predictions, supply chain optimization, and automated customer account management, addressing the longer sales cycles and operational efficiency needs of B2B transactions.

This approach works particularly well in industries where product development and customer experience are central, such as e-commerce, technology, or consumer goods.

Approach C: Group by business goal

Another way to group your AI use cases is by their contribution to broader business goals which works well with a divide-and-conquer approach. This approach ensures that all AI initiatives are aligned with the company's strategic priorities, such as increasing revenue, improving customer satisfaction, or enhancing operational efficiency.

For example:

- If the organization's top priority is improving customer retention, you could group AI use cases from multiple departments – such as marketing, customer service, and product development – under this goal. Use cases could include personalized marketing recommendations, AI-powered customer support chatbots, and improving the product recommendation engine.

- If the business goal is reducing operational costs, use cases from departments such as operations, logistics, and finance might be grouped together, including AI projects for streamlined order delivery, improved demand forecasting, and supply chain optimization.

This categorization ensures that AI initiatives remain strategically focused on what's most important to the business, regardless of which department is responsible for the execution.

In practice, you might find a combination of these approaches works best. For example, a product-centric organization might group AI use cases by product but also align certain initiatives with broader business goals, such as improving customer retention or driving operational efficiency. In the end, you'll often have a mix of these different factors, which is completely fine, as this reflects the very uniqueness of your own organization.

Building a use case backlog

Let's explore a practical example of building a roadmap by department. In the previous chapter, we explored the *AI RFP response process* use case. In our sales department, we also identified the following potential AI use cases that could be added to the department **backlog**:

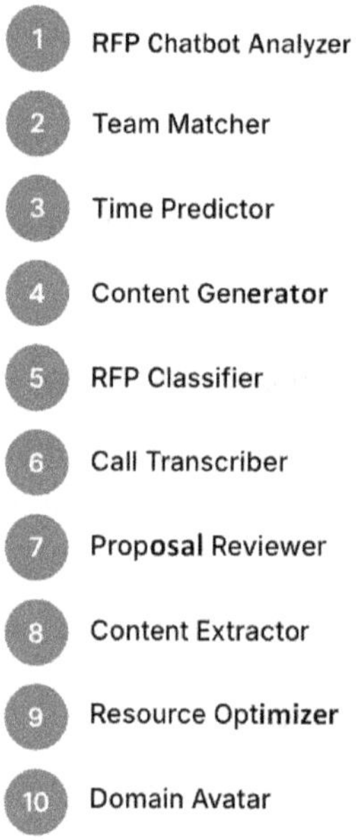

1. RFP Chatbot Analyzer
2. Team Matcher
3. Time Predictor
4. Content Generator
5. RFP Classifier
6. Call Transcriber
7. Proposal Reviewer
8. Content Extractor
9. Resource Optimizer
10. Domain Avatar

Figure 7.1: AI RFP response process backlog

This backlog includes entries like:

- **RFP Chatbot Analyzer**: AI-driven chatbot that helps answer RFP-related questions quickly and accurately.
- **Team Matcher**: AI system that suggests the best internal teams to handle specific RFPs based on skillset and experience.
- **Time Predictor**: Predicts how long it will take to complete an RFP based on past data and project complexity.

- **Content Generator**: Automatically generates proposal content by leveraging AI to draft sections based on previous successful proposals.

- **RFP Classifier**: AI system that classifies incoming RFPs and routes them to the appropriate department or team.

- **Call Transcriber**: Transcribes and analyzes sales calls related to RFPs, helping identify key insights and action points.

- **Proposal Reviewer**: AI-powered tool that reviews and provides feedback on RFP drafts, ensuring compliance and improving quality.

- **Content Extractor**: Extracts relevant information from RFP documents for easier analysis and faster response times.

- **Resource Optimizer**: Optimizes the allocation of internal resources based on project needs and availability.

- **Domain Avatar**: AI-driven *avatar* that can simulate internal domain experts to quickly gather the right knowledge necessary for submitting an RFP.

For every one of these use cases, the department has created a **use case fact sheet**.

The use case fact sheet for the RFP Chatbot Analyzer is depicted in *Figure 7.2*:

Use Case Fact Sheet: RFP Chatbot Analyzer

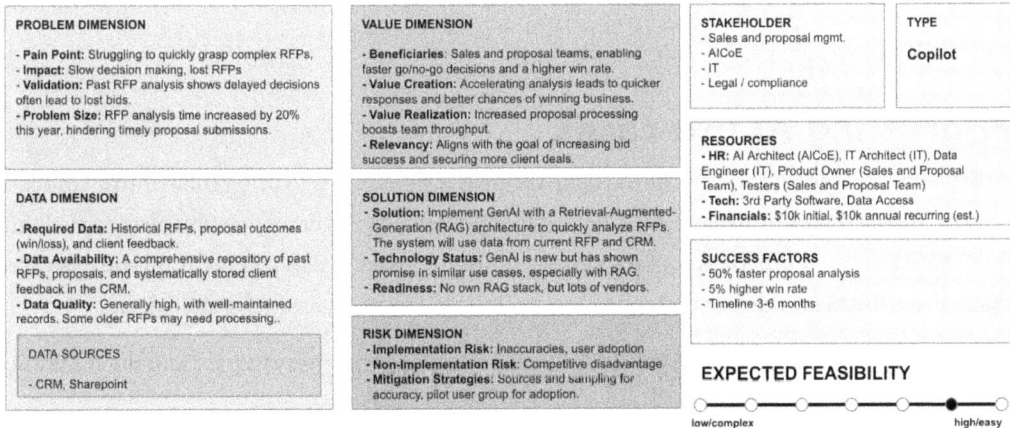

PROBLEM DIMENSION

- **Pain Point:** Struggling to quickly grasp complex RFPs.
- **Impact:** Slow decision making, lost RFPs
- **Validation:** Past RFP analysis shows delayed decisions often lead to lost bids.
- **Problem Size:** RFP analysis time increased by 20% this year, hindering timely proposal submissions.

DATA DIMENSION

- **Required Data:** Historical RFPs, proposal outcomes (win/loss), and client feedback.
- **Data Availability:** A comprehensive repository of past RFPs, proposals, and systematically stored client feedback in the CRM.
- **Data Quality:** Generally high, with well-maintained records. Some older RFPs may need processing..

DATA SOURCES

- CRM, Sharepoint

VALUE DIMENSION

- **Beneficiaries:** Sales and proposal teams, enabling faster go/no-go decisions and a higher win rate.
- **Value Creation:** Accelerating analysis leads to quicker responses and better chances of winning business.
- **Value Realization:** Increased proposal processing boosts team throughput.
- **Relevancy:** Aligns with the goal of increasing bid success and securing more client deals.

SOLUTION DIMENSION

- **Solution:** Implement GenAI with a Retrieval-Augmented-Generation (RAG) architecture to quickly analyze RFPs. The system will use data from current RFP and CRM.
- **Technology Status:** GenAI is new but has shown promise in similar use cases, especially with RAG.
- **Readiness:** No own RAG stack, but lots of vendors.

RISK DIMENSION

- **Implementation Risk:** Inaccuracies, user adoption
- **Non-Implementation Risk:** Competitive disadvantage
- **Mitigation Strategies:** Sources and sampling for accuracy, pilot user group for adoption.

STAKEHOLDER	TYPE
- Sales and proposal mgmt. - AICoE - IT - Legal / compliance	Copilot

RESOURCES

- **HR:** AI Architect (AICoE), IT Architect (IT), Data Engineer (IT), Product Owner (Sales and Proposal Team), Testers (Sales and Proposal Team)
- **Tech:** 3rd Party Software, Data Access
- **Financials:** $10k initial, $10k annual recurring (est.)

SUCCESS FACTORS

- 50% faster proposal analysis
- 5% higher win rate
- Timeline 3-6 months

EXPECTED FEASIBILITY

low/complex   high/easy

Figure 7.2: Use case fact sheet example

When a backlog is populated with fact sheet, it becomes easier for the organization to quickly identify high-priority use cases, reallocate resources when necessary, and maintain momentum even when certain projects hit roadblocks. The Use case fact sheets also ensure consistency, as each AI project can be evaluated, compared, and refined using the same set of criteria.

A backlog of use cases is not a one-time exercise – it's a living document. As new technologies emerge and business needs evolve, your backlog should be continuously updated to reflect these changes. For instance, a use case that wasn't feasible a year ago might now be within reach due to advancements in AI technology or changes in data availability.

This ongoing review process also allows you to reprioritize use cases as needed. For example, if a department achieves success with a low-complexity use case (a **Quick Win**), they can immediately move on to a higher-complexity project that's already in the backlog. By continually cycling through the backlog, you ensure that your AI efforts remain aligned with current business priorities and external opportunities.

Your AI **use case backlog** (*Figure 7.1*) is the foundation of your roadmapping process. It provides a structured, comprehensive view of the organization's AI opportunities, ensuring that each department, product team, or cross-functional team behind a business goal has a clear understanding of how AI can drive value. The backlog demonstrates a robust example of multiple AI initiatives that, when prioritized and aligned correctly, can become a well-organized roadmap.

This department could now proceed by prioritizing these use cases by business impact and feasibility and finding synergies that exist between them.

And that's exactly what we're going to do next!

Prioritizing AI use cases

With your use cases collected in the backlog, the next logical step is to bring them into an order of priority. Before diving into dependencies or overlaps between use cases, we first need to evaluate them based on their **business impact** and **feasibility**. This will help you focus on the use cases that deliver the most value and are the most practical to implement in the short term.

There are two key dimensions to consider when prioritizing: business impact and the feasibility of the use case.

Business impact

This dimension assesses the potential value a use case can bring to the organization. In earlier steps, you've already checked whether a use case clears your $10K threshold and is therefore worth considering at all. At this stage, the focus shifts to two questions: how much value the use case delivers above that threshold, and how measurable that value will be in practice. You can gather insights for this dimension from the **VALUE DIMENSION** field in your Use case fact sheets.

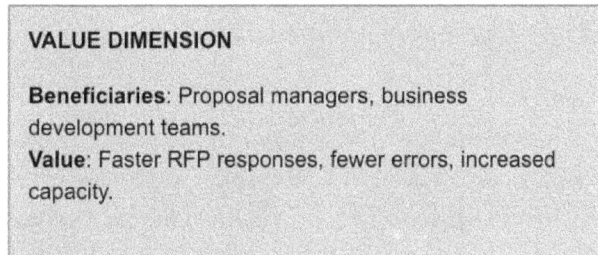

VALUE DIMENSION

Beneficiaries: Proposal managers, business development teams.
Value: Faster RFP responses, fewer errors, increased capacity.

Figure 7.3: Value dimensions to assess the business value of the project

Keep in mind that at this early stage, quantifying impact can be difficult due to many unknowns. You don't need a perfect financial model yet, but you do need a credible sense of scale and traceability for value creation.

So, instead of using arbitrary scoring systems like *T-shirt sizes* or vague categories, a more straightforward approach is to rank use cases against each other. This allows you to prioritize without overcomplicating things in the beginning.

Simply compare each use case head-to-head with another and ask yourself: Which one is likely to deliver more measurable value above the $10K threshold? You can think in terms of the following four **Value levers**:

- **Cost**: Will this use case allow us to operate more cost-effectively?
- **Quality**: Will this use case allow us to do things better?
- **Speed**: Will this use case allow us to do things faster?
- **Quantity**: Will this use case allow us to do more?

Some use cases might hit just one – others might hit all value levers. What matters, though, is the business impact overall. If one use case just has a cost lever of allowing you to save $50k per month – that is more valuable than a use case where you can do more things faster and cheaper, but the overall impact might be just $20k per month.

Continue doing this for all use cases. As you compare them one by one, you'll end up with a ranked list – highest impact to lowest – without worrying too much about the exact numbers or metrics in between.

Bear in mind that, in practice, you don't need to compare every use case against each other. For example, if we know that *Use Case 1* is more valuable than *Use Case 2*, we don't need to compare *Use Case 3* against *Use Case 1* if *Use Case 3* is less valuable than *Use Case 2*.

In our RFP example (*Figure 7.3*), we might find that **Domain Avatar** has a higher expected business impact than **RFP Chatbot Analyzer**. However, when comparing **Team Matcher** to **Domain Avatar**, **Team Matcher** might rank higher in terms of potential business value. Comparing **RFP Chatbot Analyzer** with **Time Predictor** could result in **RFP Chatbot Analyzer** taking precedence. By working through this head-to-head comparison method, you'll end up with a rough ranking of use cases by business impact, which is a great starting point to move forward.

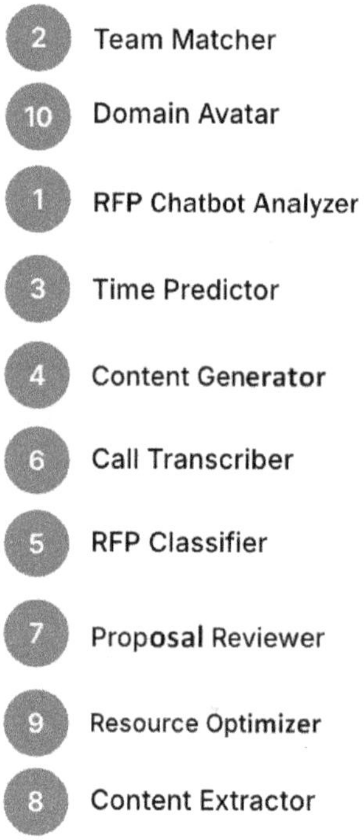

2 Team Matcher

10 Domain Avatar

1 RFP Chatbot Analyzer

3 Time Predictor

4 Content Generator

6 Call Transcriber

5 RFP Classifier

7 Proposal Reviewer

9 Resource Optimizer

8 Content Extractor

Figure 7.4: Use-case ranking of AI RFP response process

Remember, this ranking is just a rough heuristic – use it to establish an order of priority quickly, knowing that it can and likely will change as you progress and gather more insights.

Feasibility

Once you have a rough ranking of use cases by business impact, the next dimension to evaluate is feasibility. This dimension assesses how practical each use case is to implement based on available resources, data, technology, and organizational readiness - essentially, a measure of how fast and easily value can be realized.

In your Use case fact sheets, you've already made an initial guess regarding the feasibility (refer to *Chapter 6*). Refine this initial assessment now with a strong focus on the fields **Data Dimension**, **Risk Dimension**, **Resources**, and **Stakeholders** in *Chapter 6, Figure 6.20*.

Some use cases may require substantial investment in data collection, integration, or infrastructure, while others might be relatively easy to implement with the tools already available.

I use a system where I assign *complexity points* to a given use case whether it checks off a criteria or not:

Check?	Question	Complexity Points
[ ]	Does this require high automation?	2
[ ]	Does this require high integration?	2
[ ]	Is the data for this use case not available?	3
[ ]	Do we need to train an AI model for this?	3
[ ]	Are we lacking the necessary expertise?	1
[ ]	Is this use case in a regulated domain?	1

Table 7.1: Complexity points for different use cases

Whenever you check off one of these lines, add the number of complexity points to your total.

Then you can match this use case roughly to one of the following categories:

- **0-2 Points**: High feasibility
- **3-4 Points**: Medium feasibility
- **5+ Points**: Low feasibility

Feel free to adjust these questions and the complexity point system to your organization.

With this information in mind, perform a head-to-head comparison of your use cases based on feasibility, much like you did for business impact, but this time doing it within each feasibility class (low/medium/high) and through a lens of asking yourself how easily each project can be executed.

As you work through this head-to-head comparison of feasibility, you'll spread out your use cases vertically, forming a two-dimensional view. The first dimension is impact, and the second dimension is feasibility. Here's how that might look in our current example:

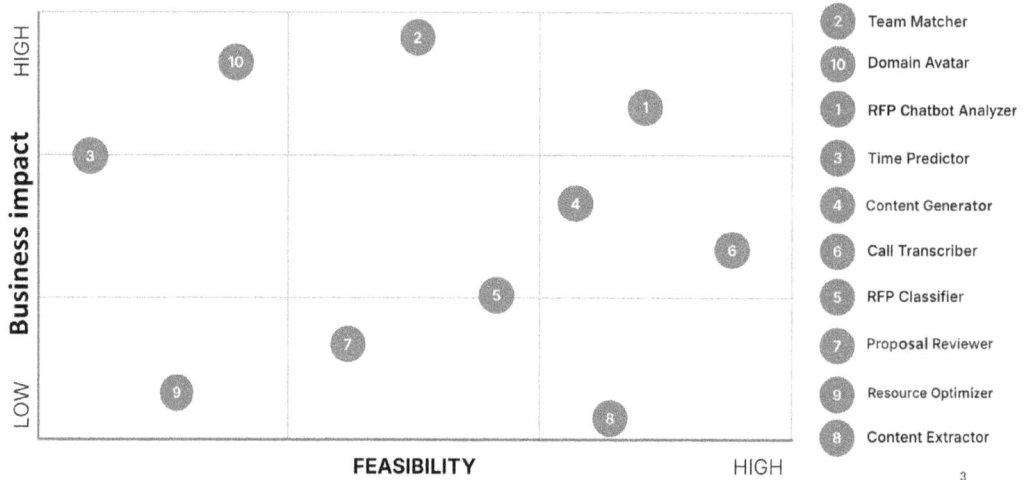

Figure 7.5: Comparing use cases – feasibility vs business impact

For example, after evaluating feasibility, you might realize that building a **Call Transcriber (6)** would be easier than implementing the more complex **RFP Chatbot Analyzer (1)**. Similarly, **RFP Chatbot Analyzer (1)** might be easier to develop than an **Automated Content Generator (4)**, which might require significant resources and advanced capabilities.

With these two dimensions in mind, we will look at a more structured method to prioritize your use cases.

Creating the Use case prioritization matrix

If you've completed this exercise, congratulations, you've just created the first draft of your **Use case prioritization matrix** (*Figure 7.5*). This matrix allows you to quickly identify where to focus your efforts and provides a structured approach for deciding which use cases to prioritize.

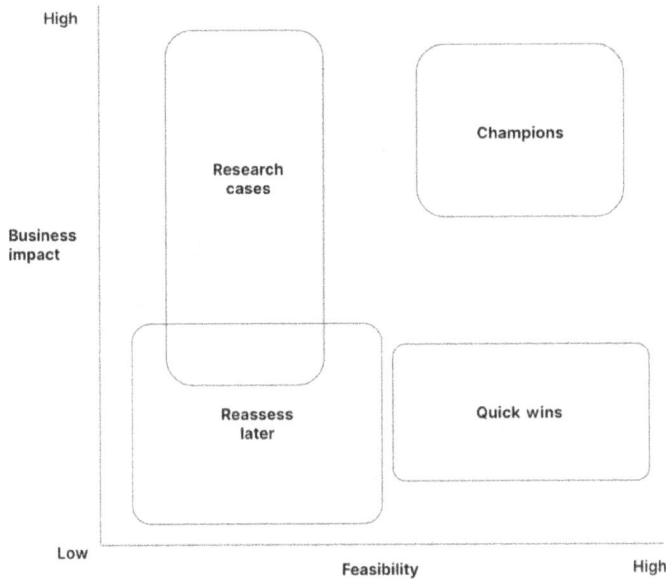

Figure 7.6: Use case prioritization matrix

The **prioritization matrix** is a great visual tool that offers a clear, objective way to align stake-holders on which use cases to pursue and ensures that resources are directed toward initiatives that deliver maximum business value. It also helps to categorize use cases into four distinct types:

- **Champions**: High-impact, high-feasibility projects. These should be prioritized as they offer the most immediate value.
- **Quick wins**: Lower-impact but high-feasibility projects. These can be implemented quickly to demonstrate early success and build momentum.
- **Research cases**: High-impact but lower-feasibility projects. These are longer-term strategic bets that will require more resources and development time.
- **Reassess later**: Low-impact, low-feasibility projects. These should be deprioritized but may be revisited later as circumstances change.

This prioritization matrix will be crucial as you move forward, ensuring that your AI roadmap focuses on the highest-value and most feasible use cases, while also maintaining a clear view of more ambitious projects that require a longer-term commitment. It will also serve as an effective tool for stakeholder communication, helping everyone stay aligned.

To be clear, you need to run this process for every use case backlog you have in each department, product team, or business goal – depending on how you grouped them. This is why scoping is critical. A good sweet spot is a backlog of around **5-15** use cases per group. This range gives you enough room to iterate while preventing you from becoming overwhelmed by too many competing priorities.

Finally, keeping track of all the different roadmaps and ensuring overarching alignment across the organization is the task of a central AI unit, such as a **Head of AI** or **AI Center of Excellence (AI CoE)**. We'll explore that topic in more depth later, in this chapter.

For now, the last missing piece is to identify how different use cases are related and if they can be combined to leverage additional synergies.

Connecting the dots: Finding synergies across use cases

In practice, a lot of *AI roadmapping* processes stop right here after the *prioritization matrix*, with teams jumping straight into developing *quick win* use cases or starting to build resources for more ambitious but less feasible projects. However, they overlook a critical step: *Connecting the dots*.

Connecting the dots means finding overlaps and identifying synergies across different use cases. The goal is to leverage insights from one use case to benefit others, transferring learnings (both successes and failures) across projects. It also enables the organization to achieve compounding gains, where progress in one area leads to improvements in others.

This process can take place:

- Within a single group (whether grouped by department, product team, or business goal).
- Between groups across all roadmaps, ensuring alignment across the organization.

While a central unit like an AI CoE or a Head of AI will ensure alignment between multiple roadmaps, business leaders and department heads of different groups are responsible for maintaining alignment within their own roadmaps. AI experts should assist in this process, but business leaders. must also develop a sense of how different use cases relate to one another. This helps them pivot as needed, adjust roadmaps on the go, and make more informed decisions.

Let's take a look at some of the common overlaps.

Common data sources and technology overlaps

One of the most immediate ways to connect the dots is by identifying shared data sources and technology overlaps across your use cases. Many AI projects require the same types of data or depend on similar technical infrastructure. By identifying these shared requirements, you can centralize efforts and reduce redundancies.

For example, in our RFP example, both the ***RFP Chatbot Analyzer*** and the ***Content Generator*** require access to the original RFP documents submitted by clients. Both use cases may share a similar data pipeline, which processes these documents and ensures that the data is formatted correctly. Streamlining this data pipeline benefits both use cases simultaneously.

If you look at the technology aspect, the ***RFP Chatbot Analyzer*** and the ***Domain Avatar*** are both ***Chat with your documents*** use cases, powered by **large language models (LLMs)**. Both use cases share a similar technological stack, meaning that advancements or improvements in one (e.g., refining LLM interactions) can easily benefit the other.

When data or technology is standardized across use cases, the benefits multiply. Enhanced data quality or improvements in your AI tech stack can elevate multiple projects at once.

Similar processes across departments or teams

Process-driven synergies often arise within a group but can also emerge between departments. Different teams might be solving similar problems, even if the specific use cases look different on the surface.

For instance, while the sales department is building an RFP chatbot to automate responses to client tenders, the internal purchasing department might face a similar challenge from the opposite angle – comparing incoming offers to RFPs they've sent out. Both departments deal with document comparison and could benefit from a shared AI platform that streamlines document processing.

Identifying these process overlaps ensures that similar AI tools can be leveraged across departments, reducing duplication and improving overall efficiency.

Shared product features or customer touchpoints

Some use cases might target similar product features or customer interactions. Recognizing these connections ensures that improvements in one use case directly enhance other parts of the customer journey or product experience.

Consider an e-commerce setting where different use cases, such as personalized recommendations or cart abandonment recovery, might all impact the checkout process in an online store. Streamlining the underlying technology powering these features ensures that multiple parts of the customer journey benefit from AI-driven improvements.

Connecting the dots between product-focused use cases allows for more consistent user experiences and helps maximize the value of AI across the entire organization.

As you connect these dots, you ensure that your AI roadmaps are not just a collection of isolated projects but a tightly integrated program of initiatives working together to drive greater business value.

But how do you find and orchestrate these overlaps in practice? There is a practical framework you can use – the **3S framework**. Let's see how you can use it.

The 3S framework: Spot, Size, Seize

Start with **Spotting the Overlaps**, which involves scanning your AI use cases for any shared data sources, technologies, workflows, or customer touchpoints. Create a shortlist of overlaps between the use cases in your backlog.

> Tip: Cluster the use case overlaps using a mind map!

Next, **Size the Overlaps** to decide which commonalities truly matter. Not every shared element is worth unifying – some might offer a limited benefit or require too much extra effort. A quick evaluation of each overlap's potential business value, feasibility, and cost savings allows you to focus on the integrations that will have the most impact.

Finally, **Seize the Overlaps** and translate these insights into concrete action. Once you know where you can consolidate effort and investment, it's time to unify those projects under a shared architecture or platform, and a timeline that avoids duplicated effort, allows smoother future integrations, and adds a quicker path to scaling.

To illustrate how applying this framework and connecting the dots looks in practice, let's revisit the RFP process we prioritized earlier.

Revisiting the RFP response process example

Which dots are there that we should connect – and how do we find them? Let's run the 3S framework:

1. **Spot the Overlaps**: Look across AI projects for shared needs in:

   - **Data**: Are multiple use cases relying on the same datasets or sources?

   - **Technology**: Do different AI use cases need similar models, APIs, or infrastructure?

   - **Processes**: Are different use cases essentially trying to solve the same type of problem in different ways?

   - **Touchpoints**: Which new AI features would impact the same customer/user journey?

   In our RFP scenario, for example, the ***Chatbot Analyzer***, ***Content Generator***, and ***Domain Avatar*** all rely on the same RFP document database and LLM-powered text generation.

2. **Size the Overlaps**: Not every dot (connection) is relevant for us. So, let's briefly evaluate which overlaps are really worth pursuing by asking:

   - **Higher business impact**: Will combining efforts create significantly better outcomes?

   - **Better feasibility**: Will merging make execution easier rather than harder?

   - **Cost-saving potential**: Will we reduce redundant AI work and save resources?

   Example: Since the ***RFP Chatbot Analyzer***, ***Domain Avatar***, and ***Content Generator*** are all ranked with high business value, it makes sense to bundle them in order to reduce cost and build technical capabilities to unlock the most complex use case (***Domain Avatar***) as we go.

3. **Seize the Overlaps**: Now that we know which synergies exist and whether it makes sense to realize them, we will define guardrails for our implementation plan accordingly.

   In our example, instead of developing separate AI tools in isolation, we could merge the ***RFP Chatbot Analyzer***, ***Domain Avatar***, and ***Content Generator*** into a single project called *Smart RFP AI Suite*. While each use case still lives on its own (and gets implemented individually), we would ensure that infrastructure, AI models, and strategic decisions are planned holistically, eliminating redundant development efforts and infrastructure costs.

Concretely, rather than purchasing an off-the-shelf *chat-with-your-data* tool that only solves the immediate chatbot use case, we choose a flexible AI platform that:

- Meets the chatbot's immediate needs, enabling rapid deployment.

- Provides built-in support (or easy expansion) for additional AI use cases, such as content generation and domain expertise simulation.

- Ensures long-term scalability by allowing seamless model updates and integration with future AI initiatives.

Figure 7.7 shows how you can connect and order the use cases for the RFP Chatbot Analyzer project.

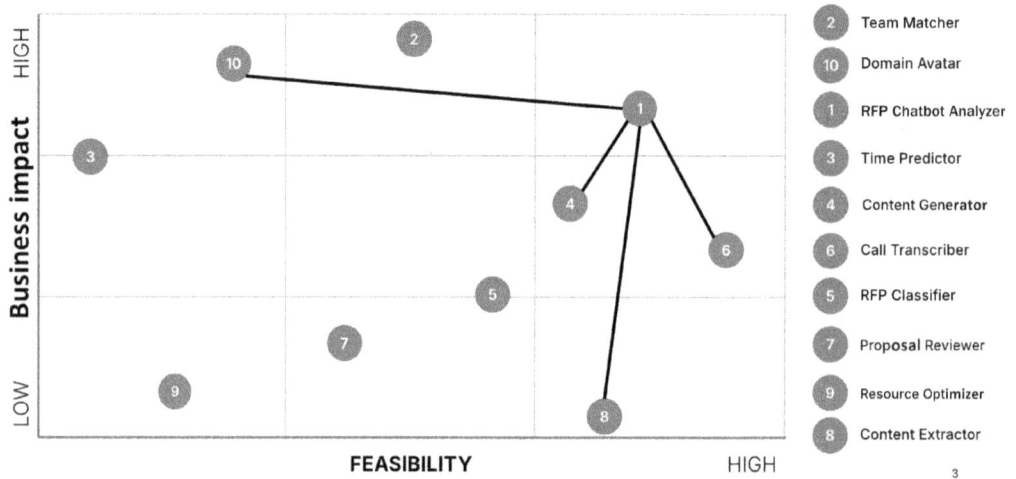

Figure 7.7: Connecting the dots for the RFP response process

This approach reduces tech fragmentation, avoids vendor lock-in, and maximizes ROI by ensuring that every AI investment serves multiple use cases over time. It also helps optimize resources and amplifies the business value of AI implementation within the department.

After grouping, prioritizing, and connecting the dots between your AI use cases, the final step is to determine the optimal sequence for implementation. Let's talk about it more in the next section.

Sequencing use cases for maximum impact

Sequencing the use cases ensures that the AI initiatives in your roadmap are tackled in the right order, balancing quick wins, strategic bets, and dependencies between use cases.

A well-thought-out sequence allows your organization to:

- Maximize resource efficiency by reusing capabilities and infrastructure across related projects.
- Deliver short-term wins while laying the groundwork for more complex initiatives.
- Mitigate risks by solving foundational issues (e.g., data readiness) early on, making larger projects more feasible down the road.

When deciding the order in which to implement your use cases, several factors should be taken into account:

- **Dependencies between use cases** : Some use cases will naturally depend on others. You need to determine which use cases must be completed first to unlock the value of subsequent projects.

  For example, in our RFP example, the ***RFP Chatbot Analyzer*** may require a well-established document processing pipeline. If the department also has a ***Content Generator*** that uses the same document inputs, it makes sense to implement both sequentially, so that the document pipeline created for the chatbot also powers the generator. In this case, the chatbot might need to be prioritized first as it helps establish the infrastructure for the other.

  By sequencing use cases with shared dependencies, you ensure smoother implementation and more efficient use of resources.

- **Quick wins versus strategic bets**: You should also balance quick wins with more ambitious, long-term projects. Quick wins demonstrate immediate value, helping build momentum and support from stakeholders. Strategic bets, on the other hand, are more complex initiatives that take longer to deliver but offer greater rewards.

  In cases where the ***RFP Chatbot Analyzer*** is a feasible quick win that could be implemented within a few months, it should be prioritized early. On the other hand, the ***Domain Avatar*** might be a more ambitious project, requiring advanced AI capabilities and a longer timeframe. While both are important, tackling the quick win first can help build organizational support and generate early value while laying the groundwork for more complex projects.

By sequencing both types of projects strategically, you maintain momentum and deliver continuous value throughout the roadmap.

- **Data and infrastructure readiness**: Before certain AI use cases can be implemented, the organization needs to ensure that the necessary data and infrastructure are in place. If foundational work is required – such as cleaning data, integrating systems, or improving data governance – these tasks should be prioritized early to unlock future AI capabilities.

  Let's consider a case where your roadmap includes an AI-driven *Proposal Reviewer* that relies on high-quality, structured data from past proposals. The first step might involve the data pipeline and ensuring that historical data is cleaned and accessible. Once the data is ready, the proposal reviewer can be developed more easily.

  Addressing data readiness early ensures that later projects are not delayed due to foundational issues.

- **Phased approach for ambitious projects**: For large, complex AI projects (what we previously referred to as strategic bets), it's often helpful to break them down into smaller, more manageable phases. This phased approach allows you to make gradual progress while minimizing risk.

  For an ambitious project like the *Domain Avatar*, you might start by implementing a simpler version of the avatar that handles basic inquiries before gradually expanding its capabilities to more complex tasks. This incremental approach allows for continuous learning and improvement while ensuring that progress is made without overwhelming the team with a large, complex project from the start.

Let's return to our RFP example to see how sequencing plays out in practice.

Sequencing the RFP Use Cases

After connecting the dots between the *RFP Chatbot Analyzer*, *Domain Avatar*, and *Content Generator*, the team has determined the following sequence:

1. **RFP Chatbot Analyzer**: This use case is a feasible quick win that can demonstrate immediate value. It also establishes the necessary document processing pipeline that other use cases will depend on.

2. **Content Generator**: Once the document processing pipeline is in place, the content generator can leverage this infrastructure to automate sections of the RFP creation process.

3. **Domain Avatar**: This is a more ambitious use case that will require more development time. By sequencing it after the chatbot and content generator, the team ensures that key infrastructure is already in place, reducing implementation risk.

Figure 7.8 illustrates this sequencing based on the two priority dimensions, Business impact and feasibility.

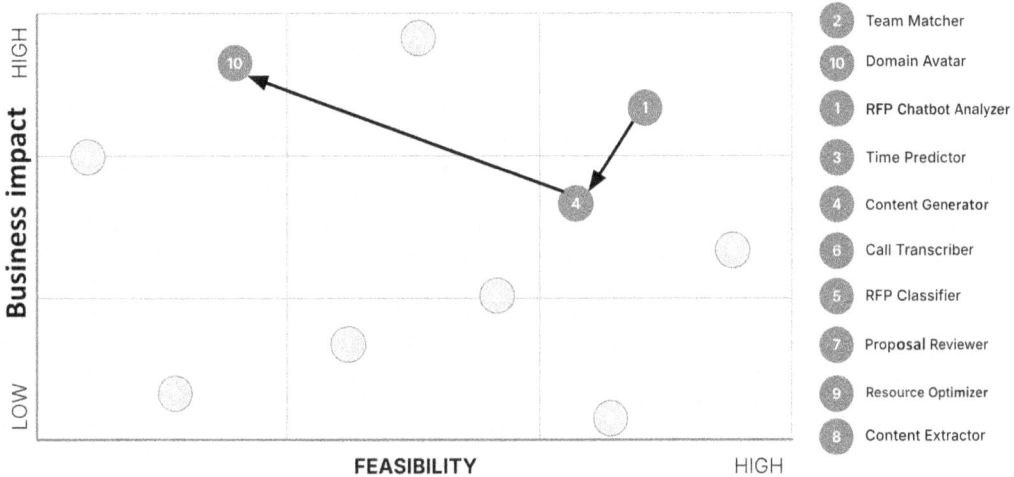

Figure 7.8: Sequencing use cases for the RFP response process

By sequencing both quick wins and strategic bets, your organization can drive immediate impact while building infrastructure and readiness for more complex projects. Phasing ambitious use cases into smaller steps allows continuous learning and prevents the roadmap from becoming bogged down by large, slow-moving initiatives. With a well-sequenced roadmap in hand, your group will be well-equipped to deliver both immediate results and long-term transformation through AI.

Next, let's wrap up by finding out how we can synchronize AI roadmaps across departments, processes, and priorities to gain maximum impact across the organization.

Aligning roadmaps across the organization

Aligning multiple department- or product-specific roadmaps ensures that every AI initiative contributes to the company's overarching objectives, while addressing specific challenges within its scope.

Decentralized ownership of AI roadmaps

One of the key elements of a successful AI roadmap is ownership. While the AI CoE or central AI team plays an essential role in coordination and strategic alignment, the responsibility for building and executing AI roadmaps should be decentralized and owned by individual business leaders or department heads.

Each business unit or department needs to take ownership of its AI initiatives, ensuring that use cases are directly aligned with its specific goals, processes, and challenges. This decentralized ownership model allows each team to move at its own pace and experiment with AI solutions tailored to its unique workflows. Business leaders must be equipped with the tools and support needed to develop their AI roadmaps. This means understanding how AI fits into their operational objectives and making informed decisions about which use cases to prioritize. By giving ownership of AI roadmaps to departments, you foster accountability – and also allow technical departments like IT, as well as AI experts from the CoE, to come in and help most effectively.

Role of the AI CoE: Driving synergy and coordination

While each department owns its roadmap, the AI CoE (if available) ensures that these roadmaps are coordinated across the organization, enabling departments to collaborate and leverage shared AI infrastructure and learnings. This balance between decentralized ownership and centralized coordination ensures that AI initiatives are both tailored to the needs of each business unit and aligned with the overall AI strategy.

The AI CoE acts as the central hub for coordinating all AI efforts across the organization. While individual departments own and manage their own AI roadmaps, the AI CoE ensures:

- Best practices and learnings are shared across departments to avoid duplication of effort.
- Data and infrastructure are unified, allowing different departments to benefit from shared resources such as data pipelines, AI models, and cloud services.
- AI projects align with the broader business objectives, ensuring that each initiative contributes to the company's overall goals.

By establishing a coordinated structure, the AI CoE makes sure that AI adoption doesn't happen in silos, but instead benefits the entire organization through collaboration and shared insights. Decentralized ownership enables teams to move at their own pace and implement solutions tailored to their unique challenges and goals. However, strategic alignment ensures that, while departments have autonomy, their efforts are still contributing to the company's larger objectives.

This balance ensures that each department can address its immediate needs while staying aligned with the organization's long-term goals.

KPIs for AI success

Finally, to ensure that roadmaps are driving the desired outcomes, the AI CoE and department heads must establish **Key Performance Indicators (KPIs)** that reflect both individual department goals and broader business objectives. These KPIs provide a clear measure of AI's success and help maintain alignment between roadmaps and the overall company strategy. Example KPIs may include metrics like cost reductions, improved customer retention, or increased revenue, depending on the goals of the specific AI use cases being implemented.

In practice, tracking AI project success with high-level KPIs is often too simplistic, as AI's impact frequently spans multiple complex dimensions. However, operating without any measurable criteria isn't feasible either, as you'd lack visibility into whether a project delivers tangible value or not.

A more realistic and actionable approach is to define *two simple thresholds* for every AI use case:

- **Value threshold:** This is the expected minimum business value or impact delivered per defined period (typically annually). It reflects concrete operational benefits, such as time savings, incremental revenue, improved customer retention scores, or cost reductions.
- **Cost cap:** A clear upper limit for the annual costs or cost share associated with an AI initiative, including all factors – software licensing, infrastructure, maintenance, data labeling, and internal resource allocation.

By clearly setting both thresholds, you create an intuitive benchmark: as long as your *value threshold exceeds your cost cap*, your AI use case is considered *net-positive*, justified, and delivering meaningful value. It's profitable.

Let's illustrate this approach concretely with our RFP Chatbot Analyzer example.

Suppose the primary benefit of your chatbot is saving sales representatives' valuable working time. You decide to set your value threshold as follows:

- **Value threshold:** Saving each sales rep at least 1 hour per week.

  With 10 sales reps using the chatbot, this adds up quickly:

  - 10 hours/week saved × 52 weeks/year = 520 hours/year
  - With each hour valued at roughly *$60/hour*, that translates into a business impact of around $31,200 per year.

- **Cost cap**: Then, let's say your total yearly cost cap for developing, deploying, and maintaining this RFP Chatbot is *$10,000*. Since your annual value (~*$31K*) significantly exceeds your annual cost (*$10K*), your chatbot is effectively looking at a payback period of under four months. As a rule of thumb, prioritize projects with payback within 12 months for use cases with medium to high feasibility.

Incorporating these simplified but effective thresholds into your AI roadmap evaluation ensures clarity around your AI project's value and viability. This approach also reduces the complexity and impracticality of overly simplistic or excessively complicated metrics. And also supports informed decision-making, strategic adjustments, and effective resource allocation – critical factors in driving AI success at scale.

As AI continues to scale throughout the organization, it becomes essential to treat AI roadmaps as living, evolving documents – regularly refining value thresholds and cost caps based on real-world performance insights, technological advancements, and shifting business priorities.

The iterative nature of AI roadmaps: Learning and pivoting

AI roadmaps aren't static documents, but living plans that need to be continuously updated and iterated based on new information, emerging technologies, and changing business priorities.

Unlike traditional project roadmaps that may have fixed timelines and objectives, AI roadmaps must be adaptive because the field of AI evolves quickly. Technological breakthroughs, such as new machine learning models or more efficient data processing techniques, can open up opportunities that didn't exist when the roadmap was first created. Similarly, business priorities can change in response to market trends, customer needs, or competitive pressures.

- Some of these changes could be external. If a new, highly capable AI model is released that drastically improves language processing, a company working on an internal document analysis AI system might decide to pivot from its original solution to incorporate this new model, thus improving performance and reducing development time.

- Internal changes based on evolving business and strategic objectives may also impact the AI roadmap. For instance, a company might be focused on an AI-driven customer support chatbot. However, if early trials show that the chatbot is struggling to understand customer queries, the organization might pivot to a text-based recommendation engine instead, while they work on refining the chatbot's capabilities.

AI roadmaps need to be dynamic to allow for these pivots – adapting to both internal learning and external technological advancements.

Hence, it is essential to be flexible about your AI roadmaps. Let's talk more about it in the next section.

Approaching AI projects in an agile way

The key to maintaining a flexible roadmap is adopting an agile approach to AI development. In **agile project management**, work is done in small, iterative cycles (**sprints**), allowing teams to continuously test, learn, and adapt. This principle is especially effective in AI, where trial and error is often part of the process.

The small and fast iterations enable breaking down AI projects into smaller, more manageable phases allowing teams to make faster progress while limiting risk. By developing small increments, like proof-of-concepts or prototypes, teams can test AI use cases quickly and gather feedback early on. You'll learn more about this in Chapter 9.

For example: Instead of building a complex AI-based customer voice bot all at once, a company could start by launching a text-based chatbot for internal use. By gathering insights and refining the chatbot's performance over time, the company can then move on to more complex iterations, such as external customer-facing bots or voice interfaces.

Summary

Throughout this chapter, we've explored how AI roadmaps provide the structure and flexibility needed to guide profitable AI adoption, from building comprehensive use case backlogs to adapting to internal and external changes. Done right, AI roadmaps become more than planning tools—they become engines of profitable transformation. To achieve this, they must be owned, aligned, and measured against clear value thresholds and cost caps.

Yet even the best-designed roadmap succeeds only through effective execution. The critical factor is empowering teams across the organization. Each department must take ownership of AI initiatives that address its specific challenges and goals. Departments that own their roadmaps are better positioned to innovate and adapt, while the AI CoE ensures alignment with the company's overall strategy, prevents silos, and optimizes resources. Empowering teams goes beyond tools and data. It requires fostering an environment of cross-functional communication, continuous skills development, and regular roadmap reviews to ensure each department can respond swiftly to both successes and challenges. When teams have the right support structures in place, they can move quickly and confidently, knowing they're contributing to both short-term wins and long-term business objectives.

With our roadmaps in place, we're now in a great spot to start building our use cases out. That's what we're going to cover in the next chapter!

Stay tuned

To keep up with the latest developments in the fields of Generative AI and LLMs, subscribe to our weekly newsletter, AI_Distilled, at `https://packt.link/80z6Y`.

Part 3

Setting Sail

With your course defined, it's time to leave the harbor and set sail. This final part of the book takes you from planning to action. You'll learn how to build effective prototypes, scale them into production-ready systems, and leverage the growing ecosystem of AI tools to accelerate your journey. Along the way, we'll cover pitfalls to avoid, strategies for sustainable scaling, and how to equip your teams with the right capabilities. By the end, you'll be ready to operationalize AI in a way that delivers lasting business value.

This part of the book includes the following chapters:

- *Chapter 8, Prototyping for Success*
- *Chapter 9, Scaling AI-Powered Systems and Workflows*
- *Chapter 10, Leveraging Your AI Toolkit*

8

Prototyping for Success

In the previous chapter, we built our AI roadmaps by identifying high-impact, feasible use cases and aligning them with broader business goals. But having a roadmap alone doesn't automatically deliver results, especially in AI, where uncertainty and rapid technological change can make planning complex.

The next step is to move from planning to prototyping. **Prototyping** validates whether your use cases can actually deliver the value you envisioned. In this chapter, we'll look at the core elements of prototyping: deciding whether you want to build or buy your AI solution, managing AI projects effectively throughout the prototyping phase, and evaluating prototypes to ensure they're on track to achieve success.

In this chapter, we'll explore the following topics:

- The make-versus-buy decision
- Managing an AI project
- Evaluating and iterating your prototype
- Developing your prototype

The make-versus-buy decision

One of the first questions that arises when you move from idea to prototype is: *Should we build everything in-house, or purchase an off-the-shelf (or partially off-the-shelf) solution?* The **make-versus-buy** question is rarely straightforward, and your choice may shift at different stages of your AI journey. It's best to think of this not as a binary decision, but as a continuum of options.

There are choices to make: whether you want to build the complete solution in-house or outsource to external vendors. Let's first give an overview of the options.

- **Fully build**: You do it all in-house, including data pipelines, model development, front end integration, and ongoing maintenance. This option offers maximum control, but also requires significant technical expertise, time, and resources.

- **Hybrid**: You might use pre-built machine learning platforms or large language models, but develop the specific application logic, integrations, and custom data pipelines in-house. This approach can strike a balance between speed and flexibility.

- **Fully buy**: In this scenario, you purchase or subscribe to an existing AI solution. The vendor handles the technical heavy lifting, and your internal teams focus on deployment, change management, and user adoption. This can accelerate time-to-value if a vendor solution matches your needs.

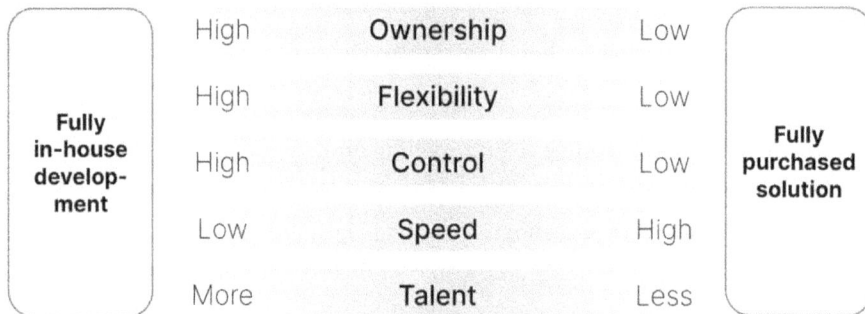

Fully in-house develop-ment	High	**Ownership**	Low	Fully purchased solution
	High	**Flexibility**	Low	
	High	**Control**	Low	
	Low	**Speed**	High	
	More	**Talent**	Less	

Figure 8.1: Continuum of the make-versus-buy decision

The decision to pick from fully build, fully buy, or a hybrid approach depends on four key factors:

- **Use case stage**: You might have to revisit this decision based on what stage your idea is at.

  - **Discovery**: During your first prototypes or proofs of concept, it's often faster and cheaper to buy or license an existing solution – especially if you're still in *learning mode*. You want to test quickly, fail fast, and iterate.

  - **Delivery**: If your prototype proves high strategic value, you may later decide to gradually internalize more of the solution or build a new version from scratch that's deeply tailored to your needs.

- **Strategic value:** Different products bring different business value. For instance, some products may help improve productivity, and some may be moonshot ideas. Hence, this decision will be driven by short- and long-term business goals.

  - **Core differentiator:** If the success of your entire business strategy hinges on a given AI use case – think autonomous driving for a company such as Tesla – it often makes sense to invest in building these capabilities in-house.

  - **Non-core but useful:** For a low-impact or routine AI task (e.g., generating basic marketing insights), it's typically more cost-effective to adopt an existing tool rather than re-invent the wheel.

- **External solution performance:** For many use cases, there might be an existing solution on the market. If bringing a vendor in is a valid option, your main focus should be on evaluating the available solutions against relevant criteria using a vendor scorecard that covers key dimensions such as *Functionality and Performance*, *Integration and Technology Fit*, *Cost and Commercials*, *Vendor Trust and Stability*, and offered *Support and Services*. Consider the following:

  - **Good enough versus perfect:** No vendor solution will fit your needs perfectly out of the box. But sometimes 70%–80% accuracy, say on the *Performance* dimension, it can still be better than the 60% you had before. If an off-the-shelf product delivers that *good enough* threshold, you might opt to buy it.

  - **Specialized requirements:** If you have ultra-specific needs, unique data, or regulatory constraints, you may find vendor solutions insufficient – pushing you closer to a *make* or *hybrid* approach.

- **Internal resources:** Who will actually be responsible for building and maintaining the AI solution? These aren't set and forget but require constant monitoring and development over time – even if it's just someone managing vendor licenses. The extent to which you have internal resources available at all is a key decision criterion.

  - **Data, infrastructure, and talent:** Even if a use case is valuable, you may not have the internal skill sets or computing capabilities to build and maintain a custom AI solution. In that case, buying or partnering can help you leap forward.

  - **Shifting over time:** As your internal **AI Center of Excellence (AI CoE)** develops or matures, you might bring more of the AI lifecycle in-house. What you buy today, you might decide to build later if the strategic importance grows – or if your internal expertise becomes strong enough.

The following flowchart helps visualize the make or buy decision:

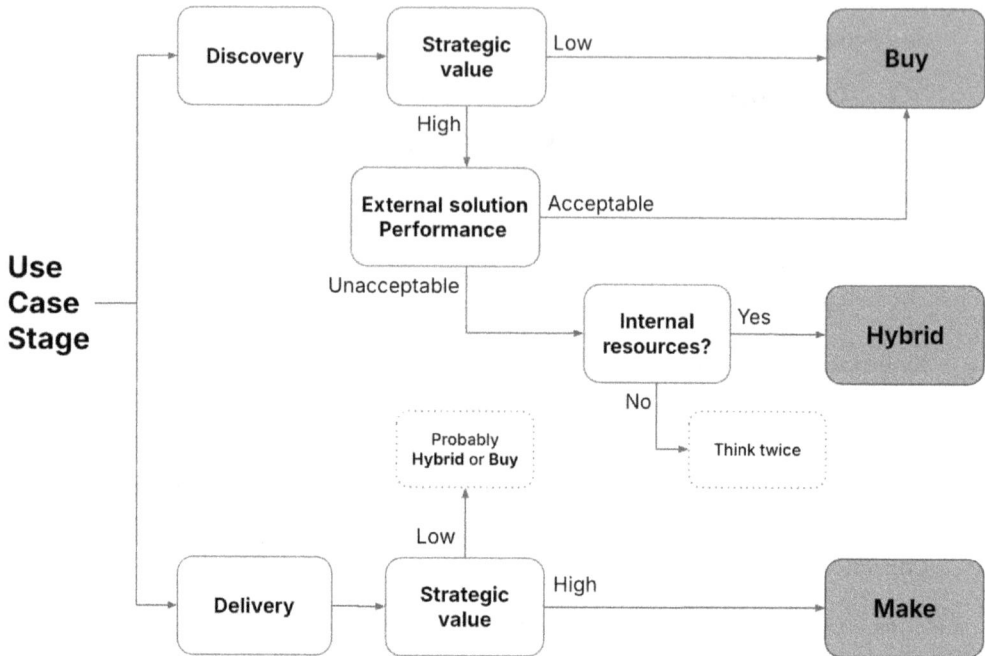

Figure 8.2: Make-versus-buy flowchart

Before we dive into a specific example, it's useful to highlight the typical situations that push organizations toward a make, buy, or hybrid approach. Prototyping is not one-size-fits-all, and the right path often depends on your organizational context:

- **Buy**: Smaller organizations, or teams just starting their AI journey, often benefit from buying off-the-shelf solutions. For example, a mid-market retailer might quickly pilot a pre-built sentiment analysis tool to understand customer reviews without hiring data scientists. The goal here is speed, learning, and minimizing upfront investment.

- **Make**: Larger organizations with deep technical expertise may view prototyping as an R&D investment. A global automaker or big insurance company might build in-house prototypes for potential AI use cases that might eventually have a strategic business impact. Even if the early versions are rough, the long-term strategic importance makes in-house ownership essential.

- **Hybrid**: Most companies actually land in the middle ground. They rely heavily on off-the-shelf solutions for things such as general AI infrastructure, but build the last mile in-house. This might involve the integration layer, user experience, or the monitoring framework for the AI solution. Ultimately, this last mile is what makes their AI solution competitive. For example, a media company might license a large language model from a vendor but build its own application layer on top to help editors write better headlines and article teasers without disrupting the editors' workflows and with adherence to the company's style guidelines. This balances speed with customization and control.

These scenarios illustrate that prototyping is not just about testing feasibility – it's also about making strategic choices where you want your use case to land – whether it should be designed as a short-term ROI initiative that quickly has to pay for itself or a long-term strategic bet (that has more of an R&D character). With that context in mind, let's look at a practical example of how this decision framework could play out.

A practical example

Let's revisit our AI roadmap from the previous chapter. Suppose you've prioritized the RFP Chatbot Analyzer, which will provide responses to users based on the RFP documents. The next question is: How? Do you build or buy? At this stage, you're typically in discovery mode – a concept we'll explore in even more detail in the next chapter. In short, value hasn't been validated yet. You're confident the use case could add value, but you don't have the data to prove it. So, for now, the goal is speed and learning: validating whether the idea works at all without committing heavy resources.

We've scoped this use case in a way that it hits a $10K per year threshold (*Chapter 5*), which immediately puts it into a tactical, not a strategic gain – which is exactly the lens under which we'll prototype it, with a clear rigor on ROI.

The anticipated $10K per year threshold basically rules out any means of hiring internal resources. That's why our first action item is to quickly survey existing *chat-with-your-documents* vendors. One vendor might offer a 14-day free trial. The team signs up and uses a limited set of RFP PDFs to test the concept quickly. Or, you choose a solution that you're already using in-house, such as Microsoft Copilot, and test whether the system can answer basic queries accurately enough to be useful. Within a few weeks, you'll know whether this approach shows promise, where it struggles (e.g., compliance-heavy documents or graphics in PDFs), and whether your sales team sees real productivity gains.

Fast-forward: if the prototype shows impact and you're ready to switch to delivery mode (more on that in *Chapter 9*), you reassess the situation. If you're still looking for tactical impact, your means of delivery could mean moving to a hybrid approach, extending the existing vendor capabilities with custom additions such as a custom data integration layer. Or, you could choose a fully make approach, developing an in-house solution for greater control over data security and long-term ownership, basically rebuilding some components that were previously offered by the vendor, from scratch. The latter makes sense if responding to RFPs is a core business activity. But if RFPs are just one sales process among many, a hybrid approach is usually the better fit. And if the vendor solution continues to meet your needs at an acceptable cost and performance level, you may even stay with a pure buy strategy for quick ROI.

This example shows how the same use case can follow different paths depending on your strategy and whether you're still exploring or already scaling. We'll dive deeper into these concepts-and how to transition seamlessly between phases in *Chapter 9*.

For now, let's recognize that for many AI use cases, especially in early prototyping phases, buying is often the simplest path, especially if your focus is more on generating ROI than making a heavy R&D investment. Later, for the few critical use cases that truly differentiate your business, you might invest in building. This dynamic approach to the *make-versus-buy* question will ensure you're focusing resources where they have the highest payoff. As a rule of thumb: default to buy for fast ROI validation; only shift toward make when the use case proves core to your strategy.

AI projects can often become unwieldy, given that you need to be agile in adapting to the dynamic landscape and developments, yet ensure that you don't go down a rabbit hole, going back and forth on your AI project. We will discuss how to effectively manage an AI project next.

Managing an AI project

Prototyping is rarely a smooth, linear journey. From proof-of-concept to pilot, you'll encounter unique challenges-unstable timelines, complex data requirements, evolving user requirements, and uncertainties around performance.

In traditional IT, strict project plans can work well (sometimes). But AI projects come with higher uncertainty. A purely waterfall approach can stifle adaptability when your model's accuracy stalls at 70%, or new data revelations require pivoting. On the other hand, a purely agile approach without business alignment can lead to *prototype purgatory* that never make it to production.

First and foremost is *balancing structure and flexibility*. For this, you can follow these steps:

1. **Define a clear scope, then embrace iteration**: Break your AI project down into small, manageable increments. Make sure the problem statement is crystal clear: What exactly are we trying to improve, and for whom? Rather than planning every detail up front, allocate time for repeated experiment cycles (sprints). After each cycle, review your results and adapt.

2. **Build a blended team**: AI prototypes benefit from a mix of data engineers, data scientists, subject matter experts, business leaders, and user-experience specialists. Recall from *Chapter 6* that frameworks such as **Responsible, Accountable, Consulted, Informed (RACI)** can help define responsibilities. If you also have an AI CoE, they can coordinate with departmental teams. Don't hesitate to bring in freelancers or consultancies if your internal capacity is lacking-especially during the early prototype phase.

3. **Plan in two horizons-near-term and mid-term**: Keep weekly or bi-weekly sprints for building prototypes, analyzing data, and refining the approach. Focus on quickly testing big assumptions. A flexible project timeline that may include a pilot test after 6 to 12 weeks works quite well in many cases (as a rule of thumb). Prepare next steps if the pilot goes well (or an exit plan if it does not).

While you define the scope and plan your projects, you will also need to be vigilant about some common mistakes that happen while implementing AI projects.

Common AI project pitfalls and how to address them

Here are the most common pitfalls you should avoid when starting to build your AI solutions:

- **The 80% fallacy**: Many AI projects start off strong, with early prototypes quickly reaching a pretty decent performance that impresses stakeholders-making it feel like the project is *already 80% there*. This often sparks excitement and gives the impression that the project is nearly complete. However, this belief is misleading. While reaching 80% in accuracy, for example, may come relatively easily, pushing that performance up to 95% is often far more difficult and time-consuming. In fact, this last stretch can take up to 80% of the total effort, despite being only 15% of the total performance range.

To give you a simple example: if your goal is to build an AI model that predicts anomalies, you could simply achieve a high accuracy by building a model that mostly predicts *no anomaly*-out of the box, this model would have 99% accuracy because 99% of all observations wouldn't be an anomaly. Yet, this model would be 0% useful. While it's easy to understand the 80% fallacy in this case, more complex AI solutions fall for the same principle. For complex AI solutions too, it's easy for the model to make some *easy* guesses, but matching the nuances is where it gets really tough.

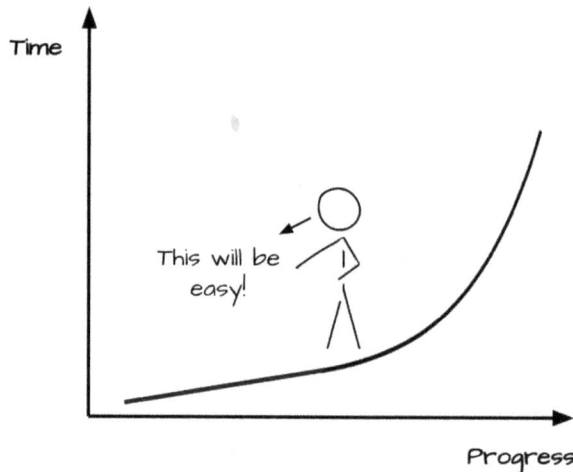

Figure 8.3: 80% fallacy-visualized

Very often, the performance gains from a prototype to a deliverable product are slow and complex to achieve, as they require rigorous experimentation, handling countless edge cases, and fine-tuning to achieve a model that works well for real-life inputs, and gains are not guaranteed.

To address this, teams need to adopt a mindset that views early success as just the beginning. The real challenge-and the real value-lies in closing that final gap in performance. Plan and resource accordingly.

- **Ignoring user experience**: It's not uncommon for AI teams to get so deep into building technically sophisticated models that they lose sight of the people who are actually supposed to use them. The result? A smart system that no one in the business understands, wants, or knows how to work with. You might end up with something that looks impressive on paper, but fails to make any real impact.

A classic sign of this is when a model is technically accurate but completely misaligned with day-to-day workflows. Maybe it delivers insights, but they're buried in a confusing interface. Or, maybe it suggests actions, but at times when no one is in a position to act. If users can't trust it or don't see how it helps them, they'll avoid it altogether.

To avoid this, it's critical to involve end users from day one. If you're building an AI tool for a sales team, for instance, show them early wireframes or rough demos. Ask how they'd use it, where it fits into their daily routines, and what would make it truly helpful. Be ready to tweak the interface, the timing, and even the model's behavior based on real feedback. Think of it as building *with* the user, not *for* the user. Embrace the concept of augmented-AI systems that support human decision-making, rather than trying to replace it entirely.

- **Spiraling costs and timelines**: What starts as a quick two-month prototype often turns into a six-month saga, burning through budget, stretching teams thin, and creating frustration across the board. This is one of the most common pitfalls in AI projects: underestimating how long things will take and failing to recognize when to cut losses.

  AI projects are, by nature, exploratory. You're often working with messy data, uncertain value, and shifting expectations. That's why it's crucial to build in decision points or clear checkpoints where you assess whether the project is still viable. Has the model reached a baseline performance level? Is it operating fast enough to be useful? Is there a clear path to return on investment? If the answer to any of those questions is *not yet, that's okay-but only up to a point*. Be disciplined about setting limits. If a use case hasn't proven itself within a defined time or budget window, it may be smarter to pause, pivot, or shut it down entirely. That frees up resources to double down on ideas that *are* working and shows stakeholders that your team makes strategic, data-driven decisions, not just sunk-cost commitments.

Now that you are ready to set up your AI project, I will share a few tips to get you started.

Practical tips for project setup

Over the last decade of building machine learning and AI projects from both internal and AI consulting projects, I have acquired some tactics that can help you set up your AI projects. Obviously, the specifics might need to be adapted to your organization and ambition level, but on a high level, they'll provide you with some guiding principles.

- **Find atomic AI use cases**: Keep the prototype scope small – something you can test within a short timeframe (e.g., under four weeks). This ensures the project team can gather real feedback quickly and either iterate or move on.

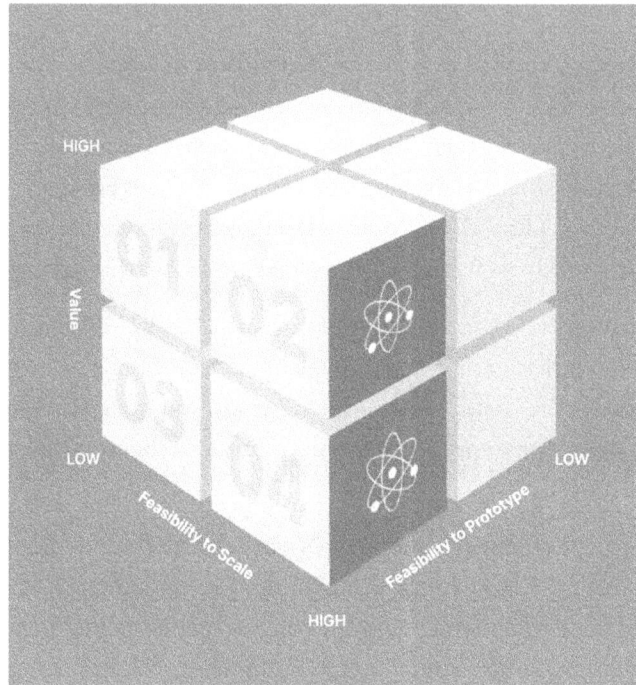

Figure 8.4: Atomic AI use cases

The idea here to create atomic AI use cases is that, besides impact and feasibility (dimensions we discussed earlier, in *Chapter 6*), we're now also looking at a third dimension: how easy is it to test or prototype a solution. If the solution can't be prototyped easily, that's a big roadblock.

I like to follow the 20-20 rule. A prototype should be shipped in less than 20 days and cost no more than 20% of the anticipated annual value threshold. For example, if your threshold is $10K per quarter (that's $40K per year), 20% equals $8K. If a prototype requires more time or budget than that, it's usually a sign the scope is too big or the business case too weak. Of course, adjust these numbers to fit your organization's size and risk appetite, but always keep them at the lower end.

- **Adopt a hybrid project management style**: In the roadmap stage, you have used somewhat *waterfall* thinking to outline timelines, budgets, and resource needs across departments. Once you start prototyping, though, it's time to switch to an ***agile*** mindset for day-to-day execution:

  - **Iterative sprints**: Plan 2-4 week cycles. Each sprint aims to deliver a tangible improvement (such as *a working data ingestion pipeline* or *model V2 that reduces error rates by 5%*).

  - **Frequent testing**: Evaluate results with real or representative data quickly. The sooner you find issues, the better.

  - **Risk reviews**: Implement short risk checkpoints. If you discover your data pipeline can't handle new file formats or your vendor solution is incompatible with your enterprise security requirements, address it now.

  - **Stakeholder feedback**: Keep relevant business owners in the loop. They can confirm whether the prototype is meeting real business needs or whether you're drifting off course.

- **Building the right team**: Most organizations still have a gap in specialized AI skill sets – particularly in older, legacy-driven companies. For an effective AI prototype, you'll want a ***blended*** team:

  - **AI experts**: Data scientists or ML engineers who are comfortable with your chosen modeling approach.

  - **Business SMEs**: People who understand the real problem inside out. They'll keep you from going down rabbit holes.

  - **Translators**: Those who speak both ***data*** and ***business***. They ensure that ROI is front and center and that AI experts build something truly relevant.

  - **IT/infrastructure**: Someone who can spin up (or procure) the environment, handle data ingestion, and plan for any security constraints.

  - **Project manager or team lead**: Coordinates tasks, monitors progress, organizes sprints, and ensures stakeholders stay aligned.

Bear in mind, these are roles, not necessarily people. For very small projects, it's not uncommon to have just 1-2 people wear these hats, which might be fine at the beginning, but as you can imagine, this won't last long.

Managing an AI project effectively means embracing uncertainty, prioritizing well-scoped prototypes, and creating a culture that allows you to pivot quickly-without sacrificing the structure
and alignment necessary to deliver business value.

The next important action item is how to evaluate and evolve your prototype, which we will
discuss next.

Evaluating and iterating on your prototype

Prototyping doesn't end once you have a *working model*. You need a systematic approach to evaluate whether it's worth further investment – and how to refine it for real-world conditions. Think
of your prototype not as a *mini product* but as a *seed* that you'll nurture into production. It might
be planted in a small test environment, but it must already consider future operational needs to
avoid dead ends when scaling.

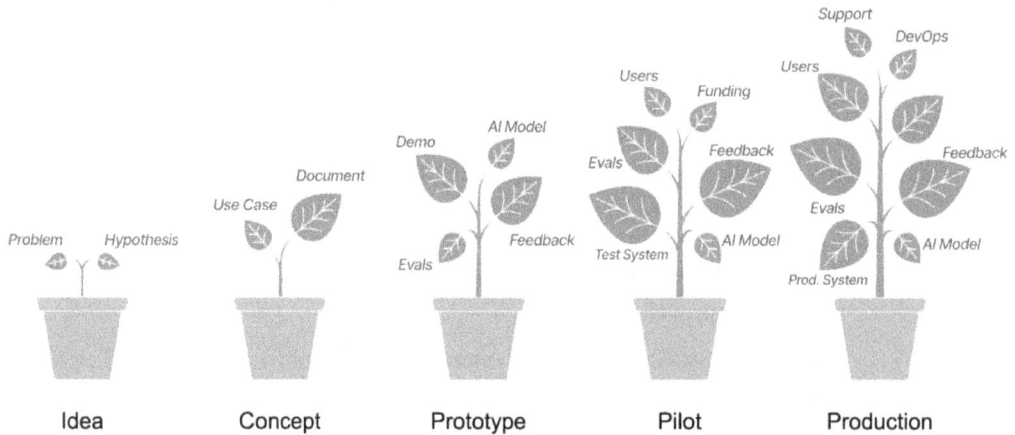

Figure 8.5: Planting the seed of a prototype-from idea to production

In many traditional software development projects, prototypes are often *throwaway* builds – quick
tests that are eventually discarded and rebuilt *the right way* for production. AI prototypes are different. The reality is that your AI prototype typically forms the seed of your final, deployed solution.
The model, data workflows, integration points, and UX decisions made during prototyping don't
simply vanish; they're carried forward (and often expanded) into production.

Thinking backwards

Because AI prototypes eventually live on as your production system, it pays to adopt a *thinking
backwards* approach. In other words, treat every prototype as if it will one day serve real users in
a live environment-because it probably will.

- **Prioritize the end goal**: Identify the ultimate business outcome and user needs even in the initial prototype phase. For instance, if your plan is to reduce call handling time by 50%, design the AI interactions (such as how a chatbot flows or how predictive suggestions appear) with that metric in mind from day one.

- **Involve real users early**: Too often, teams validate prototypes only with synthetic or carefully prepared data. But messy, real-world usage is the best litmus test. Getting your AI in front of actual end users – whether that's an internal team or external customers-reveals critical workflow issues you can fix early.

- **Build with a future in mind**: You can still keep the prototype *lightweight* but choose tools and infrastructure that won't be roadblocks when you want to scale. For example, if you pick a quick SaaS AI platform that can't handle more than a few thousand documents, you'll eventually have to rework large parts of your application if your data needs explode.

What persists and what can be upgraded

When transitioning from prototype to production, some components of your AI system are carried over, while others need to be rebuilt or added for the first time. Thinking about this upfront helps you avoid dead ends and design your prototypes in a modular way.

The following figure illustrates the core components of an AI solution at a high level:

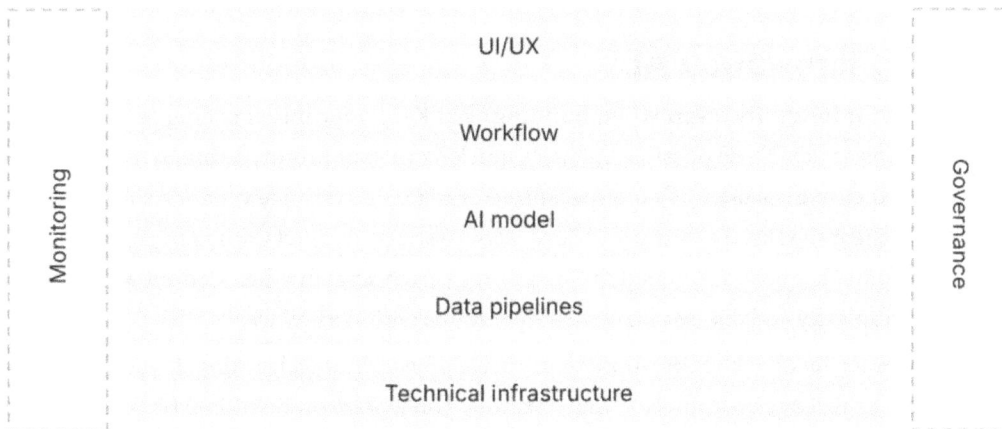

Figure 8.6. High-level components of an AI solution

During prototyping, you'll naturally focus on a few of these components - the AI model, the basic workflow logic, and perhaps a lightweight version of your data pipelines. These are the pieces you need in order to validate whether the idea works at all.

Other components, like monitoring and governance, are rarely part of early prototypes. And that's fine. You don't need a full compliance dashboard or drift detection system just to validate your RFP Chatbot Analyzer. But it's important to keep in mind that these missing pieces will eventually become critical if the solution moves into production.

Think of it as building a seed: the prototype contains the early shape of your workflows, data flows, and models, but not yet the full scaffolding of production. In *Chapter 9*, we'll look at how each of these components evolves from prototype to production and what it takes to harden them for real-world delivery.

But for now, let's highlight three key components that deserve special attention:

- **Core model:** If your chatbot or computer vision tool can't interpret data well in the prototype stage, it won't magically fix itself in production. Early design choices about model architecture, training data, and inference speed typically remain.

- **Data pipelines:** If you rely on manual data prep for a prototype, you'll need a robust data pipeline for production. That pipeline will inherit any quirks in data formatting, cleansing steps, and refresh cycles built during the prototype.

- **User adoption:** How people actually work with your AI in the prototype (e.g., providing feedback or correcting mistakes) shapes their habits in production. If the prototype's user experience is confusing, it will be doubly confusing with a larger user base later.

Avoiding throwaway AI

- **Plan for longevity, even when building fast:** Keep your initial coding or platform decisions as flexible as possible. A hacky, quick fix in your prototype might snowball into an expensive rework if it's too specialized or reliant on a single vendor's solution. I had one client that used a flashy RAG-as-a-Service start-up called Carbon to prototype their customer support chatbots. They had to start from scratch when Carbon was acquired by Perplexity and discontinued their operations within a few weeks.

- **Embrace feedback loops:** AI systems thrive on continuous learning. If your prototype ignores feedback or collects it haphazardly, you'll start production with a suboptimal model. Instead, design user-friendly ways for business owners or customers to report mistakes, supply better data, or highlight edge cases.

- **Consider operational costs:** A prototype that's impressive but too expensive to run in production (e.g., using a high-end GPU 24/7 for minimal gains) won't scale. Make sure cost factors, such as, cloud usage or licensing-are in the conversation early. You'll learn more about these cost factors in the next chapter.

- **Build (even) a minimal path to production**: Outline where your prototype will *live* if it's successful. This doesn't require full DevOps from day one, but do think about basic version control, model deployment options (e.g., a container), and how you'll monitor runtime performance. A lot of out-of-the-box AI tools and SaaS offerings simply don't provide these metrics, and you're not able to add them later on. We'll also dive deeper into this during *Chapters 9* and *10*.

Prototyping is not a disposable exercise. The work you do up front strongly influences your final product. Quality and sustainability count. Even if you're moving quickly, avoid choices that could corner you later. AI prototypes grow, evolve, and adapt in production; they don't start over.

By recognizing that your prototype is already in the gravitational pull of a real, production environment, you'll avoid the ***throwaway trap*** of traditional IT prototypes and set your AI project up for faster, smoother scaling.

Once you have a working prototype-however rough-the real learning starts. Let's see how you can refine it and create a fully functional AI product.

Developing your prototype

Prototypes are living experiments; their primary purpose is to gather feedback and guide your next steps. Evaluating them thoroughly and incorporating them helps you validate assumptions and refine your approach.

- **Define clear success criteria**: Before you let real users test your AI, set objective thresholds that indicate whether the prototype meets your business needs. These can include the following:

  - **Quantitative performance**: Does the classification model achieve a minimum precision/recall? Does the generative model produce acceptable responses 90% of the time?

  - **User adoption**: Do employees in the relevant department actually use the pilot solution? Or do they revert to manual processes?

  - **Time savings or cost impact**: Are you seeing a measurable decrease in manual work hours or an increase in sales conversions?

> **Tip**: Use the same four **Value Levers** from the previous chapter (**Cost**, **Quality**, **Speed**, **Quantity**) or your departmental KPIs for alignment.

- **Conduct fast, real-world tests**: AI results can look brilliant in contrived lab conditions but flop when encountering real, messy data. Push your prototype into a near-real environment as soon as possible, even if it's only a subset of your user base or partial data feed. This is how you spot edge cases quickly:

  - **Data gaps**: Additional data that's needed to handle certain requests.

  - **Integration hiccups**: Slow performance or errors due to incomplete infrastructure.

  - **User behavior**: Surprise user inputs or different user expectations.

- **Gather feedback early and often**: Invite direct feedback from pilot users. For instance, if your sales team is testing an RFP chatbot, ask them the following:

  - Did the chatbot reduce the time it took to prepare proposals?

  - Did the chatbot occasionally produce awkward or incorrect statements? How often?

  - Would they keep using the chatbot if it were optional?

  Leverage **observational feedback**, too. Sometimes, a formal survey might say *Everything's fine*, but usage logs show minimal adoption. That's a red flag indicating the solution might not actually fit into daily workflows.

- **The pivot or proceed decision**: After a pilot runs for a certain period (a few weeks or months), gather all your data and decide which of the following to do:

  - **Proceed**: The prototype shows enough promise that you're ready to address the last 20% of polish and move toward production.

  - **Pivot**: Some aspects need a major revamp – maybe you discovered a different vendor can do it better, or a different data approach is needed.

  - **Pause or halt**: The business impact or feasibility just isn't there. It's better to stop now than to sink more money into a dead end.

  Don't be discouraged if you must pivot or even pause. This is a natural part of the process. In fact, healthy prototypes should have a higher risk of *failing early*. This is how you preserve resources and channel them into other high-potential use cases on your roadmap.

Many times, you might want to prioritize your prototypes based on value gained. Let's talk about how you can achieve this.

Sequencing your prototypes for maximum learning

If you have multiple prototypes lined up from your backlog, consider the sequence in which you tackle them. Just as you sequence your roadmap at a higher level, you also want to optimize your prototyping schedule to gain maximum synergy:

- **Start with quick wins**: Particularly if you're new to AI or need immediate proof to get more buy-in, for example, you might pick an atomic AI use case that can be proven or disproven in just a few weeks

- **Apply learning**: The feedback and knowledge you gain from your first prototype (e.g., how to store text data efficiently or how to best interface with a vendor's API) can be reused to accelerate subsequent prototypes

- **Move to champion use cases**: Once your teams and infrastructure have matured from smaller prototypes, take on high-impact, more complex projects

Let's see how all these elements might look in practice.

Prototype-in-action: Revisiting our RFP Chatbot Analyzer example

Now, if you want to build a prototype of our RFP Chatbot Analyzer, how would you go about it? Here are a few pointers that can help you build this prototype.

- **Make-versus-buy decision**: You could assemble a team with various team players focusing on the different aspects of the prototype.

    - A marketing manager to supply real RFP data.

    - A data translator who has a good understanding of which data is needed, where it is stored, how it is stored, and how to access it.

    - An IT specialist who sets up the environment to feed documents to the vendor's API (if applicable).

    - A project manager (in a smaller company, this might be the same person as the data translator) to keep the pilot organized.

- **Test in a real environment**: Then run the chatbot on real RFP data that came in last week. At first, the chatbot gives answers that are correct in 8 out of 10 cases. But a few RFP documents have domain-specific terms that confuse it, leading to missed key facts, especially when graphics or tables are involved. In some cases, the model just times out, which particularly happens on larger PDF files.

For the uninitiated, the model development typically happens on historical data (here, RFP PDFs), and then the model can be tested on the new or latest documents to check its performance.

- **Gather feedback**: Let the sales team use the chatbot for a subset of actual RFP tasks. Have them track usage and fill out a quick survey. They discover the following:

    - The chatbot significantly reduces your team's RFP drafting time (on average by 25%) for standard proposals.

    - It struggles with specialized compliance forms.

    - The sales reps prefer the chatbot to be integrated directly into their CRM system, rather than having to log into a separate web interface.

- **Decision**: The sales team decide to *proceed* with the next iteration, exploring a partial *build* approach: hooking in a custom **large language model** (**LLM**) trained with compliance data, then reusing the vendor's interface for everything else. The factors that impacted this decision are as follows:

    - An encouraging time reduction of 25% in RFP response.

    - They see a path to solving the compliance gap by adding domain-specific data or custom fine-tuning.

By carefully prototyping in this manner, they avoid prematurely investing in a custom, fully in-house solution or blowing the budget on a vendor license that's not quite fit for purpose.

Key takeaways

Prototyping is where grand AI ideas get their first real test. By carefully balancing the make-versus-buy decision, managing your AI project with a blend of structure and agility, and rigorously evaluating each prototype's performance, you turn your strategic vision into tangible business outcomes.

Here are your key takeaways for building effective and scalable prototypes:

- **The make-versus-buy choice**: In early prototypes, don't overcomplicate things. Leveraging off-the-shelf solutions can reduce risk and deliver fast feedback. For core, high-strategic-value use cases, you may eventually lean toward building and owning the IP.

- **Effective AI project management**: Plan in small increments, but ensure each sprint aligns with your broader roadmap. Build cross-functional teams, track risks, and expect some pivots along the way.

- **Prototyping as a living lab**: Start small with *atomic AI use cases* so you can validate ideas quickly. Embrace short, iterative cycles, define success criteria from day one, and keep production realities in mind to avoid rework later.

- **Iterate, integrate, or exit**: Not every prototype will make it all the way to production. That's normal and it's good to fail fast rather than sink time and money into a dead end. For the winners (successful prototypes), refine them in a pilot and then scale confidently.

Summary

In this chapter, we focused on various aspects to consider when developing your prototypes. This included decisions around whether to create in-house solutions or buy them from external vendors. We also discussed how you can effectively manage your AI projects. We learned to evaluate and iterate on prototypes and how they can evolve as a complete solution. Through a case study of the RFP chatbot, we demonstrated how you can put these principles into practice.

In the next chapter, we'll explore how to operationalize these prototypes and manage your AI stack as it matures across the organization-so you can scale your successful AI prototypes sustainably and keep delivering tangible ROI to your business.

Unlock this book's exclusive benefits now **UNLOCK NOW**

Scan this QR code or go to `https://packtpub.com/unlock`, then search for this book by name.

Note: Keep your purchase invoice ready before you start.

9

Scaling AI-Powered Systems and Workflows

In the previous chapters, we've explored the journey from identifying high-impact AI use cases to effectively prototyping solutions and validating their potential. However, moving beyond the prototype stage to fully operational, scalable systems presents a unique set of challenges - and opportunities.

Scaling AI isn't simply about making your prototype bigger. Rather, it involves carefully transitioning from exploratory validation to robust operational delivery, ensuring your AI solutions are not only effective but also sustainable over the long term.

This chapter will guide you through the critical process of scaling your AI prototypes into production-ready systems, offering you a high-level roadmap of what to expect as you continue on your AI journey. Keep in mind, however, that while the process of discovering and prototyping AI solutions tends to be fairly standardized, scaling them effectively is heavily dependent on your specific organization.

Therefore, treat this chapter as an orientation rather than a detailed blueprint.

In this chapter, we'll cover the following main topics

- Understanding the AI product lifecycle
- Core goals of scaling AI solutions
- From prototype to production: Core components and strategies
- The five levers of scaling

- Aligning people and purpose: The organizational side of scaling AI

- Managing cost at scale

- Monitoring and metrics

- Practical steps for scaling AI solutions

Understanding the AI product lifecycle

What does **scaling AI solutions** mean anyway? In practical terms, it means actively shifting between two distinct phases of the AI product lifecycle: **discovery** and **delivery**. While these phases may seem linear, in reality, they represent distinct modes of operation, each with unique goals, methodologies, and challenges.

Let's first talk about the distinction between the discovery and delivery phases of the AI product lifecycle. What's the difference?

Discovery is the exploratory phase where your primary goal is validation. In this stage, you're actively testing your assumptions - whether your AI use case is technically feasible, generates measurable value, and effectively addresses real business needs. This is what you did in *Chapters 7* and *8*. Your focus during discovery is not on perfection or complete robustness; rather, you're aiming to rapidly prototype, experiment, learn, and adapt. Discovery embraces uncertainty and encourages quick iterations to minimize investment risks and quickly uncover critical insights.

Delivery, on the other hand, is about scaling validated use cases into robust, reliable, and operationally viable systems. In this phase, the key objective shifts from exploration and validation to stability, maintainability, and operational integration. Delivery requires a different toolkit than discovery. Instead of moving fast (and perhaps even a little chaotic at times), delivery involves careful planning, disciplined execution, and adherence to processes that ensure your AI solution meets business standards for the key delivery criteria of scalability, reliability, performance, maintainability, and security.

Transitioning from discovery to delivery is not merely a technical milestone - it represents a fundamental change in mindset and approach. Here is a quick comparison between the discovery and delivery phases.

Discovery Phase	Delivery Phase
Quick iterations	Structured planning
Experimental mindset	Rigorous governance

Discovery Phase	Delivery Phase
Minimal constraints	Defined standards
Informal processes	Formal processes
Innovation focus	Scalability focus

Table 9.1: Comparison between the discovery and delivery phases of AI solutions

Clearly recognizing this distinction from the outset will help you avoid the common pitfall of prematurely scaling exploratory prototypes into full production systems, or vice versa, accidentally applying rigid delivery frameworks to drive innovation. In other words, scaling too soon leads to brittle prototypes in production. Scaling too late leaves you stuck in *prototype purgatory*.

Checklist: Are you ready to scale?

Before we dive into the delivery phase, let's tackle one question first. How do you even know it's the right time to switch from discovery to delivery? While there's no one-size-fits-all answer, over the last years of applied AI consulting, I've developed an internal checklist that helps me identify AI solutions that are *ready* for production versus the ones that are very likely to fail real-world requirements and will likely lead to a huge resource drain. Please note that this checklist isn't a guarantee for success. It's more designed to prevent you from rushing into production too early and showing you the blind spots that are (potentially) still missing. Here's what I look for to decide whether it's time to shift gears from discovery into delivery:

Criteria	Description	How to Measure (Examples)	Red Flags
Value clearly validated	The prototype has demonstrated clear and measurable business value or impact (e.g., reduced costs, time savings, user satisfaction).	ROI model, A/B test results, KPI lift (e.g., $\geq 20\%$).	No metrics tracked; unclear benefit.
Positive user feedback	Initial users have consistently provided positive feedback or have shown strong engagement and enthusiasm for the prototype.	NPS ≥ 40, SUS ≥ 70, positive survey/ interviews.	No user feedback at all. Users are confused, disengaged, or critical.

Technical feasibility proven	Core technical questions or risks have been answered or mitigated - there's high confidence that the AI solution is technically viable.	IT approval complete; passes tech review, working prototype.	Frequent errors, reliance on future enhancements, fragile setup.
Demand is growing	Increasing user demand indicates broader organizational interest or clear potential for wider adoption.	Usage trends, waitlist, internal requests.	Use remains flat or drops. High churn. Unclear who needs it.
Leadership support secured	Senior stakeholders or decision-makers (often in the respective business unit) have explicitly signaled willingness to fund the AI solution moving forward.	Budget approved; sponsor assigned.	No sponsor. No ownership.
Ethical and compliance checks passed	While you perhaps haven't considered all ethical and compliance-relevant intricacies up to the last detail, it's clear that in general, your AI solution will meet both ethical and compliance standards of your organization.	Data protection impact assessment done, compliance check passed.	Open compliance issues; unknown risks.
Integration path understood	There's clarity around how the AI prototype will integrate within existing workflows, systems, and processes.	Interface defined; architecture and owners aligned.	Unclear how it fits into existing workflows or who owns the implementation.

Table 9.2: Checklist for assessing readiness to move from discovery to delivery

In short, there's plenty of value and fewer red flags.

As a practical example, let's say you managed to create a functional prototype of your RFP Chatbot Analyzer that is also able to handle new (unknown) proposals and meets the minimum value threshold of saving busy salespeople at least 1 hour per week. Besides the early test users, more people in your organization are now actively requesting access. Your checklist reveals clear validation of value, user enthusiasm, solid technical feasibility, and robust stakeholder support. At this stage, shifting into delivery mode is both logical and timely.

When you're ready to make this shift, remember: transitioning from a prototype to a production-ready AI solution isn't just about scaling up your prototype as we explored in the previous chapter. Usually, it involves careful assessment of what can be directly transferred, what needs enhancement, and what must be rebuilt entirely.

Now that we know whether we're ready to scale (or not), let's take a look at what *scaling* success actually looks like.

Core goals of scaling AI solutions

As we found out in the beginning of the chapter, scaling isn't just about shipping bigger software. It's about meeting five core goals that make your AI systems viable at scale. These goals include capacity, reliability, performance, maintainability, and security. Each plays a critical role in ensuring your AI system not only works technically but also remains an asset, not a liability to your business.

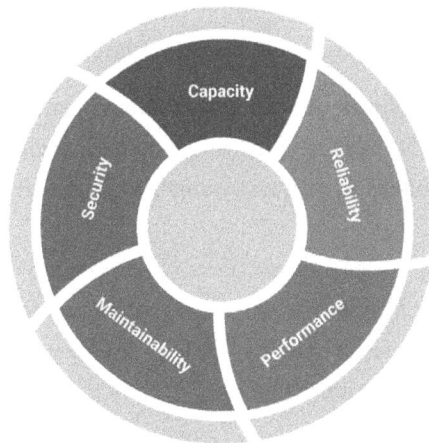

Figure 9.1: Five AI scaling goals

First, let's get a high-level overview of what these goals mean, their typical key metrics, and their milestones before we dive deeper into how to achieve these goals.

Capacity

Capacity scaling is the ability of your AI system to handle increasing volumes of data, users, and transactions without breaking down or driving costs out of control. This typically involves two dimensions: scaling up (adding more resources, such as CPU, memory, or storage to a single system) and scaling out (adding more instances or nodes that share the workload). True capacity planning balances both, ensuring growth can be supported quickly and cost-effectively.

Some examples of the key metrics and milestones for capacity scaling are as follows:

- **Load handling:** Tracking how many requests or transactions the system can support before performance degrades.
- **Latency under load:** Monitoring whether response times stay within agreed expectations as usage grows.
- **Data freshness:** Checking how reliably data pipelines deliver up-to-date inputs on time.
- **Elastic cost profile:** Watching whether costs per request or per user remain stable (or decrease) as the system scales.

Some typical challenges include:

- Over-relying on fragile prototype fixes (manual exports, scripts).
- Hitting bottlenecks in single systems (databases, queues, APIs).
- Vendor rate limits or licensing constraints not visible in early testing.
- Over-provisioning infrastructure *just in case*, leading to wasted spend.

High capacity ensures your AI solution grows alongside your business. It prevents slowdowns and outages that erode trust, avoids costly rebuilds, and protects margins by keeping scaling efficient. Put simply: strong capacity makes adoption sustainable under real-world pressure.

Reliability

Reliability is the ability of your AI system to deliver consistent and correct results under real-world conditions. A reliable system doesn't just stay online - it also produces outputs that users can trust, even as data, usage, or conditions change.

Some key metrics and milestone examples to help track reliability include:

- **System availability:** Tracking uptime against service-level agreements.
- **Pipeline success rate:** Monitoring how consistently data processing completes without errors.

- **Model accuracy** and **stability:** Measuring model accuracy, precision, recall, or other relevant KPIs over time.

- **Recovery speed:** Assessing how quickly the system recovers after failures or interruptions.

- **Consistency of outputs:** Checking that predictions remain stable across runs and environments.

The typical challenges you might encounter while building reliable systems include (but are not limited to):

- Degradation of model accuracy due to data drift.

- Silent data corruption or missing monitoring of quality.

- Overfitting to test conditions that don't reflect real-world variability.

- Infrastructure single points of failure or brittle retry mechanisms.

- Alert fatigue - too many signals without actionable prioritization.

Reliable AI systems build trust with users and stakeholders. They reduce costly downtime, prevent incorrect outputs from spreading into business decisions, and encourage widespread adoption. Unreliable systems, whether from outages or inaccurate predictions, quickly erode confidence and can become more damaging than not using AI at all.

Performance

Performance is the ability of your AI system to respond quickly and efficiently to user interactions or processing demands. A performant system delivers insights at the speed users expect, without excessive resource consumption. To measure performance, you can utilize the following key metrics and milestones:

- **Response time:** Tracking how long it takes from user request to system response.

- **Throughput:** Measuring how many requests or transactions the system can handle simultaneously.

- **Resource efficiency:** Monitoring CPU, GPU, and memory utilization relative to workload.

- **Optimization impact:** Comparing model architectures or serving techniques (e.g., smaller models, quantization) to balance accuracy and efficiency.

> Remember to include more metrics and milestones that are relevant to your organizational use case(s).

You might encounter some of these challenges as you build performant systems:

- Oversized models that are accurate but too slow or costly to serve.
- Latency spikes caused by inefficient pipelines or network bottlenecks.
- Cold-start delays when models are spun up on demand.
- Lack of optimization, leading to wasted compute and higher costs.

High performance drives user adoption by ensuring interactions feel seamless. It also improves productivity and reduces infrastructure costs. Poor performance, on the other hand, leads to user frustration, slower workflows, and declining ROI.

Maintainability

Maintainability is the ease with which your AI system can be managed, updated, and troubleshot over time. A maintainable system is modular, well documented, and designed to evolve safely as requirements and data change.

Some of the metrics and milestone examples you could track are:

- **Deployment cadence:** Tracking how often new features, models, or fixes can be rolled out.
- **Change safety:** Monitoring failure rates of new releases and how quickly they can be rolled back if issues arise.
- **Documentation quality:** Assessing whether system design, data flows, and processes are clearly captured and accessible.
- **Onboarding speed:** Measuring how quickly new team members can become productive with the system.

Here are some challenges you should be aware of:

- Entangled code, pipelines, or infrastructure that makes updates risky.
- Lack of standardized testing, leading to undetected regressions.
- Poor documentation that slows down new team members.
- Manual deployments that increase error risk and delay improvements.

Maintainable AI systems reduce operational risk and cost. They allow teams to iterate faster, fix issues safely, and adapt to new requirements. Without maintainability, AI solutions quickly accumulate technical debt, making them fragile, expensive, and hard to evolve, undermining their long-term business value.

Security

Security is the protection of your AI system's data, models, and infrastructure from unauthorized access, misuse, or breaches. As prototypes scale into production, security becomes critical for compliance, trust, and resilience.

Some of the key metrics and milestone examples include:

- **Data protection:** Verifying that sensitive data is encrypted in transit and at rest.
- **Access control:** Monitoring role-based permissions and identity management practices. **Compliance readiness:** Tracking adherence to frameworks such as GDPR, HIPAA, SOC2, or ISO/IEC 27001.
- **Model robustness:** Assessing exposure to risks such as adversarial inputs, model theft, or data leakage.
- **Auditability:** Ensuring system activity and data flows can be traced when needed.

Typical challenges you may come across are:

- Over-broad or unclear access rights that expose sensitive data.
- Shadow data copies outside of governed systems.
- Vulnerabilities unique to AI (e.g., prompt injection in LLMs, inference attacks).
- Inconsistent application of compliance standards across teams or regions.

Secure AI systems protect your organization from regulatory penalties, reputational damage, and operational disruption. Strong security practices also build user trust, enabling wider adoption of AI solutions. Weak security, by contrast, can stall scaling efforts, invite legal risk, and undermine stakeholder confidence.

Together, these five goals - capacity, reliability, performance, maintainability, and security - describe *what success looks like* when AI systems are scaled. But knowing the goals isn't enough. To actually achieve them, you need to understand how the pieces of your prototype evolve into production. Some elements carry over directly, while others must be rebuilt or hardened for real-world use. In the next section, we'll revisit the core components of an AI solution and explore the strategies - retain, enhance, rebuild, or establish - that guide their transition from prototype to production.

From prototype to production: Core components and strategies

When moving from discovery to delivery, prototypes act as the seed of your production system. The core components you assembled during prototyping don't disappear - they evolve. Some can be carried forward with little change, others need to be rebuilt for scale, and a few entirely new components must be added for the first time.

To make this evolution practical, it helps to view each component through a clear strategy: *retain*, *enhance*, *rebuild*, or *establish*. These strategies prevent waste, avoid *throwaway AI* (prototypes that can't be used in production), and ensure you focus effort where it matters most.

The following diagram revisits the core components introduced in *Chapter 8*, now overlaid with their delivery strategies:

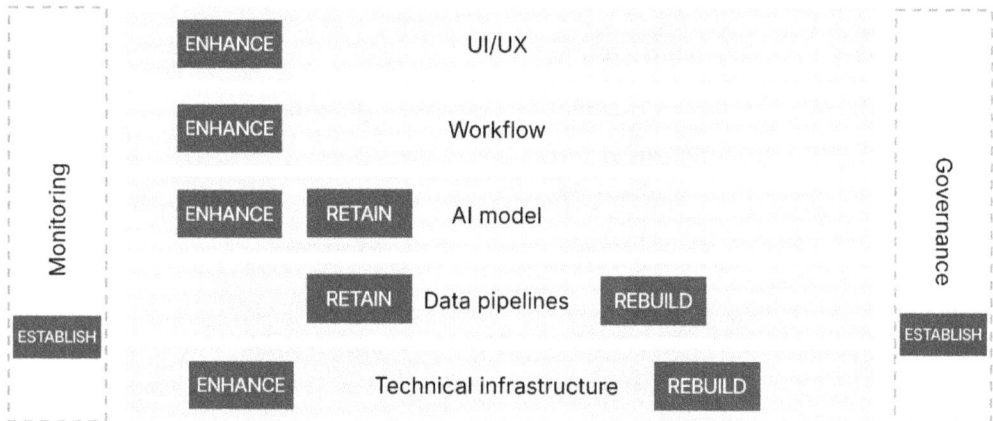

Figure 9.2: Strategies for moving AI components from prototype to production

To make this more concrete, *Table 9.3* provides a detailed view of each component - the recommended delivery strategy, an explanation of why that strategy matters, and common tactics you can use to put it into practice:

Component	Delivery Strategy	Explanation	Common Tactics
AI model core	Retain and enhance	If the trained model and its architecture worked during prototyping, you can usually build on that foundation in production. What matters most is whether performance holds up under real production data and conditions, which typically needs consistent work or tweaks, but not an overhaul of the entire model.	• Validate on larger, diverse datasets using appropriate metrics (e.g., RMSE/MAE for forecasting, precision/recall/F1 for classification, lift/AUC for ranking, pass/fail or human review for LLMs) • Establish feedback loops to capture user corrections and log edge cases • Benchmark against faster or cheaper alternatives to ensure ROI • Compare across vendors or model providers for resilience and performance • Improve prompts • Fine-tune model on additional data
Basic workflow integration	Enhance	Core workflows (user interaction patterns, how insights are consumed, etc.) remain, but integration must go deeper to allow building an enhanced user experience.	• Embed features directly into enterprise systems (CRM, ERP, CMS) via APIs or connectors • Design for convenience: Users should not need to leave their normal workflow (recall TRICUS principles in *Chapter 5*) • Involve *late adopters* early to encourage adoption beyond enthusiastic testers

Component	Delivery Strategy	Explanation	Common Tactics
Conceptual data pipelines	Retain	The design logic of your data pipeline (what data is used, how it flows, how it's transformed, etc.) should remain consistent from prototype to production. If it changes dramatically, the prototype likely didn't reflect realistic production needs. What evolves is the physical implementation.	• Preserve the overall data flow design from prototype to production • Validate that chosen sources and transformations hold true at scale • Align pipeline logic with governance rules (ownership, privacy, retention)
Technical data pipelines	Rebuild	While the conceptual flow stays the same, the technical build must be upgraded. Prototyping often uses quick fixes such as CSV exports or scripts. But these won't scale. Production pipelines must be automated, monitored, and made resilient enough for real-world data volumes.	• Automate data movement (e.g., replace manual exports with scheduled jobs) • Use orchestration tools (e.g., Airflow, Prefect, or cloud schedulers) where necessary • Add quality checks (flag missing values, duplicates, or errors before processing) • Enable logging and alerts (so failures are visible immediately) • Build resilience (retries, fallbacks, or backups to prevent small errors from breaking the pipeline)

Component	Delivery Strategy	Explanation	Common Tactics
Governance and compliance	Establish	Governance and compliance are often (deliberately) overlooked during prototyping, but they are essential when moving to production. A working AI system that ignores privacy, security, or regulatory rules can create more risk than value. In production, governance ensures your system is trusted, auditable, and aligned with legal and organizational standards.	• Restrict access with role-based permissions • Define clear policies for how data is collected, stored, and deleted • Document key decisions, such as which datasets and models were used and why • Involve legal, compliance, and security teams early to prevent late-stage issues • Align with relevant regulations (e.g., GDPR, HIPAA, SOC 2, industry-specific rules)
User experience and training	Enhance	Prototypes validate usability with early adopters. Production requires refinement for broader audiences, including *late adopters* who may resist change. Successful delivery depends on training, support, and a UX that fits seamlessly into broad, daily workflows.	• Test interfaces with a diverse user base to refine usability and accessibility • Develop onboarding and training programs to ease adoption • Provide ongoing support channels (helpdesk, in-app support, documentation) • Gather structured feedback after rollout to drive continuous improvements

Component	Delivery Strategy	Explanation	Common Tactics
Monitoring and maintenance	Establish	Monitoring rarely exists in prototypes but is critical in production. AI models degrade as data, environments, and user behavior change. Without systematic monitoring and maintenance, performance will erode over time.	• Log inputs and outputs to create an audit trail for troubleshooting • Track technical, operational, and strategic metrics (see *Monitoring and metrics* section in this chapter) continuously at different intervals • Detect model drift by comparing new data with training data • Define retraining triggers (e.g., when accuracy drops below threshold) • Establish incident response playbooks for errors or downtime
Other infrastructure	Rebuild or enhance	Expect substantial upgrades to support scaling requirements that span all of the preceding components.	• Replace trial setups (laptops, SaaS accounts) with enterprise-ready environments • Migrate workloads to cloud, on-prem, or hybrid infrastructure depending on security and scale requirements • Implement CI/CD pipelines for reliable deployment of updates (see the later AIOps section) • Plan for resilience with backups, failover, and disaster recovery based on the criticality of your application.

Table 9.3: Overview of transitioning components from discovery to delivery

This nuanced approach - clearly identifying what to retain, enhance, rebuild, or establish - is critical. The key to successful scaling lies in balancing validated elements from your prototype with the new operational demands that arise only in production.

In short, transitioning from prototype to production is less about *scaling up* and more about scaling thoughtfully. By deliberately distinguishing between the discovery and delivery phases, and by methodically managing this transition, your organization lays the groundwork for reliable, sustainable, and impactful AI deployments.

With this foundation in place, the next question is: *what enables these strategies in practice?*

To scale thoughtfully, you need the right enablers across people, processes, data, technology, and operations. These are the five levers of scaling, which we'll explore next.

The five levers of scaling

Scaling AI is hardly achieved by technology alone. Even with clear goals and well-defined component strategies, success depends on the organizational muscle that brings them to life. These muscles take the form of **five key levers: people, processes, data, technology**, and **AI operations (AIOps)**.

Each lever plays a distinct role:

- *People* provide the skills, leadership, and adoption needed for delivery.
- *Processes* give structure without suffocating agility.
- *Data* fuels every AI system.
- *Technology* provides the infrastructure to serve models securely and efficiently.
- *AIOps* ensures that once deployed, AI systems remain accurate, trusted, and valuable over time.

Individually, these levers strengthen specific aspects of scaling. Together, they compound to give you even greater leverage in successfully moving AI prototypes into solutions that are sustainable, governed, and aligned with business needs - as best described by the following figure.

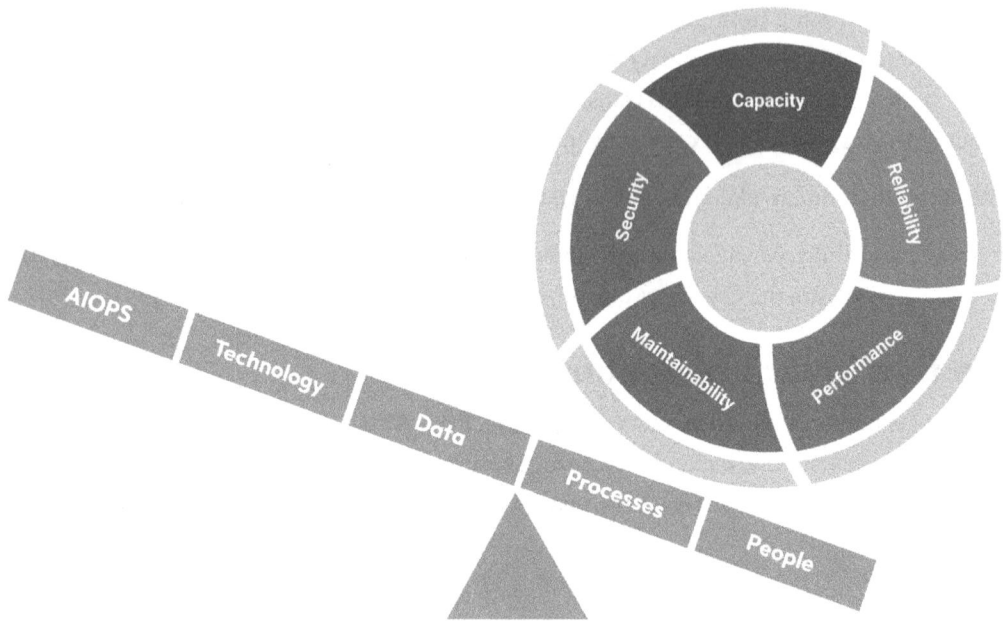

Figure 9.3: Key levers to realize AI scaling goals

Let's explore these critical enablers in more detail.

People

During the discovery phase, you likely relied on a small, agile team following the Two-Pizza rule
(`https://aws.amazon.com/executive-insights/content/amazon-two-pizza-team/`). Team
members probably wore multiple hats, taking on varied responsibilities ranging from data science
to infrastructure management, and from business analysis to informal stakeholder communication.

However, when transitioning from discovery into the delivery phase, it's time to reconsider your
team's structure and scale. Instead of two pizzas, you should prepare to order the *full buffet*. Scaling your AI solution into production involves expanding both the size and diversity of your team,
assigning clearly defined roles and responsibilities, and ensuring you have the right depth of
expertise across critical domains.

As you scale, your team naturally evolves from a tight-knit innovation unit into a broader
cross-functional group that collectively possesses the diverse capabilities required to achieve
scalability, reliability, performance, maintainability, and security. In many cases, that might
involve handing the project off to a completely different delivery team entirely.

This delivery team will typically include dedicated data scientists or AI specialists who ensure the accuracy and reliability of your models, ML and data engineers who manage scalable data infrastructure, and IT infrastructure specialists who maintain system performance and security at scale. You'll also involve dedicated business domain experts or product owners, ensuring that the AI solutions stay closely aligned with real-world business needs and continue to generate value.

While prototyping often operated with minimal formal oversight, scaling to delivery means explicitly aligning with your organization's internal frameworks, governance policies, and regulatory compliance requirements. Collaboration with internal teams such as data governance, IT security, enterprise architecture, compliance, legal experts, or works councils (employee representative bodies) becomes daily business.

Engaging end users will also become more structured and formalized. Regular user training sessions, comprehensive documentation, and ongoing support systems are crucial for driving widespread adoption. This also involves getting consistent buy-in for your solution. Not every user might be happy to work with AI - some might fear getting replaced or training an AI model that will replace their job in the future. Anticipating these fears and actively engaging users will become more important.

As you involve more people and stakeholders, communication and management become increasingly vital, which we'll explore in more depth later in this chapter.

But how exactly do you keep all these people connected, aligned, and moving in the right direction? That's where the next critical lever - processes - comes into play.

Processes

Just as your team structure must evolve from prototyping to production, your approach to processes also needs to mature.

In the discovery phase, agility was essential but likely informal. Rapid iteration, minimal constraints, and loosely structured sprints allowed your prototype team to innovate quickly and pivot easily when facing new insights or challenges.

However, as you transition into the delivery phase, maintaining agility becomes more complex. You're now coordinating larger teams, managing multiple stakeholders, and aligning to established internal policies, all while delivering predictable outcomes. In delivery mode, agility doesn't mean working without structure. Instead, it means embedding agile principles within frameworks that provide the clarity, consistency, and governance necessary to manage complexity effectively.

In practice, this typically involves adopting frameworks such as Scrum (`https://www.scrum.org/`), Kanban (`https://www.atlassian.com/agile/kanban`), or scaled agile methodologies such as the Scaled Agile Framework (SAFe) (`https://scaledagile.com/`). Such frameworks formalize agility by defining clear roles, structured planning cycles, and systematic processes for collaboration, enabling multiple teams to work in an agile manner while maintaining coherence across the broader organization. Regular sprint cycles now become more systematically planned, reviewed, and adapted. Additional roles such as Product Owners, Scrum Masters, and Agile Coaches guide teams, facilitate cross-team collaboration, and continuously realign priorities and expectations.

What kind of process framework you adopt heavily depends on your organization, and in particular which IT delivery processes have already been established there.

For example, if your organization still operates with a predominantly classical (waterfall) IT delivery model, introducing a fully agile AI project from the start may create confusion or resistance. Teams accustomed to fixed scopes, rigid timelines, and sequential workflows can find agile delivery methods unfamiliar or disruptive. In this case, a more effective approach may be to start with a smaller, self-contained AI initiative that doesn't require broad organizational change. Alternatively, you can frame the AI delivery to align with existing stage-gate or milestone-driven processes while embedding agile cycles - such as iterative model development or experimentation - within those phases. This hybrid approach respects the organization's delivery culture while introducing agility where it adds the most value.

Data

While agile processes help you manage team collaboration and task coordination, your AI system's effectiveness still hinges on another critical dimension – *data*. Without clear, robust, and scalable data pipelines, even the most structured agile process won't enable effective AI delivery.

During the prototyping phase, data handling is often a hands-on, ad hoc activity. Teams work with small, curated datasets - sometimes extracted manually, cleaned offline, or gathered just once to test an idea. This is acceptable in the discovery phase because the goal is to prove feasibility, not optimize for scale or reliability.

However, once you enter delivery, these makeshift pipelines quickly become a liability. Production systems need automated, resilient, and secure data flows that can operate continuously and handle real-world messiness such as irregular inputs, missing fields, version mismatches, and scale fluctuations.

In other words, while the conceptual logic of your data pipeline may transfer from prototype to production, the technical implementation almost always needs to be rebuilt. The prototype might have worked with a manually uploaded CSV file and a few hundred records. Your production system must now pull data automatically from cloud warehouses, CRM systems, or real-time APIs - and be ready to process perhaps millions of rows per day.

This transition raises a few key questions that you need to resolve early in the delivery phase:

- Is your data refresh cycle well defined and automated?
- Do you have a consistent schema and version control for inputs?
- How do you handle anomalies or incomplete data in real time?
- Where is the data stored, and who has access?
- Are your data sources future-proof for scaling across use cases or regions?

The answers to these questions don't just impact performance, but also affect security, compliance, and maintainability. As your system scales, so does your exposure to regulatory risks, especially if your data includes personal or sensitive information. In delivery, you'll need to work closely with data governance and compliance teams to ensure your pipelines meet internal and external requirements, such as GDPR, HIPAA, or industry-specific standards.

Another key consideration is **data lineage**. In prototyping, no one usually asks where the data came from or how it was transformed - so long as it works. But in production, you need to trace and audit data flows from end to end. If a model starts behaving unpredictably, you'll need to determine whether the issue lies in the model logic or in a subtle change to an upstream data source. Many organizations implement data lineage using tools such as OpenLineage (https:// openlineage.io/) or vendors such as DataHub (https://datahub.com/), which can be integrated with modern data platforms such as Airflow, Spark, or dbt.

Lastly, don't underestimate the value of **standardization**. Prototyping is often fast and dirty - tailored scripts, custom file formats, and one-off data fixes. At scale, this creates **technical debt**.

Delivery should aim for standardized preprocessing logic in the form of reusable ETL components and shared data contracts across teams and applications:

- **Reusable ETL components** are modular **Extract-Transform-Load (ETL)** building blocks that can be applied across projects instead of writing custom data ingestion scripts each time. **Reusability** improves consistency, reduces errors, and speeds up onboarding. For example, a reusable ETL component might be a standardized function for cleaning time-series data or loading customer records into a data warehouse. You can learn more about ETL concepts in this Azure guide (`https://learn.microsoft.com/en-us/azure/architecture/data-guide/relational-data/etl`).

- **Shared data contracts** define the structure, format, and expectations of data exchanged between teams or services. They act as formal agreements (like APIs for data) and help ensure that producers and consumers of data stay in sync. For example, a contract might specify that a customer ID field must be a non-null string of a certain format. Tools such as Protocol Buffers and Apache Avro, or tools supporting the data contract paradigm (e.g., DataHub, OpenMetadata), help enforce these. Learn more about data contracts with this DataHub blog post: `https://datahub.com/blog/the-what-why-and-how-of-data-contracts/`.

These practices not only reduce rework, but they also enable more teams to build on top of each other's work without introducing brittle dependencies. Making data a first-class citizen in your delivery approach ensures your models have the foundation they need to thrive in production.

> **Technical debt**
>
> Technical debt refers to the hidden cost of taking shortcuts in software, data, or system design in order to deliver something quickly. Just like financial debt, it can accumulate interest over time - in the form of increased maintenance burden, reduced agility, and greater risk of failures.
>
> In AI projects, technical debt often shows up as undocumented scripts, manual data pipelines, or even vendor lock-in.
>
> While these might be acceptable in a prototype, if not addressed, they become obstacles to scaling, reliability, and collaboration.

With the right people in place, agile processes formalized, and production-grade data pipelines taking shape, the next enabler for successful AI delivery is your technology stack. Let's talk about it now.

Technology

While technology played a supporting role during prototyping, it becomes a central pillar in the delivery phase to meet the aforementioned scaling goals.

In the discovery phase, your team probably worked with lightweight environments. Maybe someone spun up a virtual machine manually, trained models in a Jupyter notebook, and shared results through ad hoc dashboards. These setups were perfect for learning and fast experimentation - but in many cases, they don't scale. That means moving from temporary setups to well-structured, monitored, and governed environments that are integrated into your broader enterprise infrastructure.

This transition typically raises three key questions:

1. *Can your infrastructure scale with your AI workloads?*

   AI systems often require a very different resource profile than traditional software applications. From GPUs for model inference to autoscaling containers for serving APIs, your delivery infrastructure must be able to adapt dynamically to workload spikes. It's not just about throwing more compute at the problem - it's about managing compute efficiently, ensuring resource elasticity, and avoiding cost blowouts. The key principle here is **adaptability**. You want a system that can scale quickly enough to meet demand without over-provisioning resources that sit idle and inflate costs. What *scaling quickly* means - whether a few milliseconds or a few days - depends entirely on your use case. For many internal applications, it's often more practical to add a bit more server capacity manually if needed than to invest significant effort upfront in building a fully automated Kubernetes setup from day one. The key is that you're actually able to scale as workloads grow.

2. *Do your tools and platforms support operational handover?*

   Tools used during prototyping (e.g., local dev environments, SaaS APIs) often lack the access controls, monitoring, or integration hooks required in production. In delivery, your stack should support at least version control (e.g., Git), likely CI/CD automation, and definitely robust monitoring and logging. The right choices depend entirely on your use case. Real-time systems, for example, typically demand more automation and observability than batch workloads. What matters most is that your tooling enables a smooth handoff from development to operations, without adding unnecessary manual patchwork.

3. *Can you minimize rebuilds?*

   While some components of your prototype may need to be re-engineered, try to minimize unnecessary rebuilds. If your prototyping tools are compatible with your production platform (e.g., using Azure ML Studio or Vertex AI), you may be able to reuse model endpoints or pipeline configurations. That's why choosing the right tools from the beginning - ones that support both experimentation and delivery - can significantly smooth your scaling journey.

Another important consideration in this aspect is **modularity**. Delivering AI at scale doesn't mean building one monolithic system. Instead, modular architectures allow you to isolate components - models, APIs, pipelines, and dashboards - and evolve them independently. This makes it easier to swap out technologies, upgrade individual components, and reduce risk when something breaks.

Security also becomes tightly linked with your tech stack. The infrastructure decisions you make, such as your cloud provider, access architecture, or data storage format, will directly influence how easy (or difficult) it is to meet internal security and compliance requirements. Work closely with your IT and InfoSec teams to choose technology that aligns with both operational needs and regulatory expectations.

So while technology may have taken a backseat during prototyping, in delivery, it becomes a key enabler. The choices you make here will either accelerate your AI adoption or become roadblocks that limit scale, increase cost, or introduce unnecessary risk.

AIOps

Once your AI system is live, running in production, and delivering value, your job isn't done; it's just the beginning of a continuous cycle of monitoring, maintenance, and optimization. AI models naturally degrade over time due to data drift, evolving user expectations, or changing business conditions. That's where our next enabler comes in: AIOps.

AIOps refers to the set of operational practices, tools, and processes that ensure your AI models remain accurate, useful, and trustworthy over time. It's like **DevOps**, which focuses on deploying and operating traditional software reliably, but extends these practices to the unique challenges of AI - such as monitoring model accuracy, detecting data drift, and managing retraining cycles.

During prototyping, model performance was probably measured in quick evaluations: a test dataset, a few metrics, and some informal stakeholder validation. But in production, you need rigorous, *ongoing monitoring* - because everything from user behavior to upstream data sources to market dynamics can shift unexpectedly. The most critical role of AIOps, therefore, is to continuously monitor your AI systems and alert your team when things go off track. This includes:

- **Model performance monitoring**: Are metrics such as accuracy, precision, recall, or other KPIs drifting below acceptable thresholds?
- **Data drift detection**: Are the characteristics of incoming data changing over time that might require you to update or adjust your models or prompts?

- **Pipeline health**: Are all systems - from ingestion to inference - running smoothly, or are there bottlenecks or failures?

- **Latency and availability**: Are your AI services responding fast enough to support users and workflows?

Well-structured AIOps will automatically flag issues when they arise, enabling quick investigation and resolution. This is less about avoiding every issue, but rather catching them before they snowball into bigger problems.

A healthy AIOps setup, therefore, also includes mechanisms for feedback and iteration. This means that beyond flagging issues, you're able to apply corrections and retrain models with updated data over time. Many organizations make the mistake of treating model deployment as a one-time event. In reality, AI models are like living systems that require updates, retraining, version control, and, occasionally, full replacement. AIOps gives you the structure to manage this lifecycle sustainably.

In order to achieve this and make the right decisions, you need clear ownership. *Who is responsible for checking model performance next month? Who's notified if the model suddenly produces errors?*

In a good AIOps setup, it's clear who's going to do what and overall who's accountable for the AI system's health. If you don't yet have a dedicated MLOps or AIOps function, start small: implement performance dashboards, automate drift detection, and define what *acceptable performance* means for each use case. Then, evolve those practices as your AI footprint grows.

Together, these five enablers - people, processes, data, technology, and AIOps - give you the organizational muscle and structural resilience needed to scale AI thoughtfully and successfully.

Practical example: Scaling the RFP Chatbot Analyzer

To make these concepts more tangible, let's revisit our RFP Chatbot Analyzer prototype from earlier chapters and see what happens when it's scaled thoughtfully into production:

1. **Applying the checklist**: Let's say the chatbot prototype demonstrated measurable value. Feedback was enthusiastic, demand was spreading beyond the initial test group, and leadership secured the budget for the next steps. The readiness checklist was effectively completed: value validated, technical feasibility proven, and an integration path understood. *Table 9.4* shows an example of the applied checklist:

Criteria	Evaluation	Red Flags/Concerns
Value	• Salespeople with access processed RFPs ~10+ hours faster per month each; ~10K hours/year saved. • Higher throughput without higher costs, faster response time.	None.
User feedback	Early tester feedback was very positive	Broader survey still pending. UI still needs enhancements.
Technical feasibility	• IT review completed. • Performance is already good enough to be useful.	• GenAI stack still new. Platform decisions still pending.
Growing demand	Early testers enthusiastic but not encouraged to promote the project internally yet.	Wider demand signal pending.
Leadership support	• Head of sales agreed to sponsor the first year of implementation and assign a budget. • IT assigns a PM.	None.
Ethics	Legal/compliance review still pending, but no initial blockers identified.	Final sign-off WIP.
Integration path	Embed in CRM/SharePoint workflows.	Integration testing not yet completed.

Table 9.4: The readiness checklist for RFP Chatbot Analyzer

2. **Defining scaling goals**: With delivery on the horizon, the team clarified the five scaling goals:

   • **Capacity**: Ensure the chatbot can handle at least 10 active RFPs in parallel without slowing down.

   • **Reliability**: Maintain at least 90% accuracy (9 out of 10 chat requests handled with complete, truthful information) and ensure the system is available during critical bidding cycles.

   • **Performance**: Keep response times under 10 seconds, even for large, complex proposals.

   • **Maintainability**: Allow effective monitoring and testing of new models, with update cycles expected every 6 months.

- **Security**: Protect sensitive RFP data with encryption, access controls, and auditability.

3. **Applying component strategies**: Using the framework from *Table 9.3*, the team mapped prototype elements to their delivery strategies:

   - **AI model core (Retain)**: The existing model approach was kept, but tested even more rigorously with additional, compliance-heavy documents.

   - **Workflow integration (Enhance)**: Instead of a separate interface, the chatbot was embedded directly into the CRM so salespeople could use it in their daily workflow.

   - **Technical data pipelines (Rebuild)**: Manual PDF uploads were replaced with automated connectors pulling RFPs directly from shared drives.

   - **Governance and compliance (Establish)**: Logging was added to track document access, and compliance officers reviewed policies for handling sensitive data.

   - **Monitoring and maintenance (Establish)**: Dashboards were set up to track accuracy, latency, and usage, with alerts for failures or anomalies.

4. **Leveraging the five enablers**: Scaling required more than technology. The organization pulled the five levers to support the transition:

   - **People**: A new cross-functional team was assembled, led by a dedicated product owner and supported by IT and sales specialists.

   - **Processes**: Agile sprints continued, but with more formal testing, documentation, and release gates.

   - **Data**: Pipelines were automated, and governance teams defined retention and privacy policies.

   - **Technology**: The prototype moved from a trial setup to a cloud-hosted solution. The team picked a customizable vendor solution that was compatible with their CRM out of the box (hybrid approach).

   - **AIOps**: Within IT, continuous monitoring was implemented to detect data drift, track adoption, and trigger retraining. The product owner was in charge of controlling these KPIs.

5. **The outcome**: By following this structured approach, the RFP Chatbot Analyzer scaled into a production-ready system that:

   - Saved thousands of hours annually across the sales organization and allowed faster RFP responses.

- Maintained stable accuracy even as new document formats were introduced.
- Operated securely within the company's compliance framework.
- Achieved widespread adoption thanks to seamless CRM integration.
- Laid a critical foundation for other AI use cases to be developed.

As a result, the organization ended up with a solution that extended the value proven in the prototype, fit naturally into existing workflows, and gained traction with a broader set of users.

Of course, scaling an AI solution is rarely as straightforward as this example makes it seem. Every organization encounters its own friction points, trade-offs, and surprises along the way.

From a process perspective, embedding agile delivery practices into a sales-driven environment might create friction, especially if business stakeholders expect rigid timelines or immediate results. Data pipelines may also turn out to be fragile - especially for new RFPs that might come in unexpectedly.

On the technology side, integrating the chatbot deeply into systems such as a CRM or SharePoint could raise implementation issues or cost debates as this might affect other teams as well. Measuring adoption, accuracy, and cost trends can turn out to be complicated too - a spike in usage could quickly inflate inference costs beyond initial projections. And on the people side, adoption could slow once the chatbot reaches less tech-savvy or skeptical sales teams, requiring stronger training and change management.

To unpack these challenges further, we'll now zoom in on three particularly sensitive areas of scaling: the people who fund, use, and approve what you're building; the costs of running AI solutions at scale; and your ability to monitor what's happening as your AI footprint grows across the organization.

Aligning people and purpose: The organizational side of scaling AI

So far, we've talked a lot about technical enablers that allow you to scale AI systems across your organization. But all of this will amount to little if your people aren't on board.

Implementing AI requires buy-in from the very employees whose work AI is meant to enhance. This organizational readiness needs to be in close sync with the technical readiness, as shown in the following diagram:

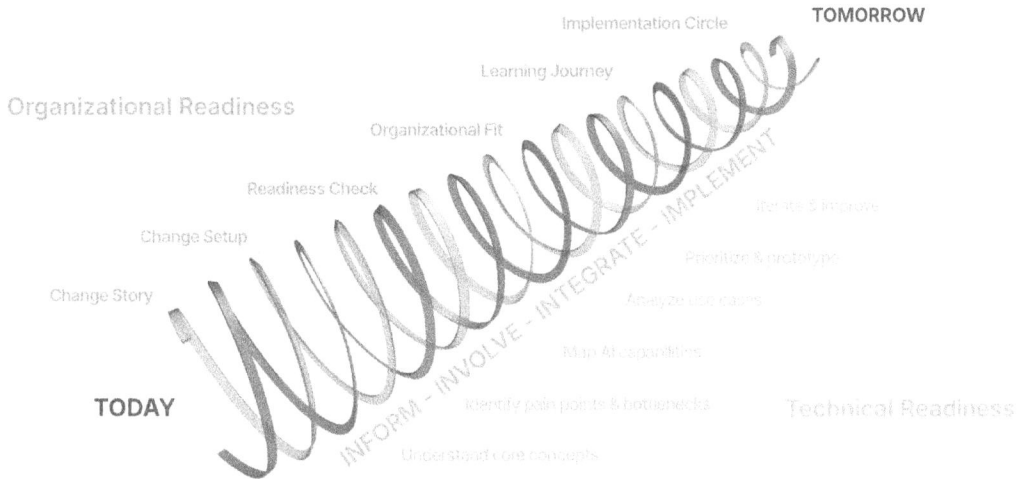

Figure 9.4: Synchronizing technical and organizational readiness

Figure 9.4 illustrates the crucial balance between technical and organizational readiness when scaling AI solutions. Successful AI implementation requires both robust technical systems and engaged, prepared employees. Technical advancements (such as developing AI models or infrastructure) alone are insufficient. Simultaneously, the organization needs to adapt and change, ensuring employees understand and embrace the new AI tools. This involves addressing employee concerns, providing training, and integrating AI into existing workflows.

In simple words: no matter how advanced your solution is, it simply won't deliver results if the people expected to use it don't believe in it. Integrating AI into day-to-day operations is not a purely technical exercise - it's a cultural shift. A transformation. One that touches how people work, how they make decisions, and how they see their role in the organization.

Employees rarely resist AI because they fail to understand its benefits. They resist it because they're not convinced those benefits apply to them. Why should they support a system that might disrupt their job or rewrite familiar processes? Why should they even embrace a future where an AI system might perform part of their work better than they themselves?

AI anxiety is real - and so is the instinct to resist change when the *why* is unclear or unconvincing.

That's why organizational readiness must evolve hand in hand with technical readiness. The preceding diagram shows how these two forces must grow together over time. One without the other creates friction, resistance, and, ultimately, failure.

The further you move along your AI journey, from understanding core concepts to rolling out real use cases, the more your organization must evolve in parallel. You're not just implementing software but instead guiding people through a mindset shift: helping them understand how AI fits into their work, what it changes, and why it matters.

Unfortunately, this is where many initiatives stumble. The most common pitfalls are surprisingly consistent: vague strategic narratives, overhyped promises, lack of training, missing change support, and no mechanisms for feedback. They focus on delivering the model, not on supporting the people around it.

A people-first AI transformation flips this logic. It doesn't start with the algorithm. It starts with the employee.

The focus shifts from *"What can this model do?"* to ***"How will this help someone do their job better?"*** and ***"How do we explain this solution to our workforce?"***

It means aligning the pace of technical progress with the pace of change your organization can actually absorb.

This doesn't mean putting everything on pause until the whole organization is *ready*. But it does mean recognizing that AI success is built on two foundations: the maturity of your systems and the *readiness* of your people. And just like your technology stack, organizational readiness can (and should) be developed incrementally, step by step.

That journey starts with a compelling change story that explains not just what is changing, but why. It continues with dedicated teams guiding the transformation, a structured learning journey that equips employees to engage with AI meaningfully, and constant feedback loops to make sure the organization is evolving with the solution.

Put simply: no company has been transformed by AI just because they had the fastest models or the cleanest data. Transformation happens when people feel empowered, not displaced, by the tools they're asked to use. That's what turns capability into impact. And that's why scaling AI is, in the end, just as much about psychology and trust as it is about infrastructure and algorithms.

Next up, we will talk about how to manage costs when you scale your AI solutions.

Managing cost at scale

Adding all the elements we have discussed so far will obviously increase the cost of your AI solution. So once your AI solution scales in production and starts to rack up costs, one question will come up again and again, from finance, from leadership, from your own team: *Is this still worth it?*

The answer depends on whether you're prepared for how *AI projects behave differently from traditional IT projects*, especially when it comes to cost.

Take a look at the following simplified illustration:

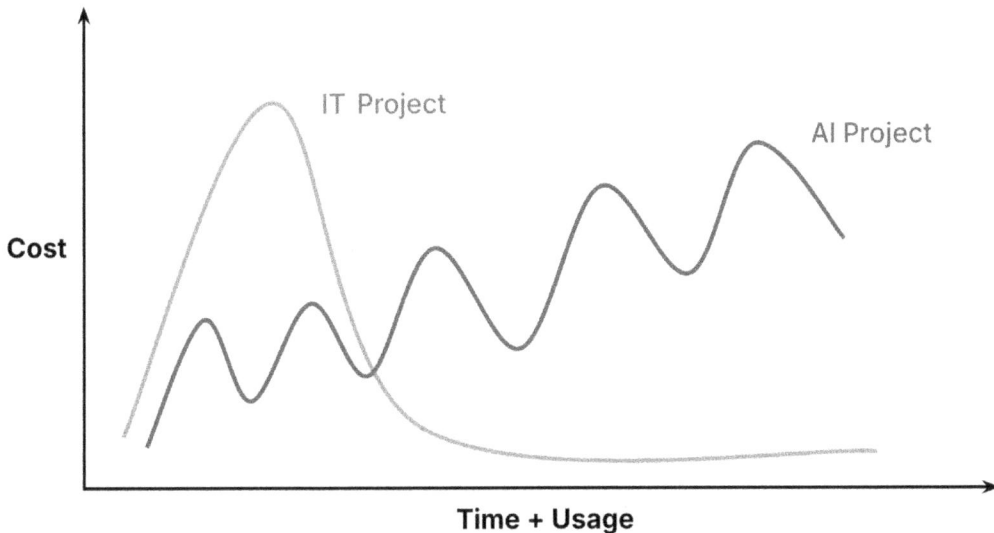

Figure 9.5: IT project cost versus AI project cost

What you see here is a common pattern.

In classical IT projects, most costs are typically front-loaded. You invest heavily during implementation - building systems, integrating software, and training users - and then costs typically flatten out over time. Whether you have 100 users or 10,000, the cost per user stays largely stable (aside from software licensing, which might be usage-based).

AI projects follow a very different rhythm.

While early development costs may be lower - especially if you start with off-the-shelf components - AI introduces oscillating and scaling costs that emerge as the solution grows. Model retraining, fine-tuning, and general model maintenance introduce a cyclical cost block that will reappear over time, causing maintenance costs for your AI solution (more or less predictable) to go up and down periodically. This makes budgeting the solution hard since you always need to keep some reserves in case things go wrong unexpectedly, for example, due to underlying data changes.

On top of that, AI costs typically scale more noticeably with usage. A model that handles 50 queries a day might be inexpensive to run. But when you scale that same model to handle 50,000 daily requests across multiple business units, inference costs, compute load, and latency-handling infrastructure can drive up costs rapidly. What looked efficient in the pilot can become surprisingly expensive at scale - especially when response time and model accuracy need to be preserved under load. This is because AI models often rely on specialized infrastructure such as GPUs or high-performance CPUs, which are much more expensive than your average IT stack.

So, how do you tackle that?

Don't try to model every edge-case cost from the beginning. Instead, I recommend a more practical and scalable approach: the value threshold and cost cap model that we introduced earlier in *Chapter 7*.

Here is a quick recap of these approaches:

- A *value threshold* is the minimum business value an AI use case needs to generate - typically defined as time savings, increased conversion, cost avoidance, or another business-relevant metric

- A *cost cap* defines the maximum annual budget allocated to developing, deploying, and maintaining that solution - including infrastructure, licensing, and internal resources

If your AI use case stays below the cost cap and above the value threshold, it's considered a net positive - justified, and delivering business value. If either side of that equation changes, your governance process should force a reevaluation: either raise the threshold or optimize the system to bring costs back under control.

Let's look at a simple example.

Suppose your AI system is used by customer support agents to automatically summarize complaint emails:

- The *value threshold* might be defined as: saving at least 3 hours per agent per week.

- With 50 agents using it, that's 150 hours per week × 52 weeks = 7,800 hours per year.

- At an average internal rate of $50/hour, that's $390,000 in annual value.

- If the total cost (infrastructure, vendor fees, and maintenance) is capped at $100,000 per year, the solution is well within bounds. But if compute costs spike due to an increased volume, that would likely push the annual cost above $300K. You now need to reassess: Can you raise the value threshold by showing that more departments are benefiting?

- Or do you need to reduce cost (e.g., by using cheaper models, more caching, or asynchronous processing)?

AI economics requires active management. Your AI solution isn't a *deploy once and walk away* system. It's a living product that needs regular cost-performance evaluations. Without them, you risk creeping infrastructure costs, unmonitored vendor bills, or inefficient workflows eroding your ROI over time.

That's why this simple cost/value framing is so powerful. You don't need perfect accounting models. You just need clarity about what success looks like, how much you're willing to invest to achieve it, and when the balance tips too far.

In other words: don't obsess over the exact value. Make sure your AI solution consistently exceeds a real, tangible threshold (which you have defined in *Chapter 4*). When costs begin to rise, as they almost inevitably will, treat that as a checkpoint for smart, strategic recalibration.

In the next section, we will talk about practical approaches for defining and measuring business impact, employing clear and actionable metrics to maintain alignment with organizational objectives.

Monitoring and metrics

We've touched on monitoring at several points already - as a dedicated component in your AI solution, as a critical part of AIOps, and even during prototype evaluation when you measured model accuracy. Each mention reflects the same reality: monitoring isn't a single step or tool, but a thread that runs through the entire AI lifecycle.

What changes at scale is the scope. Monitoring moves from being an occasional check or a technical safeguard to becoming a structured discipline in its own right - one that ties together system health, user behavior, cost signals, and business outcomes.

This includes not just traditional metrics such as latency or accuracy but also **guardrails against unsafe outputs**, tracking for potential **Personally Identifiable Information (PII) leakage**, and detection of jailbreak attempts in generative models. These privacy and security dimensions are as critical as performance or reliability because they directly influence trust, compliance, and user safety.

So far, we've mostly looked at data as the fuel that powers our AI - data we ingest, clean, and feed into models. But once our AI solution is live and in use, it starts producing its own data, such as usage data, performance metrics, and operational logs. This new layer is just as important as the data we used to train the system in the first place. In other words, AI systems don't just consume data; they generate it. Scaling AI successfully means knowing how to use that data to track what's working, what isn't, and where your next optimization should happen.

In that sense, monitoring isn't just something you do to catch failures, but a sophisticated form of analysis that - if done well - lets you answer questions such as:

- Are users actually engaging with the AI solution?
- Are we able to keep performance high at all times?
- Are we seeing less helpful outputs over time?

As you can see, there aren't just engineering concerns - they're business concerns. If a model silently loses relevance or accuracy, users will stop trusting it. If compute cost per inference is rising without a corresponding increase in value, you may be on the path to negative ROI.

A minimum monitoring setup for AI in production is shown in *Table 9.5*:

Monitoring Criteria	Description
Usage metrics	Number of predictions made, queries processed, active users, peak usage hours, and API response times.
Performance metrics	Model-level statistics, such as, accuracy, precision, recall, or business-specific equivalents (e.g., number of complaints resolved, proposals accelerated, conversions influenced).
Cost metrics	Inference cost per user, per API call, or per department. Compute spikes. Scaling patterns.
Feedback data	User corrections, thumbs-up/thumbs-down scores, and flagging behavior. Anything that gives insight into real-world model quality.
System health	Pipeline reliability, latency, error rates, retraining intervals, and success/failure rates of data ingestion.

Table 9.5: Minimal set of metrics to monitor in production

Of course, it's not enough to just collect this data - you need to put it to work. That's why dashboards shouldn't be built just for data scientists, but for business users and product managers alike. Align your metrics to the **value threshold/cost cap** framework. If performance dips below a defined KPI, that should trigger investigation or retraining. And likewise, if usage spikes without a value increase, it deserves your attention.

And don't forget: AI can help here, too. For example:

- Use AI anomaly detection to flag sudden drops in model accuracy
- Predict when the cost per user is likely to exceed the budget cap
- Suggest strategies for enhancing user engagement based on user feedback

To keep track of the growing complexity, here's a straightforward way to organize your monitoring criteria by breaking it down into three connected layers:

Layer	Focus	Example Metrics and Signals
Technical	Infrastructure and system health	• Pipeline uptime and failure rates • Inference latency • Data ingestion success/failure • Infrastructure usage (CPU/GPU/memory)
Operational	Solution performance and user interaction	• Number of predictions per day • Active users/departments • Model accuracy, precision, recall • Cost per prediction or per user • Retraining frequency • Feedback loop activity (e.g., flagged results, thumbs up/down)
Strategic	Business impact and alignment	• Value threshold achieved (e.g., time saved, conversions influenced) • Cost cap status (e.g., projected spend versus budget) • Usage trends over time • ROI signals per department or process area

Table 9.6: Framework for organizing monitoring metrics

This layered approach ensures you're not only keeping the system online (technical), but also ensuring it remains useful (operational) and valuable (strategic). As you scale your AI solutions, this kind of structured, multi-layered monitoring becomes essential - not just to prove that your systems are working, but to continuously optimize, adapt, and steer them toward what matters most.

We will now shift our focus to applying our learnings in practice. The next section focuses on how you can take incremental steps to scale AI.

Practical steps for scaling AI solutions

Scaling AI can be quite overwhelming. Yes, it's complex. Yes, it's cross-functional. So, how do you move forward without overextending your resources or losing focus?

One proven approach is to work in **complete, contained increments** - very similar to delivering atomic AI use cases during the prototyping phase. Think of each increment as a mini-project with a clear boundary: it can be delivered from end to end, shows tangible value, and generates lessons for the next round.

A strong increment typically includes:

- **A specific use case or feature**: Narrow enough to complete, but meaningful enough to matter
- **A defined value threshold and cost cap**: Keeps the business case visible at all times
- **A monitoring plan**: Tracks both technical performance and business impact
- **A clear change narrative**: Explains the *why* to affected users
- **A learning plan**: Equips people with the knowledge and support to adopt the solution

These increments can then be developed sequentially or in parallel (*Figure 9.6*) depending on the resource constraints and priorities of your organization.

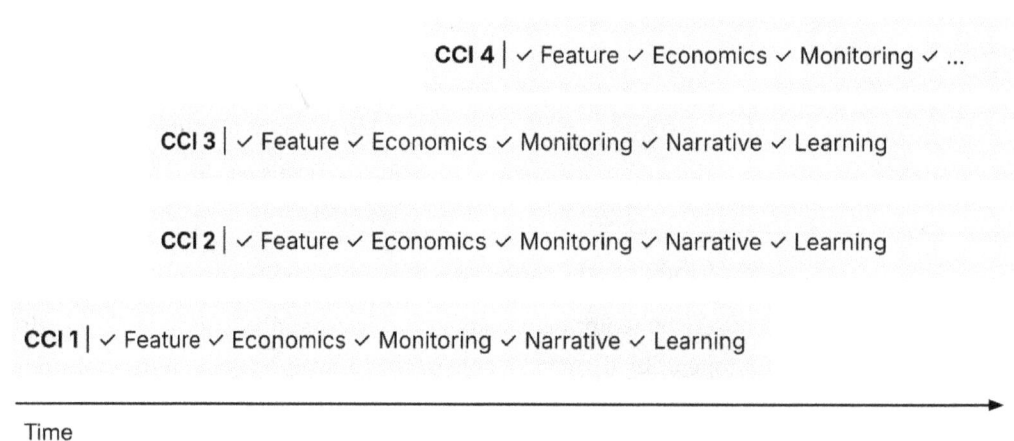

CCI 4 | ✓ Feature ✓ Economics ✓ Monitoring ✓ ...

CCI 3 | ✓ Feature ✓ Economics ✓ Monitoring ✓ Narrative ✓ Learning

CCI 2 | ✓ Feature ✓ Economics ✓ Monitoring ✓ Narrative ✓ Learning

CCI 1 | ✓ Feature ✓ Economics ✓ Monitoring ✓ Narrative ✓ Learning

Time

Figure 9.6: Development of complete contained increments over time (schematic)

This approach works because each increment is small enough to manage risk, but complete enough to build trust and momentum.

Let's revisit our RFP Chatbot Analyzer example and how you can build complete, contained increments.

Example: Scaling the RFP Chatbot Analyzer in increments

Here's how the RFP Chatbot Analyzer could grow step by step:

1. **Increment 1**: Extend to one more sales team:

   - **Use case**: Deploy the chatbot beyond the original pilot team.
   - **Value threshold**: Save at least one hour per week per salesperson.
   - **Monitoring**: Track accuracy on new RFP formats, usage per rep, and time saved.
   - **Narrative**: *We're rolling out to another team to see whether the benefits hold at a larger scale.*
   - **Learning**: Collect adoption feedback and refine onboarding materials.

2. **Increment 2**: Embed in the CRM:

   - **Use case**: Move from a standalone interface into the CRM.
   - **Value threshold**: Increase adoption rate by 20% through better workflow integration.
   - **Monitoring**: Compare usage between standalone and CRM-integrated versions.
   - **Narrative**: *Now you don't need a separate login - the chatbot meets you where you already work.*
   - **Learning**: Document integration challenges and create reusable patterns for future AI apps.

3. **Increment 3:** Add compliance document handling:

   - **Use case**: Train or fine-tune the chatbot on compliance-heavy RFPs.
   - **Value threshold**: Reduce manual compliance review time by 30%.
   - **Monitoring**: Track accuracy specifically on compliance-related sections.
   - **Narrative**: *We're extending the chatbot's reach into one of the toughest areas: compliance.*
   - **Learning**: Strengthen processes for handling sensitive data and working with compliance officers.

Each increment is complete on its own: it defines success upfront, includes adoption planning, and delivers lessons that inform the next cycle.

Each increment builds confidence, sharpens alignment, and gives you a tangible outcome to learn from - whether it's a new department using a chatbot, an upgraded model powering a workflow, or an improved retraining pipeline that reduces downtime.

Increments as agile epics

If you're familiar with agile methods, you can think of these increments as epics: larger units of work that can be broken down into smaller stories or tasks but still deliver meaningful value on their own. Each epic has a clear objective, success criteria, and learning outcomes - just like the increments described here. Check out this website if you'd like to learn more about agile development and epics in particular: https://resources.scrumalliance.org/Article/epic-agile.

This also ties back to the *processes lever*. While prototyping often relied on loosely structured sprints, scaling requires more disciplined planning and coordination. If you already know how to handle agile projects from other initiatives, you're at an advantage. By treating each scaling increment as an **epic**, you give teams a shared container that balances agility with structure: flexible enough to adapt, but formal enough to align stakeholders and track progress.

In practice, this means:

1. **Define increments as epics:** Each epic focuses on scaling one outcome (e.g., CRM integration for the chatbot).

2. **Break into stories and tasks:** Technical teams handle integration work, governance teams define policies, and training teams prepare onboarding - all within the same epic.

3. **Close the loop:** At the end of each epic, revisit your alignment points (value threshold, cost cap, adoption, learning) before starting the next.

Step by step, this incremental approach allows you to scale AI sustainably and responsibly. Each cycle delivers real value while also strengthening your organization's readiness - technically and culturally - for what comes next.

To give you a real-world example: one B2B company I worked with had a support team that prototyped a simple customer support chatbot. In discovery, they built three chatbots across different products and proved the concept: the bots could answer around 80% of customer questions, reduce ticket volume, and free up project managers (who had been handling support on the side) to focus on their actual jobs.

Instead of rushing to roll out chatbots everywhere, they treated scaling as a sequence of **self-contained increments**:

1. **Increment 1: Establish a platform**

   With more than 30 products to cover, the team realized they needed a shared hub to manage chatbot knowledge centrally while allowing per-product adaptations. They chose a chatbot platform vendor rather than building one from scratch, and defined their first increment as setting up the platform with basic monitoring, feedback loops, and governance features such as team-based access. This gave every future chatbot the same foundation: visibility into performance, a way for users to flag issues, and a process for continuous improvement.

2. **Increment 2 and beyond: Add bots one at a time**

   Once the platform was in place, they added one chatbot per product line (website). Each bot was its own increment - small enough to monitor adoption and impact, but complete enough to deliver value to a specific customer segment. Only after validating usage and accuracy did they move on to the next.

The result was a layered scaling approach: platform first, then incremental bot updates. This kept risks low, allowed fast learning cycles, and ensured each expansion built on proven foundations. After 8 months, the company had 20 different chatbots live, handling more than 10,000 messages per month and saving thousands of support hours in first-level customer service.

Summary

In this chapter, we explored what it really takes to move from prototype to production, beyond just technology.

We looked at several aspects. The first was the shift from discovery to delivery, and what needs to be rebuilt versus reused. We also talked about the five key enablers of scaling AI (people, processes, data, technology, and AIOps). An important aspect of scaling AI that practitioners must really focus on is how to engage the people who approve, use, and operate your AI solutions. We looked into how value thresholds and cost caps can help you manage AI-specific costs. The chapter also stressed the importance of generating, tracking, and acting on monitoring data to drive continuous improvement. Scaling AI is never just about performance benchmarks or technical uptime. It's about creating a system - of technology, people, and processes - that learns, adapts, and delivers value as it grows. Because at scale, AI isn't just something you deliver; it's something you live with.

In the next chapter, we'll look at how you can successfully scale AI to deliver meaningful business impact.

Unlock this book's exclusive benefits now

UNLOCK NOW

Scan this QR code or go to `https://packtpub.com/unlock`, then search for this book by name.

Note: Keep your purchase invoice ready before you start.

10

Leveraging Your AI Toolkit

You've come a long way.

You now understand what modern AI really is. You have identified high-impact AI use cases, designed and prioritized them, built working prototypes, and even explored how to scale these prototypes across your organization. But there's still one major piece missing - and it's not more theory. It's, finally, tools. Not the kind of tools that require six-month procurement cycles or cross-functional IT alignment, but the kind that teams can start using today to solve real problems, test real ideas, and build real value.

In this final chapter, we'll shift into practical enablement, showing you how to bring AI directly into the hands of your employees, teams, and business units. Not through massive overhauls or moonshot bets, but through everyday tools that are increasingly powerful, surprisingly accessible, and designed to slot into your organization's existing workflows.

To make sense of these tools, we'll use a framework we introduced earlier in this book: the **Integration-Automation (IA-AI) Framework** - a practical lens for evaluating what an AI tool can do, how it fits into your operations, and what kind of ROI you can realistically expect.

In this chapter, we will cover the following main topics:

- Revisiting the Integration-Automation framework
- AI assistants: Easy entry tools
- Copilots: Deep integration into workflows
- Autopilots: Business workflow automation tools
- AI agents: Autonomous task handling

- Framework for AI tool adoption
- AI Tool Map: A practical guide

Revisiting the Integration-Automation framework

Before we begin, let's have a quick refresher on the IA-AI framework we discussed in *Chapter 6*. This framework classifies AI projects by their levels of system integration and task automation. It defines four progressive use case types, in four quadrants, as follows:

- **Assistants** are low-integration, low-automation tools such as ChatGPT - perfect for writing, summarizing, ideating, or just experimenting.
- **Copilots** are deeply integrated but still require manual input - think Microsoft 365 Copilot in Word or Excel.
- **Autopilots** are highly automated but loosely integrated - such as a chatbot that works 24/7 without touching internal systems.
- **Agents** are the most advanced quadrant - they combine high integration and high automation to take on full tasks across your business with minimal human input.

Let's take another look at this framework (*Figure 10.1*).

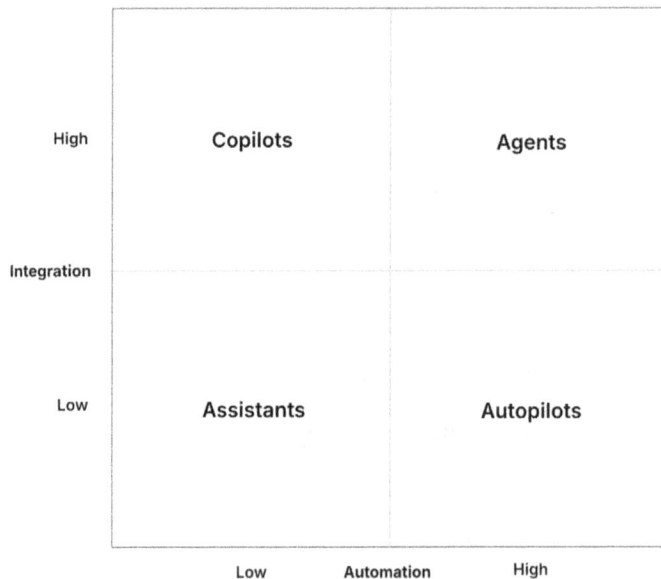

Figure 10.1: Integration-Automation Framework

Each quadrant supports a different phase of the AI journey. The best organizations aren't trying to leap straight into agentic complexity - they're sequencing tools thoughtfully, matching them to real-world maturity, and gradually building capability across teams.

This chapter will walk you through:

- Which tools to explore (and which ones to ignore)?
- Where each tool fits into your AI enablement roadmap?
- What capabilities they unlock, and for whom?
- How to roll them out without overwhelming your organization?

Whether you're an individual contributor responsible for steering your company's AI efforts, a team lead, or an executive guiding enterprise AI strategy, this chapter gives you the **practical blueprint to put AI in motion** - starting with the tools your teams can open tomorrow.

Let's start with the first quadrant: assistants.

AI assistants: Easy entry tools

If you want to start building AI capability inside your business, this is the quadrant to begin with.

AI assistants are **low-integration**, **low-automation** tools. That means they don't touch your internal systems, and they don't take autonomous action on your behalf. But what they *do* offer is immediate value with almost zero friction. These tools are your entry point into building AI literacy across your organization - without a single API call or opening an IT ticket for every mini use case.

There are several tools that fall in this quadrant, such as **ChatGPT (OpenAI,** `https://openai.com/`**), Claude (Anthropic,** `https://claude.ai`**), and Poe (Quora's multi-model chat wrapper,** `https://poe.com/login`**).** Besides the big names, there are plenty of smaller variations that focus on different areas, such as **Langdock** (`https://www.langdock.com/`), which puts a heavy emphasis on data sovereignty and control. Many larger enterprises have also started to build their internal version of these tools.

These tools are often built around a simple chat interface, such as the one popularized by ChatGPT.

Figure 10.2 shows Claude's chat interface.

✴ Evening, Tobias

How can I help you today?

+   ⇅   🔍 Research BETA   Claude Sonnet 4 ⌄

✏ Write   📖 Learn   </> Code   🍳 Life stuff   ⊞ Connect apps NEW

TZ

Figure 10.2: Chat assistant interface (here, Claude)

You feed the assistants with prompts, and they generate responses. That's exactly why they're so powerful - they're *generalists*. They don't need a fixed integration point or a clearly scoped workflow. They're just there when you need them.

These assistants can:

- Summarize dense documents in seconds
- Rewrite and personalize emails
- Brainstorm headlines, titles, or product names
- Draft job descriptions, briefs, or proposals
- Extract structured data from messy text
- Translate text or adjust tone and complexity
- Generate ideas, outlines, or talking points on demand

These are tasks that eat up time, drain energy, and rarely justify a full-blown project. But with a capable assistant, you can offload the *mental heavy lifting* and move on faster. For individuals across virtually all business functions, this is like having a hyper-fast research assistant, writer, analyst, and project collaborator all in one tab. For example, a sales manager uses ChatGPT to write first drafts of client proposal emails, then runs them through a custom GPT to check tone and clarity against company guidelines. A task that would easily have taken considerable effort can now be completed in significantly less time - with higher consistency.

Out of the box, these tools don't connect to your internal systems, which keeps the technical barriers to adoption virtually zero. That's exactly why they're so effective as a first step.

Why they work

The real power of assistants isn't so much what they do, but what they normalize. Assistants are the easiest on-ramp to AI fluency. They do the following:

- **Encourage experimentation**: There's no setup or commitment - just ask a question and see what happens.
- **Create instant productivity wins**: Even a single prompt can save an hour.
- **Democratize AI use**: No training required. Anyone who can use a search bar can use an AI assistant.
- **Start the habit**: Once people get one win, they keep coming back - and that consistency builds momentum.

Once a few team members start using a general-purpose AI assistant regularly, others follow. You'll notice people:

- Asking colleagues for prompt templates
- Comparing output quality between models
- Creating their own internal GPTs or workflows
- Sharing wins from saved time or improved drafts

This is the beginning of small *AI habits*, where people build their own intuition about when to delegate to AI, when to trust it, and when to refine it. It's the foundation of AI fluency.

These tools also spark bottom-up innovation. Unlike top-down software rollouts, assistants let curious individuals explore on their own terms. Often, this leads to unexpected process improvements or prototype ideas that would never come from a strategy deck. Some of the most valuable AI use cases in mature companies started not as top-down initiatives, but as a clever workaround one employee created using ChatGPT and a shared prompt library. I saw one particularly striking example where two editors of a leading German media company started to collect well-working prompts for everyday tasks such as improving headlines, creating article summaries, or writing preview texts and sharing these with colleagues. The best version of these prompts is now used by thousands of editors across the entire organization in the form of an *Article AI Tool* that quickly became an everyday companion nobody wants to miss anymore. And these assistants aren't standing still. Especially on major platforms such as ChatGPT and Claude, new features are rolling out fast, such as Tasks in ChatGPT (`https://help.openai.com/en/articles/10291617-tasks-in-chatgpt`), which let you schedule prompts to run automatically (e.g., tracking news mentions every morning). Claude, on the other hand, doubled down on shipping lots of connectors (`https://www.anthropic.com/news/connectors-directory`) to tools such as Jira, Confluence, or Google Drive, plus a convenient way to add custom connectors leveraging their **Model Context Protocol (MCP)**. *Figure 10.3* shows Claude's integration of several tools using its Connectors.

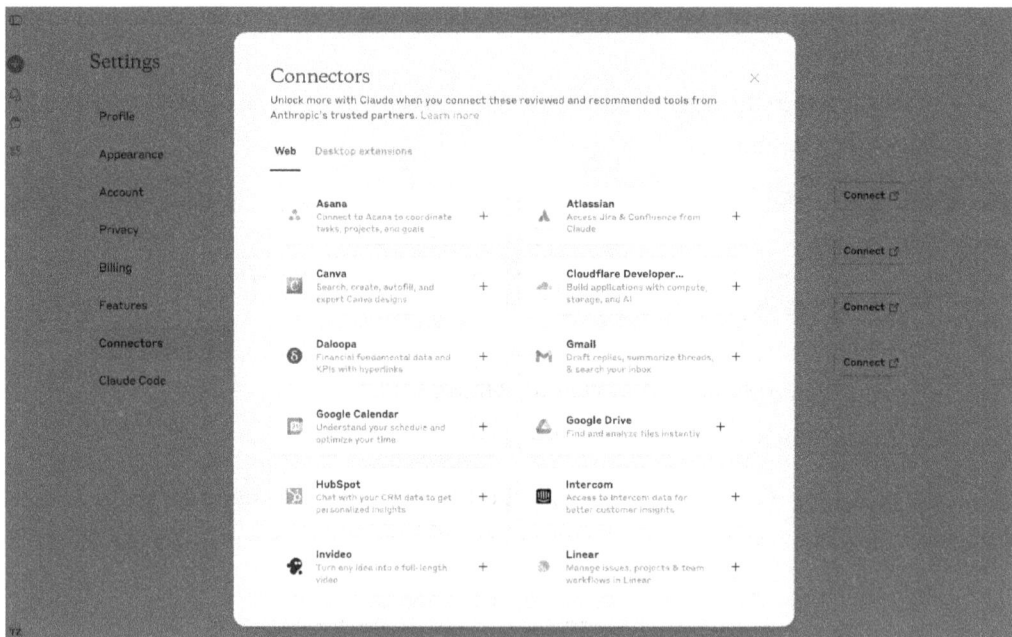

Figure 10.3: Connectors in Claude for deeper integration

That means some of the classic limitations of this quadrant - manual copy-paste, lack of context, limited integration - are starting to erode. While assistants will never fully replace more embedded or automated solutions, they're quickly becoming powerful bridges to them.

Before you roll out AI assistants, you would need to introduce support mechanisms and establish rules and guardrails to ensure their safe and effective usage. Let's look at how you can do it.

Organizational considerations for AI assistants integration

While AI assistants are easy to adopt, they still benefit from light governance. This includes:

- **Usage guidelines**: Provide a clear *dos and don'ts* list. For example, don't paste sensitive data. Do use it to improve drafts or summarize complex material.

- **Prompt libraries**: Create templates or example prompts tailored to your team (e.g., *Structure this presentation using the Pyramid Principle framework for the board meeting*).

- **Curated access**: Some organizations opt to centrally manage logins or licenses (e.g., ChatGPT Pro accounts) to track usage and simplify budgeting.

- **Lightweight enablement**: Run live demos, short workshops, or office hours. Even a short 15-minute video of a use case walkthrough can help to turn unaware or skeptical users into curious ones.

  The key principle here is lightweight. Every employee today has access to ChatGPT from their personal phone or browser. The more friction or restrictions you impose on internal tools, the more likely employees will default to using their personal version - a phenomenon often called **shadow AI**, a term borrowed from *shadow IT*, where employees bring their own AI tools without organizational approval or governance. And shadow AI is exactly what you want to avoid. Not just for data privacy, but because it disconnects usage from organizational learning. You don't just want people using AI, you want to learn *how* they're using it, and help them get better over time. This shifts the cultural conversation from "*Can we use AI?*" to "*How could we?*".

Leadership impact

AI assistants might start as individual tools, but their broader influence depends heavily on how leaders respond.

For department heads and team leads, the goal is less to micromanage usage, but to channel it. Encourage teams to share their favorite prompts, highlight time saved, or host informal *Prompt Fridays*, where employees demo clever use cases. This builds momentum from the bottom up.

For executives - especially CAIOs, CDOs, or digital transformation leaders - AI assistants are an early opportunity to signal cultural change. Not through bold declarations, but through small acts of enablement:

- Sharing a prompt you personally found useful.
- Forwarding a document with a note: *Tried summarizing this with Claude - surprisingly good.*
- Asking *"What are you using ChatGPT for these days?"* in team check-ins.

These micro-signals matter. They show that AI isn't just tolerated, but you're actively inviting employees on the journey. And when leaders treat AI tools as an everyday part of work (not just as a moonshot or risk vector), it gives others permission to do the same.

Next, we'll explore the second quadrant: copilots - AI tools that embed intelligence directly into your existing productivity apps.

Copilots: Deep integration into workflows

Where assistants often live in a browser tab, *copilots* live inside the tools you already use all day. They bring a layer of intelligence into familiar environments - you'll find copilots directly inside your docs, sheets, inboxes, notebooks, and meetings. That's what makes them so powerful: they already live where the work happens.

Yet, Copilots are, by definition, rather passive. They suggest, sometimes even proactively, but they don't take action on your behalf (that's another quadrant we'll get to soon). For copilots, the human is not only in the loop, they're in the driver's seat.

You've probably seen a few of these by now:

- **Microsoft 365 Copilot** writing meeting summaries or rewriting your 500-word update into something your boss might actually read.
- **Google Gemini** popping up in Gmail with a *"Help me write..."* button.
- **GitHub Copilot** suggesting code, commenting it, or catching that one missing bracket before you waste 15 minutes.

The deep integration allows Copilots to thrive on context. They typically know what you're working on right now:

- In **Excel**, you can say, *Turn this into a waterfall chart*, and it just builds it.
- In **Outlook**, you can highlight an email and prompt, *Tell Jen I prefer option 2*, and it will know what *option 2* means from a previous email.

- In **Docs**, you can add a new line and say, *Wrap up with a conclusion*, and the Copilot has read everything before in this document already.

- In **PowerPoint**, you can upload a product brief and get a 10-slide deck - in your custom **corporate identity** (**CI**).

- In **VS Code**, you can say *Call the weather_forecast function here*, and the Copilot knows which parameters this function expects.

The following table gives you a list of popular Copilots, their typical user surface, and what value they add:

Suite / Tool	Typical Surface	What It Adds
Microsoft 365 Copilot	Outlook, Word, Excel, PowerPoint, and Teams	Draft replies, rewrite paragraphs, build pivot tables, and auto-generate slides
Copilot Studio/ Power Automate	Low-code canvas	Build your own domain-specific chat or form bots, and connect to Dataverse or SharePoint
Google Workspace + Gemini	Gmail, Docs, Sheets, Slides, and Meet	"Help me write…" buttons, data-cleaning helpers, slide themes, and call transcripts
GitHub Copilot	VS Code and JetBrains IDEs	Predict next lines, generate tests, explain code, and suggest refactors
Google Colab (Gemini pane)	Jupyter-style notebook	Inline code generation, cell explanations, and one-click data-cleaning steps

Table 10.1: Popular Copilots in comparison

Together, these tools bring generative AI onto familiar work surfaces without forcing users into new environments.

Why they work

Copilots eliminate a lot of the copy-paste work we used to have with assistants and enable much more seamless AI-augmented workflows. When used right, copilots can be incredibly effective for organizations already using platforms such as Microsoft 365 or Google Workspace that offer copilot integrations out of the box. This extends existing workflows without requiring any larger behavioral change and meets users where they already are, making AI adoption smoother and less intimidating than asking people to learn a new platform.

Still, let's talk expectations, because this is where many teams trip up.

The most common feedback I hear when Copilot rolls out is *Is that it?* People often expect something closer to a magic button, not a helpful nudge. And that's fair. For all the bold marketing and splashy demos, most copilot interactions are surprisingly... quiet. They don't rewrite your entire spreadsheet. They won't deliver a final product. What they do is give you a faster starting point, a smarter suggestion, or a cleaner draft.

That's not a letdown - it's the point. Copilots won't do the work for you. They're helping you make your work smoother. And once you get used to that, it's hard to go back.

Let's now talk about key considerations that you need to factor in before rolling out copilots in your organization.

Organizational considerations

Despite their convenience, copilots aren't always plug-and-play. Because they touch sensitive systems and live inside core business workflows, they require thoughtful rollout and governance:

- **Licensing and cost expectations**: Microsoft Copilot, for example, can come priced per user per month, often significantly more than standard Microsoft 365 licenses. Many organizations start with limited pilots to evaluate ROI before wider rollout.

- **Data access controls**: These tools can access everything a user can - shared drives, inboxes, and calendars. It's critical to review what documents and systems are accessible by default, especially if Copilot-generated output might surface confidential info.

- **Training and enablement**: Most copilot users don't fail due to lack of functionality - they fail from unclear expectations. Short demos and prompt starter packs can dramatically improve adoption and perceived value.

- **Performance expectations**: These tools are powerful but not magic. Teams need to understand the strengths and limits of copilot models. For example, M365 Copilot may struggle with nuanced Excel analysis unless the underlying data is well structured.

- **Vendor lock-in**: Another dimension to consider is the risk of vendor lock-ins. Many companies go with the copilot integration of the platform they already use, and then call AI integration a day. However, copilots should be framed as a starting point, not the end goal. For lower-value workflows, some copy-paste effort here and there will just be enough. For more specialized or advanced workflows, power users often still prefer higher customization or automation with less human-in-the-loop involvement. But before we talk about these, let's shine a light on the leadership impact of copilots.

Leadership impact

Business leaders play a critical role in the rollout and implementation of copilots across their teams - a role that spans more than just greenlighting the budget for additional licenses.

Unlike general-purpose assistants, copilots are embedded into your workflow by design, which means they have the potential to accelerate real business processes. But only if you decide who gets access, how it's rolled out, and where it actually makes sense to use.

This isn't a case of *Switch it on and let everyone figure it out*. Copilots can do a lot - but not everything they do is equally valuable. For example, Microsoft Copilot in Outlook can write full email replies. But should your sales team really use it to respond to clients? Probably not - at least not without oversight. In that context, a rushed AI-generated email can damage trust more than save time.

A better leadership move might be to define what Copilot is for in your org:

- In Outlook, use it to draft internal updates, not external communication.
- In Excel, use it to spot trends or clean data, not build final forecasts.
- In Word, use it to restructure rough notes, not generate proposals from scratch.

Leaders should clearly communicate these expectations. Not because people need hand-holding, but because clarity drives smarter adoption.

Also important: decide early **who gets Copilot first**. You don't need a perfect rollout plan - but you do need a strategic one. Prioritize high-leverage roles:

- Sales ops teams buried in forecasting sheets.
- Strategy analysts wrangling slides and Excel.
- Internal comms or HR drafting company-wide updates.

Give them early access. Set a time frame (e.g., 8 weeks). Then, collect feedback: quantitative by measuring performance between similar teams who had access to copilot and those who didn't, or qualitative by surveying participants in the pilot. Don't just ask, *Did you like it?* but:

- What did it actually replace?
- What do you trust it with?
- What still feels manual?
- Is it worth the extra expense?

This helps you separate novelty from real ROI and lays the groundwork for a broader rollout that's grounded in actual workflows, not assumptions.

For digital leaders, CAIOs, or transformation officers, Copilots are also an early litmus test for your org's data readiness. One of the hidden values of Copilots is that they expose where your internal knowledge is weak. If a Copilot can't generate a good proposal because your materials are scattered across 15 documents with no consistency, that's not the tool's fault - it's an insight about documentation debt.

Leaders who treat Copilots not just as tools but as reusable building blocks for knowledge work will see the real return. That's where the compounding value begins.

Now, let's look at the next quadrant: autopilots - where tasks don't just get easier to complete, they start to complete themselves.

Autopilots: Business workflow automation tools

If copilots help you work faster, *autopilots* aim to help you work less by letting systems take over entire tasks.

Autopilot tools are **high-automation** and **low-integration**: they can run processes with minimal human input, but don't necessarily sit inside your day-to-day apps. Instead, they often run in the background, like a digital operations team handling repetitive work quietly and consistently.

This is the quadrant where business process automation meets AI. Instead of prompting a tool to help you rewrite something, you can automate the entire content workflow - such as listening for a new sales lead in your CRM, extracting company names from emails, and generating personalized follow-ups based on that data. While autopilots can, of course, entirely be built from scratch, this is a category where no-code workflow builders shine. The most popular examples include:

- **Zapier** (https://zapier.com) is a category king of no-code automation tools. Offers the most integrations and connects common SaaS integrations (e.g., *When a form is submitted in Typeform, send a Slack message and write to a Google Sheet*).
- **Make** (https://www.make.com/) is similar to Zapier, but offers a simpler UI and a more competitive pricing model with slightly fewer integrations.
- **n8n** (https://n8n.io) is an open-source alternative that supports AI-powered logic and agents, with scriptable flows.

Take a look at the n8n support ticket classification workflow in *Figure 10.4*.

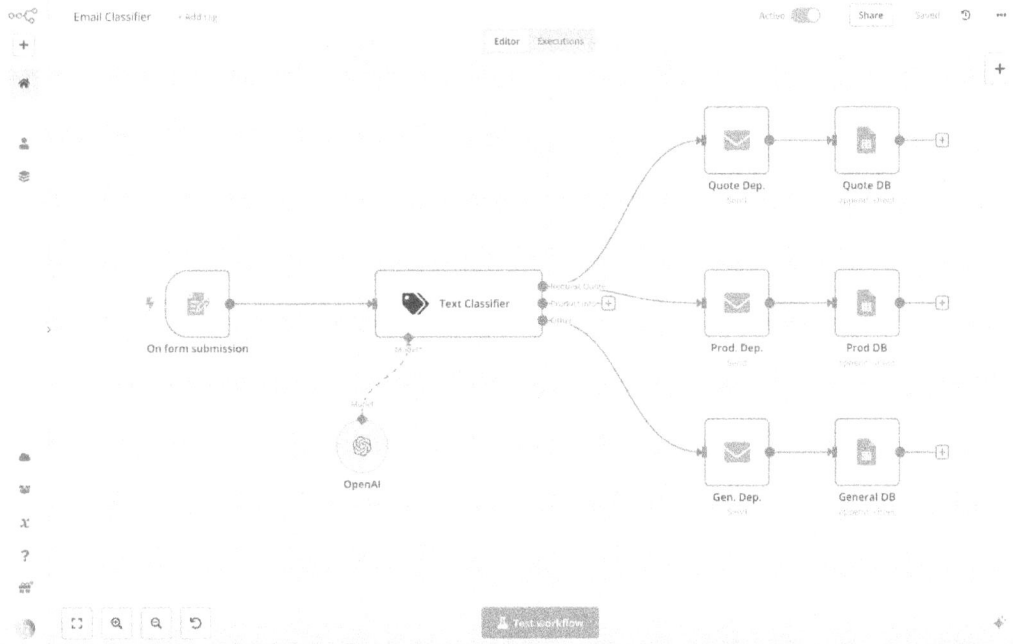

Figure 10.4: LLM-powered ticket classification workflow in n8n

This classification workflow is a good example of how classical **no-code workflows** interact with AI capabilities. The workflow is executed from left to right. In this case, the workflow is triggered when a website form is submitted. In the second step, the form content is parsed by an AI text classifier that sends a prompt to an LLM - in this case, from OpenAI. The result of the LLM is a classification that can be one of three support ticket categories. n8n routes the form depending on the content, forwards it to the respective email address, and updates a record in a support ticket database.

While discussing these tools in detail would be beyond the scope of this book, the following table gives you a brief overview and comparison:

Tool	Founded	Strengths	Limitations
Zapier, San Francisco, USA	2012	• 7,000+ integrations • Simple UX and stability • Strong error handling	• Expensive at scale • Weak developer extensibility • Limited sharing/ collaboration

Tool	Founded	Strengths	Limitations
Make, Prague, EU (part of Celonis)	2012	• Cheaper than Zapier • Visual editor for non-tech users • Supports import/export • GDPR compliance (European provider)	• 2,000+ integrations • No native code blocks
n8n, Berlin, Germany	2019	• Self-hostable, open source version available • Native Python/JS scripting • Excellent for AI integration • GDPR compliance (European provider)	• Smaller integration library • More technical interface
Microsoft Power Automate, Redmond, USA	2019	Fully integrated into the Microsoft ecosystem	• Risk of vendor lock-in • Steep learning curve

Table 10.2: Comparison of popular no-code platforms

While tools such as Zapier, Make, and n8n started as general-purpose automation platforms, they've increasingly embraced AI integrations to stay relevant. These platforms now support everything from basic LLM actions to more intelligent, AI-powered workflows.

But there's another class of tools - those that were built with AI as the foundation, not as an enhancement.

These are **AI developer platforms**, built from the ground up to develop, deploy, and run AI-powered workflows, applications, and agents (to which we'll get in a bit). Every major cloud provider has a version of these AI platforms. As an example, here's a quick look at Microsoft's Azure offerings, which are a popular choice for businesses that are already invested in the Microsoft ecosystem:

- **Azure AI Foundry** (`https://ai.azure.com/`): A central hub that allows you to build GenAI-powered apps such as custom copilots or customer-facing chatbots in one place.

- **Azure Machine Learning Studio** (`https://azure.microsoft.com/en-us/products/machine-learning`): Focuses more on classical ML and AutoML workflows - think churn prediction, demand forecasting, or regression modeling.

- **Other cloud providers** offer similar AI suites, such as Vertex AI (`https://cloud.google.com/vertex-ai`) on Google Cloud and SageMaker (`https://aws.amazon.com/sagemaker/`) on AWS.

Outside of major cloud providers, there's also a growing ecosystem of lightweight, SaaS-friendly GenAI platforms targeting specific domains or use cases. A few worth noting are:

- **Chatbase** (`https://www.chatbase.co/`): Lets you turn documents or websites into chatbot interfaces in minutes. Especially useful for onboarding bots, internal helpdesks, or searchable knowledge bases.

- **Harvey AI** (`https://www.harvey.ai/`): AI platform specialized in use cases around legal documents and contract work. Comes with an integrated workflow builder.

- **Synthesia** (`https://www.synthesia.io/`): Uses GenAI to generate avatar-based videos from text input. Widely used for automating video content for training, onboarding, or marketing.

Think of it this way: If Zapier and n8n are automation platforms that have added AI, tools such as Azure AI Foundry are AI platforms that have added automation. SaaS tools such as Chatbase and Harvey have pre-built a lot of things for you, given a certain use case, and allow for (often limited) customization.

Which one you choose depends on your team's technical depth, infrastructure needs, and broader goals. But they all point in the same direction: the shift from *AI as a helper* to *AI as the system*. Still, these tools usually don't hook deeply into your IT systems right away. You can often start with just a file upload or a webhook, and build out integrations as you go.

My recommendation is to pick one platform that lets you quickly test (and potentially scale) use cases that were discovered and validated in an assistant form. Whether this means bringing in a no-code workflow builder such as n8n, extending an existing Zapier license you already have, or giving your developers access to an AI platform such as AI Foundry really depends on your organization. The possibility of getting quick access to a versatile platform is more important than the tool itself. Another benefit of having a central platform is that you can quickly probe how much better (or feasible) a custom integration performs over a domain-specific vendor solution such as Harvey. In the end, this is another make-or-buy decision. If you'd like to dive deeper into that, I wrote an article about AI make or buy here: `https://blog.tobiaszwingmann.com/p/ai-make-vs-buy`.

So where do these autopilots fit in? You might already be familiar with some typical workflow automation use cases: auto-sending emails, routing form data, and syncing data between systems. But adding AI into the mix expands the value significantly. You can use AI to enhance several tasks, making the automation better, cheaper, faster, or just more scalable. Some of them are listed as follows:

- **Customer onboarding**: Parse a new client's submitted documents, extract relevant meta-data using an LLM, populate internal systems, and notify the account manager.

- **Content repurposing**: Watch a Google Drive folder for new content, extract insights with AI, generate LinkedIn posts and summaries, and queue them in Buffer or HubSpot.

- **Lead scoring and enrichment**: When a lead enters your CRM, enrich it with data from LinkedIn, analyze the job title with an LLM, and assign it to the right sales pipeline based on keywords.

- **Internal reporting**: Summarize support ticket data weekly and post a plain-English trend report in a Slack channel.

- **Survey analysis**: Use an LLM to categorize free-form feedback from customer surveys and flag urgent issues.

A classic autopilot use case is a first-level support chatbot - an AI system that automatically handles routine customer questions on your website, acting like a smarter, interactive FAQ.

There are several ways to build this:

- Use **n8n** to create a custom LLM-powered chatbot that connects to your knowledge base and runs via a web UI. This gives you control, but requires manual data prep.

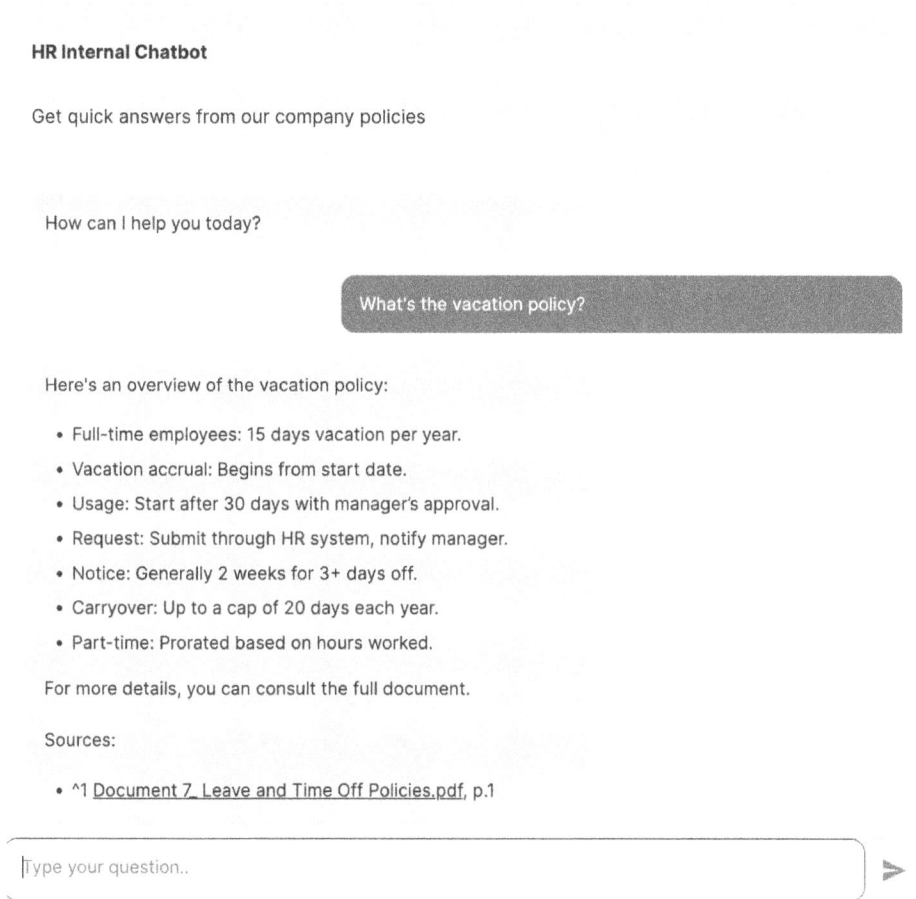

HR Internal Chatbot

Get quick answers from our company policies

How can I help you today?

What's the vacation policy?

Here's an overview of the vacation policy:

- Full-time employees: 15 days vacation per year.
- Vacation accrual: Begins from start date.
- Usage: Start after 30 days with manager's approval.
- Request: Submit through HR system, notify manager.
- Notice: Generally 2 weeks for 3+ days off.
- Carryover: Up to a cap of 20 days each year.
- Part-time: Prorated based on hours worked.

For more details, you can consult the full document.

Sources:

- ^1 Document 7_ Leave and Time Off Policies.pdf, p.1

Type your question..

Figure 10.5: Simple HR chatbot autopilot built with n8n

- Use **Azure AI Foundry** to build a custom chat app that connects to enterprise data sources and other Microsoft apps.

- Use a vertical platform such as **Chatbase** to spin up a chatbot in minutes - just upload a few PDFs or link your help center, and it generates a usable bot right away (*Figure 10.6*).

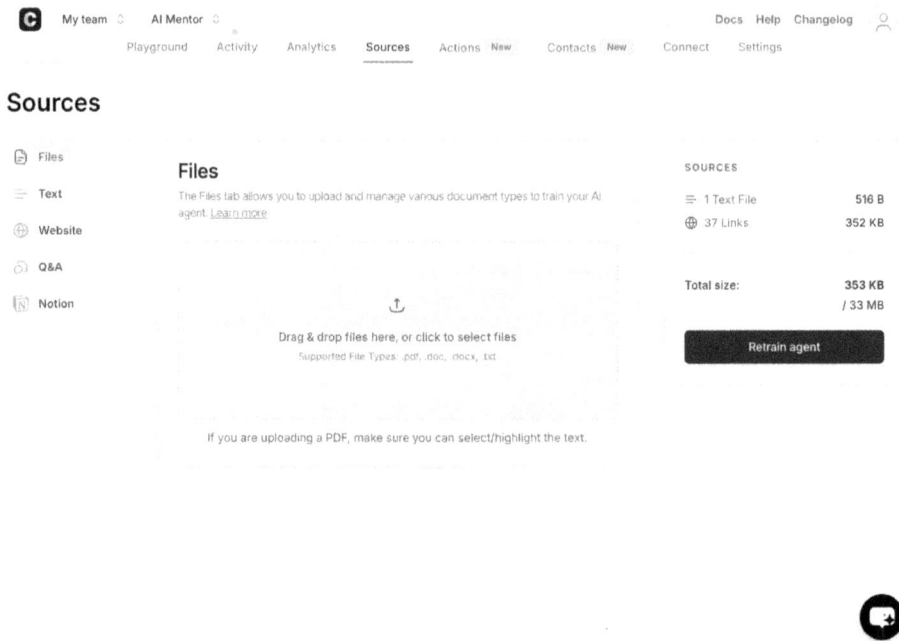

Figure 10.6: An interface for adding files to Chatbase

Each approach automates the same task - handling FAQs without human involvement - but with different trade-offs between control, speed, and integration.

And that's exactly where autopilots shine: they're easy to bring in, flexible to adapt, and powerful enough to turn one-off wins into always-on systems. Whether you start with a drag-and-drop chatbot builder or a fully custom flow, these tools make it possible to automate real work without calling IT every time.

Why they work

Autopilots don't just save time. They change *how* work happens - by turning ad hoc manual tasks into scalable, hands-free workflows. Here's why they stick:

- **They start small**: Many workflows begin with a single prompt or one-time task. With autopilot tools, that initial success can be turned into a repeatable, automated flow with minimal effort.

- **They free up headspace**: The magic isn't just speed - it's focus. Autopilots handle the boring, brittle, or brain-dead tasks so your team can focus on what actually matters.

- **They create leverage**: Small workflows save minutes. But when they run 50 times a day across five teams, you start reclaiming days.

- **They scale without scale**: Most tools here are built for business users - not just developers - so you don't need to grow your IT team to grow your automation footprint.

Unlike copilots, which assist and suggest, autopilots act. They don't wait for you to click **Go**; once set up, they're running, routing, transforming, updating, summarizing, or chatting around the clock.

That's why it's smart to start with assistants or copilots first: they help you learn where AI adds value, where it breaks, and where automation is safe. Once that understanding is in place, autopilots are the logical next step - but they require more structure and oversight, because when software starts doing things on its own, it's time to think even more about ownership, accountability, and governance.

Organizational considerations

Because of their high degree of automation, often triggered by data events or system activity, autopilots require more oversight than assistants or Copilots:

- **Define automation boundaries**: Not every process benefits from full autonomy. For example, routing support tickets to the right team can be safely automated, but automatically sending refund approvals without human oversight may expose you to financial or compliance risk. A good practice is to categorize processes into *safe-to-automate*, *human-in-the-loop*, and *never automate*. Some organizations even run *automation reviews* for new workflows, much like a lightweight code review.

- **Audit and logging**: Ensure that automations - especially those that involve LLMs - are tracked. You'll want visibility into what was generated, when, and for whom. When workflows run in the background, invisibility can quickly become a liability. Imagine an autopilot that categorizes thousands of incoming survey responses every week: if the categorization logic drifts or breaks, you may not notice until a major decision has already been made on flawed data. Proper audit trails - logging which workflow ran, what inputs it received, and what outputs were generated - allow you to backtrack and troubleshoot. In regulated industries (such as healthcare or finance), these logs may even be mandatory.

- **Cost control**: Some automations, especially with high-frequency triggers or complex AI calls, can easily rack up surprising bills. For instance, a Zapier workflow that calls an LLM every time a Slack message is posted in a channel can spiral into thousands of calls per week. Consider techniques such as batching (e.g., processing messages hourly instead of instantly), caching (storing common outputs to avoid repeated API calls), or usage caps (stopping workflows after a daily threshold) to keep costs predictable. For workflows with a potentially high workload, consider running a cost simulation on a small sample before deploying a new automation to estimate its financial footprint.

- **Shadow automation risk**: Just like with *shadow IT*, it's easy for employees to start building unmonitored workflows. While this shows initiative, it also creates risk. To balance innovation with governance, you might consider setting up a workflow registry where employees log their automations. Others create *automation groups* or internal communities of practice where power users share templates, get feedback, and avoid reinventing the wheel.

A note of caution

Don't over-AI your workflows. Just because you *can* use an LLM doesn't mean you should. Many automation steps are better handled by basic logic (e.g., if/then, regex, lookup tables). Keep AI for the steps that require judgment, nuance, or text transformation.

Leadership impact

Autopilots often emerge from *grassroots innovation* - a power user who wires something together on a weekend and shares it with the team. But leadership has a big opportunity to take those bottom-up breakthroughs and systematize them.

As a leader, your role is to:

- **Spot repeatable wins**: See what one team automates and ask, *Who else could use this?*
- **Invest in reuse**: Help teams turn individual workflows into shareable templates or internal libraries.
- **Support tool access**: Provide licenses for no-code tools such as n8n or Make, and empower non-engineering teams to use them safely.
- **Create a feedback loop**: Ask teams what is being automated, what's still manual, and what broke last week. This creates a healthy automation culture - one where people build, refine, and share.

Most importantly, normalize the automation mindset. When a new process is created, ask *Can this be automated?* Not to avoid ownership, but to ensure your smartest people aren't stuck doing robotic work.

And for digital top leadership (CAIOs, CTOs, or ops heads), autopilots offer a unique angle on AI enablement. They bridge the gap between strategy and execution - letting your org experiment, learn, and optimize without waiting for centralized roadmaps or major IT investments.

In fact, some of your highest-ROI AI use cases may not come from LLM research or vendor partnerships, but from a clever automation that turns a 20-minute task into a 2-second one, every day.

Next, we'll step into the final quadrant: agents - where AI not only automates work, but begins to decide, adapt, and act across systems on your behalf.

AI agents: Autonomous task handling

If autopilots automate tasks, *agents* take it a step further: they decide, act, adapt, and even improve over time. This is where AI stops being a passive helper and becomes an operational actor.

Agents combine deep system access with autonomous execution. They don't wait for manual instructions. They act - based on goals, data, or triggers - and can carry out multi-step workflows across tools, departments, and decisions. They don't assist with work. They run the work.

You've probably seen the early stages of this already:

- An AI system that summarizes meetings, tags action items, and automatically creates Jira tickets in the respective projects.
- A chatbot that not only answers FAQs like the autopilots did, but also authenticates users, resets passwords, fetches shipping details, and escalates support tickets.
- A sales agent that researches leads, drafts personalized emails, and updates CRM records.

Most agentic AI tools essentially rely on the following four building blocks:

- **LLMs** for reasoning and decision-making.
- **Tools or function-calling** frameworks for interaction with real-world systems (e.g., OpenAI functions, LangChain).
- **Memory** or task history to access knowledge and stay context-aware across steps.
- **Automation runtimes** to coordinate workflows.

This makes agents extremely powerful, but also complex. They require careful design, testing, monitoring, and often a blend of AI and traditional logic to perform reliably. Hence, they're often not the best place to start, as we discussed before.

Agent tooling isn't for everyone. But if your team has basic scripting skills or technical staff, these tools can help you deploy your own agents. These tools are not where most teams begin. But for organizations with technical staff or advanced prototypes ready to scale, they offer serious leverage. You can typically build AI agents on top of AI no-code tools that you've seen under autopilots above. In this case, an agent simply becomes a separate node in your workflow.

Here's an example from a lead enrichment workflow in **n8n**, where the heavy lifting is done by an AI agent node, can use an LLM from OpenAI to control a web scraping tool, which adds relevant information to a company, and then stores the output in a Google Sheet document:

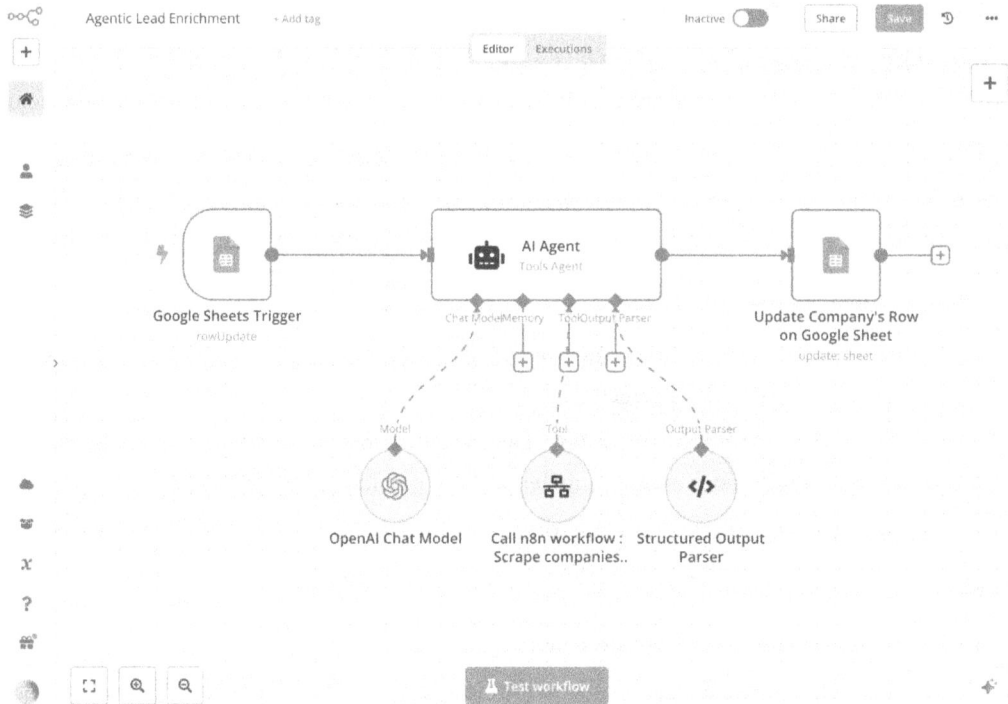

Figure 10.7: AI agent in n8n for a lead enrichment use case

As you can see, this workflow looks relatively simple because we don't have to wire up complex rules, such as which website to scrape, and what happens if a website is not provided or if no relevant information is found on a website. These are all things handled by the agent based on the prompt we gave it.

Besides building on top of existing workflow automation tools, another effective way to build AI agents is to use agent frameworks that are more targeted to developers, such as CrewAI(`https://www.crewai.com/`) and LangGraph (`https://www.langchain.com/langgraph`). The benefit of these is that they typically offer more customizability, but they often don't provide the kind of comprehensive routing and automation logic you get from tools such as n8n or Zapier, which have over a decade of experience automating workflows at scale. That's why even simple conditional logic or basic things such as HTTP requests often have to be coded manually.

Agentic frameworks like these shine in situations where you need to run multiple agents in parallel - for example, a multi-agent system where one *agent* does research, another generates a summary, and a third QA-checks the result before publishing. Ultimately, figuring out which parts work better as static automation and which ones should be handled by an agent is part of the learning journey, and usually involves a lot of trial and error.

When they work

In this quadrant, the right question isn't *Why do they work?* The value is obvious. If you can run entire workflows that figure out the steps, choose the tools, execute them, adapt on the fly without human involvement, and do it at near-zero marginal cost, the upside speaks for itself. It's the operational dream: scale without scale. Automation that adapts. Work that happens while your team sleeps.

No, the real question is: **when** do agents actually work?

In practice, agents are hard to crack. They're more sensitive to workflow messiness, edge cases, permissions, context ambiguity, and tool access than any other class of AI system in this book.

Unlike Copilots, which live neatly inside productivity tools, or autopilots, which follow clean *if-this-then-that* flows, agents must navigate dynamic environments and make real-time decisions - often with incomplete or inconsistent information. That level of autonomy demands more than just good tech. It actually requires having all scaling levers in place, which we discussed in *Chapter 9*:

- **People:** You need owners who take true responsibility for the agentic process, even if it spans company silos. Around them, you need a team ready to monitor, refine, and improve agents over time (see AIOps below). Treat agents less like tools and more like digital colleagues.

- **Processes:** You can't plan an agent in a waterfall-style way because you'll never anticipate all the edge cases they'll hit. Agents will explore unknowns by themselves. That means agile delivery - short sprints, fast feedback loops, and iteration - so you can adapt quickly when they behave in unintended ways.

- **Data:** Agents rely on structured, permissioned, and accessible data that provides enough context to act reliably. And no, spinning up an MCP server won't fix this. Data maturity comes first; easy connectors come later.

- **Technology:** Provide a safe runtime - APIs, connectors, and sandboxed environments - before exposing agents to production systems. Reliability, observability, and guardrails are non-negotiable at this point.

- **AIOps:** Of all AI solution types, agents require the heaviest monitoring, logging, and intervention. If your team has never shipped at least a Copilot or autopilot implementation before, you're likely not ready for agents.

Most importantly, you need to resist the temptation to hand your entire business process to a digital Swiss Army knife and expect magic.

Most failures happen when teams ask agents to do too much, too soon, in environments that aren't ready. The best agents do one thing well. They're a capability you earn by delivering working AI solutions in easier formats with higher human-in-the-loop involvement, such as assistants or Copilots. This will inform you naturally which tasks or workflows are ready for more *AI handoff*.

And in that context, the *agent tool* itself? Honestly, it's the easiest part.

Organizational considerations

Deploying agents isn't just a technical decision - it's an organizational shift. You're giving software the authority to act on behalf of your business. That changes the dynamics of ownership, oversight, accountability, and trust.

Unlike assistants or Copilots, which augment human users, agentic systems can operate without constant supervision. And that means you need to treat them less like tools and more like digital team members. They need policies, scopes, escalation paths, and quality assurance.

Here are four critical shifts organizations must make to operationalize agentic tools:

1. **Define boundaries**: Not every task should be automated. Not every tool should have access to sensitive systems. Teams need clear guidelines on what agents are allowed to do - and where human input is non-negotiable. This includes:

- Which workflows can be fully automated versus partially agent-led?
- When agents should request human confirmation before proceeding?
- What data sources or systems they're permitted to access or update?

Think of it like access permissions for a new hire. You wouldn't give an intern unrestricted database access on day one. Your agents should be treated with the same discipline.

2. **Implement safety nets**: Because agents operate autonomously, they need built-in safeguards. These include:

   - Rate limits to avoid spamming external systems or overloading APIs.
   - Guardrails on output quality (e.g., validating generated content against business rules).
   - Fallback behaviors when something goes wrong (e.g., alerting a human rather than retrying indefinitely).
   - Isolation environments (sandboxed agent testing before rollout).

Ensure that operational procedures are in place to monitor and control the agentic solutions in production.

Safety nets give you the confidence to roll out your agents beyond the experimentation stage and gain trust from users.

3. **Ensure observability**: One of the biggest organizational risks with agents is invisibility. If a workflow breaks or behaves unexpectedly, will anyone notice? Effective agent adoption requires:

   - Logging and audit trails for every action.
   - Version control for agent logic and prompts.
   - Dashboards or alerting for runtime errors, decision branches, or *edge cases*.

Without observability, you're not in control - you're guessing.

4. **Establish ownership**: Here's the most overlooked piece. Every agent needs a human owner. Someone who:

   - Monitors the system.
   - Reviews and improves its behavior.
   - Decides when to retire, retrain, or escalate.

Without clear ownership, agents become *ghost processes* - nobody knows how they work, why they do what they do, or when they were last updated. That's a fast path to risk, failure, or abandonment. Organizations that succeed with agents treat them like living systems: they evolve, adapt, and need care.

Leadership impact

For leaders, AI agents are both a powerful opportunity and a real test of your digital maturity. Why? Because agents don't just require a tool rollout. They require a true culture shift. You're asking teams to trust a system that makes decisions. You're introducing AI not just as an enhancer, but as a participant in business processes.

And that changes everything.

Here's what effective leadership looks like in an agent-driven environment:

1. **Set the trust bar**: Teams will mirror your attitude. If you constantly question the reliability of agent tools, expect widespread hesitation. If you overhype them, expect disappointment. But if you openly explore where agents make sense - and where they don't - you give people a balanced, usable playbook. Trust doesn't start with technology. It starts with leadership behavior.

2. **Normalize iteration over perfection**: No agent system will be perfect out of the box. The goal isn't to build flawless autonomy - it's to learn what kind of autonomy works in your environment. Leaders should create psychological safety for teams to test, iterate, and improve agents over time. That means rewarding learning velocity, not just delivery speed. Ask, *What did this agent do right? Where did it struggle? What did we learn?* This turns experimentation into improvement - and failure into progress.

3. **Shift your operating model**: Agent adoption changes the rhythm of how work gets done. Approvals happen faster. Tasks get delegated to workflows, not people. Turnaround time compresses. But if you keep your old processes wrapped around these new capabilities, you'll smother the value. Leaders must reimagine team structures and expectations:

    -   Can roles be redesigned around higher-value oversight?
    -   Can SLAs change because automation speeds up delivery?
    -   Should performance metrics shift to reflect agentic workflows?

In other words, don't just plug agents into your org. Organize for them. Ultimately, agentic systems are less about fancy AI and more about designing workflows for scale, resilience, and autonomy. When your teams no longer think *What can I do with this tool?* and start asking, *What can this tool do on behalf of me?*, you're in the agents quadrant.

Now that we have explored the different categories of AI tools - from entry-level assistants to advanced autonomous agents - it's time to think about how your organization can practically adopt them.

Framework for AI tool adoption

A natural question when you begin evaluating AI tools and their applications for your organization is: *Where should you start?*

This section presents a framework that provides a structured path for evaluating your current AI tool landscape, identifying opportunities for advancement, and embedding AI adoption into your broader tool strategy.

Instead of focusing on abstract maturity labels, this framework grounds your **AI tool adoption journey** in concrete stages that directly impact day-to-day work.

Let's explore these stages in detail:

1. **Diagnose your current state**: Begin with a simple self-assessment across the departments or products you've examined during your roadmapping process.

   - Which tools are we using today - AI assistants, copilots, autopilots, or AI agents?
   - What behaviors or examples back that up?
   - Where are our blind spots?
   - Which tools are required as per the use cases on our roadmap?

   This doesn't need to be overly formal. A quick workshop, internal poll, or department lead sync can surface honest, directional insights. Even covering just 3–5 key areas can reveal major gaps and opportunities.

   The goal isn't perfection; it's awareness. What matters most is achieving a *shared understanding of where you stand* today.

2. **Identify the *next-level moves*:** Once you know where each team is, define what moving up **one tool level** would look like:

- **From AI assistants to copilots:** For example, a support rep shifts from casually using ChatGPT for email drafts to having a copilot embedded in their ticketing system, suggesting replies and summaries.

- **From copilots to autopilots:** For example, the support team begins automating entire workflows, such as AI handling ticket triage and routing without manual intervention.

- **From autopilots to AI agents:** For example, rethinking the support model entirely so that autonomous AI agents handle common issues end-to-end, escalating only the edge cases to human reps.

I recommend framing these moves in terms of behaviors and outcomes and not buzzwords. You may start by asking:

- What process could we automate further?
- What decision could we accelerate?
- What tasks could AI take on directly?
- What would the business impact be?

3. **Prioritize with purpose:** Not every team member should advance at once. Use the model to prioritize where investment and support will yield the biggest impact:

- Where is demand already emerging (people experimenting, building small prototypes)?
- Where are manual processes creating major bottlenecks?
- Where is leadership most open to change?

Focus on 3–4 *pilot* areas for the next phase. Equip them with the right tools, track the results, and then scale learnings across other areas. Start with *units that already show signs of AI fluency and have high operational impact* (like Support or Ops).

4. **Turn it into an ongoing conversation**: This framework isn't a destination - it's a journey. Use it to:

    -   Set quarterly AI adoption goals by team

    -   Guide enablement and upskilling initiatives

    -   Track cross-functional progress

    -   Celebrate wins (for example, *Marketing just shifted from copilots to autopilots!*)

    Over time, this becomes your shared language for AI maturity.

5. **Embed in strategic planning**: Finally, link AI adoption directly to your business goals. For example:

    -   If your goal is to *reduce time-to-hire*, ask: What would moving Recruiting from assistants to copilots do for that metric?

    -   If the objective is to *improve customer resolution time*, ask: What would moving Support from copilots to autopilots unlock?

    When tool adoption becomes part of how you talk about **business performance**, AI is no longer a side project. It becomes a natural driver of competitiveness and strategy.

Now that you've seen how teams evolve in capability, let's bring it all together with a quick tool reference you can use to support that growth.

AI Tool Map: A practical guide

Every day, there's a new AI tool launching - and every day, another quietly disappears.

Trying to track them all is pointless. But in some situations, a high-level view of the landscape helps, especially when you're guiding experimentation or supporting teams with tools they'll actually use.

That's why I've created the AI Tool Map, which you can see in *Figure 10.8* and download using this link (`https://github.com/PacktPublishing/The-Profitable-AI-Advantage/blob/main/ch10/AI_Tool_Map.xlsx`); this gets updated as the tools evolve. The AI Tool Map groups different AI tools by function, shows where they fit in your AI journey, which quadrant of the Integration-Automation AI Framework they fit in, highlights real use cases, and flags what to watch out for.

AI Tool Map

Tool Category	Example Tools	Quadrant	Primary Use Case	Recommended Maturity Fluency Level	Risk / Watchout	Ownership / Enablement
Chat-Based Assistants	ChatGPT (Custom GPTs), Claude	Assistant	Draft, rewrite, summarize, explore ideas	Capable	Hallucination; missing internal context	CAIO, comms, individual users
Office Copilots	Microsoft 365 Copilot, Google Gemini	Copilot	Rewrite emails, clean data, generate slides	Adaptive	Cost per seat; expectation gap	IT, CAIO, team enablement leads
IDE Copilots	GitHub Copilot, Amazon CodeWhisperer	Copilot (Dev)	Complete code, refactor, generate tests	Adaptive	Hallucinated code; trust calibration needed	Dev enablement, engineering leads
AI-Native IDEs	Cursor, Replit AI	Adv. Copilot/ Agent	Generate full apps, multi-step workflows, agent chaining	Transformative	Less stable; lacks enterprise controls	Innovation teams, advanced dev groups
Workflow Builders (No-Code)	Zapier, Make, n8n, Azure Prompt Flow	Autopilot	Form automation, lead enrichment, FAQ bots	Adaptive	Fragile logic; cost at scale	Ops, marketing, support teams
AI Developer Platforms	n8n, Azure AI Foundry, Azure ML Studio, Google Vertex AI, Amazon	Autopilot / Agent	LLM chaining, agent logic, AutoML pipelines	Transformative	Setup time, governance complexity	CoE, platform teams, AI product owners
BI / Analytics Copilots	Power BI Copilot, Tableau Agent, Veezoo Platform, Google Colab, ChatGPT	Copilot / Agent	Conversational charts, dashboard summaries, ad-hoc analysis	Adaptive	Needs structured models; limited NLP depth	BI leads, data analysts
Internal Search / RAG Tools	LlamaIndex, Azure Cognitive Search	Copilot/ Autopilot	Internal Q&A, doc parsing, search over knowledge	Transformative	Requires data engineering + governance	Data platform teams, search engineers

Figure 10.8: AI Tool Map

Think of it as your shortcut through the hype, so you can focus on what to use, when to use it, and who should own the rollout.

The purpose of this section was to show you how to reframe AI adoption from a tools-first mindset to an intentional, fluency-first approach. The most successful organizations aren't the ones chasing every new app but the ones building consistent, team-level fluency across functions in a way that drives real business impact. Using the framework above, you can guide progress and choose tools intentionally, one step at a time. The goal isn't perfection, but visible, shared, and strategic movement toward real transformation.

Summary

You've seen the frameworks. You've studied the use cases. You've built prototypes and explored how to scale them.

But in the end, it's the tools that turn your AI strategy into tangible business results. Not because they're magical, but because they're usable. Today.

Some tools - such as ChatGPT and GitHub Copilot - deliver quick, personal wins. Others - such as n8n and Azure AI Foundry (or the service ecosystem on Azure) - unlock even more scalable automation and system-level transformation.

But they all share one thing in common: they only work when placed in the hands of people who are empowered to explore, enabled to execute, and equipped to share what works.

Whether it's a marketer using ChatGPT to rewrite an email, a product team wiring up an LLM-powered assistant, or your ops lead automating reports in n8n, AI shifts from a future concept to a functional lever.

The companies that win won't be the ones with the most tools. They'll be the ones that learned to use a few of them well - early, often, and across the org. The real edge isn't an impressive tech stack. It's an organization that knows how to learn, adapt, and build with AI every day.

You don't need a big launch. You just need to start and build your roadmap as you go. Because AI transformation doesn't begin with a keynote.

It begins with a single prompt, a working workflow, and a team willing to press **Run**.

Thank you for joining me on this journey. I hope this book empowers you to identify opportunities, prioritize initiatives, and scale AI across your business - and build your *Profitable AI Advantage*.

Stay tuned

To keep up with the latest developments in the fields of Generative AI and LLMs, subscribe to our weekly newsletter, AI_Distilled, at `https://packt.link/80z6Y`.

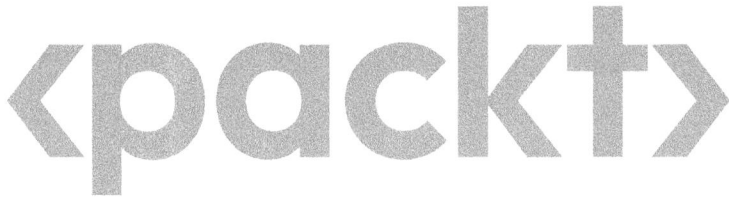

‹packt›

Other Books You May Enjoy

If you enjoyed this book, you may be interested in these other books by Packt:

<packt>

THE CHIEF AI OFFICER'S HANDBOOK

Master AI leadership with strategies to innovate, overcome challenges, and drive business growth

JARROD ANDERSON

Foreword by Jeff Winter, VP of Business Strategy, Critical Manufacturing

The Chief AI Officer's Handbook

Jarrod Anderson

ISBN: 978-1-83620-085-7

- Develop and execute AI strategy as a CAIO, ensuring ethical compliance
- Master agile AI project management from ideation to deployment
- Apply deterministic and probabilistic AI concepts through case studies
- Design and implement AI agents for autonomous system optimization
- Create human-centered AI systems using proven design principles
- Enhance AI security through data privacy and model protection measures

EXPERT INSIGHTS

**Building
Agentic AI Systems**

Create intelligent, autonomous AI agents that
can reason, plan, and adapt

Forewords by
Matthew R. Scott Chief Technology Officer, Novel a
Dr. Alex Acero Member of the National Academy of
Engineering, IEEE Fellow

Anjanava Biswas | Wrick Talukdar   ‹packt›

Building Agentic AI Systems

Anjanava Biswas, Wrick Talukdar

ISBN: 978-1-80323-875-3

- Master the core principles of GenAI and agentic systems

- Understand how AI agents operate, reason, and adapt in dynamic environments

- Enable AI agents to analyze their own actions and improvise

- Implement systems where AI agents can leverage external tools and plan complex tasks

- Apply methods to enhance transparency, accountability, and reliability in AI

- Explore real-world implementations of AI agents across industries

Packt is searching for authors like you

If you're interested in becoming an author for Packt, please visit `authors.packtpub.com` and apply today. We have worked with thousands of developers and tech professionals, just like you, to help them share their insight with the global tech community. You can make a general application, apply for a specific hot topic that we are recruiting an author for, or submit your own idea.

Share your thoughts

Now you've finished *The Profitable AI Advantage*, we'd love to hear your thoughts! Scan the QR code below to go straight to the Amazon review page for this book and share your feedback or leave a review on the site that you purchased it from.

`https://packt.link/r/1836205899`

Your review is important to us and the tech community and will help us make sure we're delivering excellent quality content.

Index

www.ingramcontent.com/pod-product-compliance
Lightning Source LLC
Chambersburg PA
CBHW081056220326
41598CB00038B/7115